present at the past episode (biographical self-disclosure) introduces the listener to information about the speaker and his or her world (Cohen, 1998), while sharing memories with someone who was present serves more of a social-bonding or intimacy function (Fivush, Haden, & Reese, 1996).

Directive

Despite some claims of the primacy of social functions, the directive function of AM is also seen as important. For example, Cohen (1989, 1998) has described the role of AM in solving problems as well as in developing opinions and attitudes that guide one's behaviour. AM allows us to ask new questions of old information in order to solve problems in the present, and to predict future events (Baddeley, 1987). A hypothesised function that may be seen as both directive and social, is to use our own past experience to construct models that allow us to understand the inner world of others, and thereby to predict their future behaviour (Robinson & Swanson, 1990). Similarly, Lockhart (1989) has argued that the major function of AM is to provide flexibility in the construction and updating of rules that allow individuals to comprehend the past and predict future outcomes. That is, by comparing different past events, and by comparing events with developed rules, individuals are able to test hypotheses about how the world (not just the social world) currently operates, and to make predictions about the future. Similarly, in several studies individuals report remembering past events and the lessons they learned from them as useful in guiding present or future behavior (McCabe, Capron, & Peterson, 1991; Pratt, Arnold, Norris, & Filyer, 1999). David Pillemer has reviewed a variety of directive functions of AM in his book, *Momentous Events, Vivid Memories*, and details some of these in his contribution (Pillemer, 2003 this issue). Thus, the directive function of autobiographical memory, use of the past to make plans and decisions in the present and for the future, has also received some attention.

In sum, theoretical work in the AM literature supports three functions of remembering the past: self, social, and directive. Most researchers agree that the self and AM are intimately linked, and many suggest that the social function of AM is an important, if not the most important, function.

The directive function of memory is seen as a crucial way in which individuals use the past as a resource for present and future behaviour.

Until quite recently, little empirical work directly addressed the functions of AM (but see Hyman & Faries, 1992). The authors contributing to this special issue are all researchers who have made important contributions concerning function: each has developed methods, in some cases full programmes of research, or provided creative theoretical guidance. By bringing together these empirical and theoretical contributions we hope to focus a research spotlight on why people remember what they do about the experiences of their lives, and what use it is to them.

Next, I introduce each of the contributions. We begin with an examination of function from a historical, socio-cultural perspective: the paper explores whether the functions of AM are universal and consistent over time. Next, there are papers that investigate each of the three major functions: self, social, and directive. This organisation into three functions does not suggest that three is the magic number. A secondary aim of this special issue of *Memory* is to stretch our consideration to allow that more or fewer categories of function may be more parsimonious. In this regard, Webster's contribution (2003, this issue) calls us to question the adequacy of the current trio.

THE FUNCTIONS OF AM IN HISTORICAL PERSPECTIVE

Shifting roles of individual and collective memory narratives

Katherine Nelson's paper analyses both self and social functions of autobiographical memory as embedded in an evolutionary and socio-cultural timeframe. Although it focuses on self and social functions, her conceptualisation of memory, based on Tulving's and others' views, is that memory is a knowledge structure that is "not about the past but about the future" (Nelson, 2003 this issue). Although she doesn't explicitly frame it this way, I believe that the directive function is therefore seen as implicit in, and part of the definition of, autobiographical memory. That is, the job that humans need done is to explain the world in which we find ourselves in order to predict and plan for the future. In questioning whether there are three basic functions of AM, I believe it is a challenge to consider that the directive function may underpin both self and social functions (see also Pillemer, 1998).

Given that explaining the present and thereby predicting the future is a basic human need, Nelson's article focuses on examining how that is done: what is the balance between the roles that the individual plays and the role that the greater society plays in providing explanations and predictors. She argues that a basic recording of temporally sequenced self-related events has developed as part of the memory system through evolution. In addition to that basic memory system, however, in historical periods that assume cyclic continuity (continuity through repetition of old patterns) between past and future there is little that individuals must do to predict the future. In such periods, cultural- and societal-level stories of continuity suggest that individuals' future will be just the same as their own past, and the past of their mothers and fathers. However, in modern or post-modern society, in which change not continuity is the norm, there is an imperative for the *individual* to forge a unique identity based on a unique life history that will allow them to explain and predict their future role in an ever-changing world.

Nelson makes a complementary argument concerning cross-cultural variation in the use of AM: in cultures that value and therefore encourage common values and group (as compared to individual) identification, the individual's best strategy for explaining the present and predicting the future is to look to common cultural myths and narratives. In individualistic societies, like the United States, a common narrative no longer exists and the *individual* has the freedom and the burden of creating a unique life story both to serve their own needs for self-continuity (self function) and to present themselves to others (social function).

Nelson concludes that the current emphasis in modern American society on personal narrative is a result of this being a socio-historical time point in which individuals (and thereby individuals' memory), more than collective society, are charged with forging a unique identity. The central importance in contemporary America of using AM to serve self and social functions is reflected in parental and institutional emphasis on nurturing children to recall their own personal past at an early age (see also Fivush et al., 2003 this issue), and to begin developing a life story that will carry them into adulthood (see also Habermas & Bluck,

2000; McAdams, 1985). Nelson's paper reminds us that the functional approach is based on adaptation occurring through the person–environment interaction. As that relationship changes, so might the way that memory serves its functions, and possibly (across evolutionary time) also the functions that memory is called upon to serve. Keeping that in mind we will, given our current time period, fall back on the three broad functions that have been defined in the current literature, beginning with the self function.

SELF FUNCTION

Self-enhancement and coherence: Time is on our side

Wilson and Ross revisit the notion of the interdependence of, and reciprocal relations between, the self and autobiographical memory in their contribution (see also Bluck & Levine, 1998; Brewer, 1986; Webster & Cappeliez, 1993). This link has long intrigued psychologists, and the authors remind us of William James' (1890/1950) remark that, were an individual to awake one morning with all personal memories erased, he or she would essentially be a different person. Most of us would agree with James' statement, but thinking carefully, what would change and what would stay the same in such a "memory-free" person? That is, when James says this would be *essentially* a different person, it raises the question, to what extent is AM not just an interrelated part, but a truly essential aspect, of self? Self and memory are not completely overlapping sets, that is, they are not simply the same thing. Instead, taking an ecological approach to memory (Neisser, 1986), we are guided to answer the question of how essential memory is to the self by identifying the functions that memory serves for the self.

Although this dynamic link between self and memory has often been the object of theoretical consideration, it has received less empirical attention. The programme of research described by Wilson and Ross provides an operationalisation of two functions that memory plays for the self: providing a coherent view of self and a largely favourable view of the self. Their work sheds light on how memory allows us to say "I am the same person as I was before—but better."

In various studies these authors have found that people self-enhance by evaluating past selves as inferior to their current one. This work highlights the truly autobiographical nature of auto-biographical memory. That is, although we often think of memory as a series of events, it is also a record of a series of selves, or a record of the self across time—an autobiography. The current self can enhance its stature by devaluing the past through remembered selves who were not as sweet or kind, as motivated or intelligent, as the current one. This is an important though fairly straightforward point.

What comes next is less intuitive. The authors detail how individuals use memory to push the past away, or to pull it forward in time, in order to better serve the function of self-enhancement. They show that people can rid themselves of past negative selves by pushing them into the distant past, so as to make them no longer relevant to the current self's well-being. As well, they discuss how favourable events can be pulled forward in time so that we can continue to take credit for past successes as part of our current identity. As a second process by which memory serves self-enhancement functions, the authors discuss point of view in memory, particularly how a third-person perspective on our own negative life events may allow us a distance from those events that promotes health and well-being.

In turn, these remembered events also have implications for the current self: for current affect and feelings of satisfaction, although not in a straightforward fashion. Remembering positive events from the past often results in one's current mood being elevated, but not always. So we can't say that the function of remembering past episodes is always to feel better in the present. Sometimes contrast effects occur in which remembering a happy past makes one feel worse about one's current woes. The piece added to this picture by Wilson and Ross is, again, time (see also Clark, Collins, & Henry, 1991). That is, mood enhancement is likely to occur when recalling recent positive events of the self, whereas contrast effects are more likely to occur when recalling events of a distant past self. Overall, the authors' programme of research suggests that autobiographical remembering serves a self function, that is, to maintain a coherent but still largely favourable present self (see also Greenwald, 1980). They briefly allude to the idea that there could be tension between functions of coherence and enhancement.

This seems an idea worthy of further consideration. I have mentioned that multiple functions may be served at one time, but what about the case in which serving one function inadvertently hinders another? For example, if as Wilson and Ross suggest, self-enhancement occurs through pushing remembered selves back in time ("I'm different now"), evaluating past selves poorly ("I'm not just different but better"), and seeing the past self in the third person (objectifying old selves), might this self-enhancement in the most extreme case lead to a sense of self based very much in the present, and one that recruits only positive past events to be part of the current self? Does this imply that, were an individual to awake one morning with all negative memories erased, he or she would essentially be what memory works for us all to be?

Emotion regulation as a function of AM: Self meets social

Although Pasupathi presents work on emotion regulation, we see again here, the tendency to employ memories in a manner that aids current well-being, this time not an enhancement of one's view of self, as in Wilson and Ross's work, but of one's current mood state. This paper focuses on a ubiquitous aspect of memories of the self—that is, that we tell and retell them to other people. The series of studies Pasupathi presents suggest that the emotional intensity of a memory for an initial everyday event is different from memories of times that we retold the event to another person. This difference in remembered affect is seen as a means by which humans engage in emotion regulation, which has been seen as one subtype of the self function of AM (Cohen, 1998; Pillemer, 1992). Thus, her work shows how a self function such as emotion regulation is served in a social context, that is, conversational remembering. Of course, the conversation may at the same time be serving social functions (e.g., eliciting empathy) and it is here we see that self and social functions are likely not, in reality, discrete categories.

The pattern of findings in Pasupathi's paper show the constancy of positive emotion between memories of an initial event and its retelling, and the diminishing of negative emotion between initial event and retelling. That is, we see that individuals can (to quote Bing Crosby) "accentuate the positive and eliminate the negative". Well, maybe not eliminate the negative, but at least diminish it, in the stories they tell to others. This seems to occur for the sample in general but even more so for men. In terms of a functional approach, the question is whether the transformation of negative emotion is due to autobiographical memory—that is, that people and especially men remember negative events in a way that helps to down-regulate negative emotion (see also Walker, Vogl, & Thompson, 1997). The alternative is that these individuals remember the negative emotion just as much but feel that it is not functional to display it, so they regulate what is said (not necessarily what is remembered).

My latter interpretation of this work suggests that emotion regulation may not be a primary function of AM but instead could be viewed as an important mechanism by which primary functions (e.g., self, social, directive) of autobiographical memory are served. So, for example, retelling a difficult situation but not retelling the negative emotion one experienced may result in presentation of a self-enhancing (strong, courageous) memory to the listener of the story. Another example, this time using emotion regulation to help AM serve a social function, is that women may include more negative affect than men when retelling an event in order to serve the function of eliciting or providing empathy.

The importance of Pasupathi's paper, and more generally her programmatic work in this area (e.g., Pasupathi, 2001; Pasupathi, Stallworth, & Murdoch, 1998), is that she highlights the role of emotion in how memory may serve important functions. She also reminds us that in everyday life, functions are often served in a social context in which both characteristics of the listener and the speaker may affect how successfully memory can be recruited towards certain ends. The paper that follows, by Alea and Bluck, further elaborates the role of social context in how AM serves its functions.

SOCIAL FUNCTION

Why are you telling me that?

Alea and Bluck's contribution focuses exclusively on how social functions are served when individuals share memories with another person. Noting the paucity of empirical work on all functions of AM, including the social, the authors attempt to help remedy this situation by providing a conceptual model that can be used to generate research questions. Although noting that such models could eventually be useful for each broad function, in the current paper they limit their scope to providing a conceptual model of the variables and processes that are involved when AMs are shared to serve social functions.

The authors provide two interrelated definitions of their model's outcome variable, that is, social function. The first is a taxonomic definition of function as use: what different types of social uses is memory put to in different situations (e.g., intimacy maintenance, teaching, eliciting empathy)? The second is a stricter idea of function that implies adaptive level: to what extent is a certain type of social function actually served under various conditions (e.g., does intimacy show an increase after memory sharing)?

The conceptual model then identifies developmental, individual–level, social, and qualitative memory variables that, according to their literature review, should affect what social uses memory is put to, and how well it serves them. At the broadest level, all variables are nested in a lifespan contextual frame. The reasons why people reflect on the past, and share memories with others, is seen as varying with their life phase. Within that developmental frame, characteristics of the person sharing the memory (e.g., gender) and characteristics of the listener (e.g., level of familiarity of the listener and speaker) are also considered. Both speaker and listener characteristics can influence what memory is used for (e.g., women may be more likely than men to use AM for intimacy development), as well as the extent to which a social function is served. Social variables such as the length and quality of the relationship between the speaker and the listener, and personal responsiveness between the listener and the speaker in a particular exchange, are also discussed as factors that are likely to affect how well AM serves social functions in dyadic exchanges.

Besides developmental and social variables, qualitative memory characteristics, such as amount of detail and emotion shared, can influence how well AM serves a particular social function. For instance, sharing an emotional AM with another person may lead to increased intimacy with that person (a social function of AM) that may not have occurred if the memory was purely informative (had lots of details) with little emotion.

The paper offers a rich framework for interpreting empirical contributions such as those made by Fivush et al., and Pasupathi, in this issue. It allows us to map the sub-field of the social functions of AM to see where contributions are substantial enough to provide guidance in generating new hypotheses, and also to identify crucial gaps that are really in need of further exploratory development.

"What happened then, Mom?" Telling as teaching

The paper by Fivush et al. examines particular variables and relations in the conceptual model of social functions detailed by Alea and Bluck. Their model illustrates that in considering the social functions of AM, we need to take note of the content (information and valence) of the memory being shared and who is doing the telling and the listening. Certainly, the functions AM serves may be moderated by what is being remembered and the relationship between those sharing the memory.

Fivush et al. explore a fundamental relationship for development, that between mother and child. One question that frames their paper is why do parents (in this case, mothers) reminisce with their children? What is the function of such exchanges? More than that, however, this work examines AM (as opposed to other information that parents might share with children) because it seeks to describe how not only the past, but *emotionally-charged* information about the past, is treated in conversation. Several complementary functions of sharing past emotional experiences with children are put forword. For example, parents influence children's developing self-concept through the way that they engage in emotional past talk with them. They also influence the way that the child sees him or herself in relation to others, and how they see emotion as an integral part of social relations. Finally, another function is to teach and inform, or socialise children about how to express, and maybe even how to experience, or cope with their own emotions (i.e., to regulate emotion, see also Pasupathi, 2003 this issue).

This latter function is nicely elaborated in the paper. It is argued that socialisation in emotion regulation (through memory sharing) may be particularly important for dealing with the negative emotional experiences in a child's everyday life. That is, mother–child talk about past situations in which the child experienced sadness, anger, or fear may serve the function of guiding children's understanding of each of these negative emotions in ways that are socially sanctioned. Sharing and rehearsing past negative events may thereby help socialise the child in their cultures' norms concerning expression and experience of different types of negative emotions, partly depending on their gender-appropriateness.

The researchers present data collected using a naturalistic method—conversations between mothers and their sons and daughters about actual everyday negative events. Their analyses show that mothers elaborate and evaluate different aspects (e.g., what happened during the event, how it was resolved, how the child was feeling at that time) of memories of sadness, anger, and fear to differing extents. This work suggests that when considering the functions of AM one should be attentive to the lifespan developmental stage of the partners in the social sharing. Teaching and informing is certainly a social role that parents are charged with, and memory-sharing may be one way in which adults socialise children about their own emotions, particularly negative ones, and what to do with them. In turn, this may influence the child's growing sense of self as an emotional being.

DIRECTIVE FUNCTION

Drawing on the reservoir of personal experience

Pillemer's contribution focuses on the directive function of AM. The central point of his article is to demonstrate the importance, and in his words, "the *guiding power* of the specific episode". He recruits examples of everyday and traumatic memories to first demonstrate the phenomenon. That is, he shows that people really do recollect specific moments or events and use their memories of both traumatic and pedestrian experiences to guide them towards successful functioning and away from repeated failure. Given the importance of using memories as directives it is perhaps surprising that this function has received less attention, and sometimes less support, in the small empirical literatures on the functions of AM and reminiscence (for a review, see Bluck & Alea, 2002).

Pillemer's reanalysis of the available data on directive functions (including some new data of his own) leads us to the conclusion that using memory as a directive has more support in the current literature than is readily apparent. In addition, he points out that this function may be underrepresented because of some confusion concerning its conceptualisation (does it refer only to current problem solving, or to the larger issue of guiding and planning future behaviour, or both?), and difficulty with its measurement. He argues that measuring memory directives is especially difficult using self-report measures (like the Reminiscence Functions Scale; Webster, 1993), because the use of memory to direct future behaviour may be less subject to awareness than the use of memory in the service of self and social functions. This brings us back to the implicit message in Nelson's paper, that using the past to explain the present and predict the future (i.e., as a directive) may underlie the use of personal memory to serve functions in both self and social domains.

Pillemer's contribution revitalises research on how individuals, whether consciously or not, use specific personal memories to guide and direct their behaviour. An additional area for future investigation is whether different levels of AM, that is not only the specific episode, but life domains and life themes (Bucks & Habermas, 2001; Conway & Pleydell-Pearce, 2000), or the life story (McAdams, 1996) have similar power in directing individuals' future plans and behaviour.

IS THREE THE MAGIC NUMBER?

The contributions reviewed thus far each provide evidence for one or more of the three broad functions of AM. It appears that self, social, and directive functions of AM have some credibility. The challenges of inventing new and creative methodologies for their further study, and sorting out some complex theoretical issues, are still before us. The final paper in the special issue challenges us in a still different way: Webster's work links two rather distinct literatures to probe whether self, social, and directive are exhaustive categories of function.

Linking with the reminiscence literature

Webster is one of a few authors who are working to tie together research on memory from the reminiscence tradition with research stemming from an autobiographical memory approach. A few papers have already been written that attempt to bridge these substantively similar but traditionally different literatures (see also Bluck & Levine, 1998; Fitzgerald, 1996; Webster & Cap-

peliez, 1993). His contribution to this special issue, development of a circumplex model for mapping reminiscence functions and relating them to the broad AM functions, provides a crucial linking of literatures that will move forward the discussion and understanding of the functions of personal memories in human lives.

Webster's circumplex model provides a good conceptual framework not only for uniting the literatures but also for utilising the strengths of each. His earlier work focused on the development and validation of the only scale in the literature to measure memory functions—that is, the eight-factor Reminiscence Functions Scale (RFS; Webster, 1993). In his contribution to this special issue, he employs theoretical work on the three broad functions from the AM literature to suggest analyses that organise the eight RFS factors into a conceptually meaningful circumplex model. The model is composed of a self-social dimension and a proactive/growth–reactive/loss dimension. The model is newly developed and its acceptance clearly awaits further statistical testing. Even at this point however, it provides a useful heuristic for viewing specific, empirically based functions of reminiscence, such as problem solving, and teaching and informing others, within the broader theoretical framework of major adaptive functions of autobiographical remembering (self, social, and directive functions).

His circumplex model also highlights how different traditions, even within one discipline (i.e., psychology), can sometimes provide such complementary convergence but can also arrive at quite different conclusions. For example, in the AM literature the notion of a directive function (using the past to plan for the future, solve problems in the present) has been repeatedly suggested, but the idea of the individual being directive in response to a negative context (e.g., being reactive) versus in order to move towards desired goals (i.e., being proactive or growth-oriented) has not been given special attention.

The reminiscence literature has its early roots in psychodynamic (e.g., Butler, 1963) and other therapeutic literature (Birren & Deutchman, 1991), especially in relation to older adults' supposed predilection for reminiscence. Issues of dealing with loss and striving for optimal human development are central themes. It is unsurprising, given these roots, that the reminiscence literature, particularly Webster's work, calls our attention to the necessity of including such reactive functions as boredom reduction, and revival of bitter memories, in our consideration of the functions of remembering the personal past (see also Pillemer, 1992, for a psychodynamic function). This may require examination of function that is not related only to immediate positive outcomes (e.g., eliciting empathy from a listener, developing intimacy in a given encounter) but to long-term adaptivity such as working through the loss of a loved one, which may require repeated processing of negative memories (e.g., Janoff-Bulman & Thomas, 1989; Suedfeld & Pennebaker, 1997). The task Webster presents us is to incorporate reactive (as well as proactive) uses of memory into the broader framework of how memory serves adaptive functions in everyday life. His own analysis sets us well on the way to doing that, while challenging AM researchers to broaden their scope both in the literature we read, and possibly in the way that we define adaptive function.

SPOTLIGHTS AND HIGH BEAMS: FUTURE DIRECTIONS AND CONCLUSION

I began with the metaphor of using this special issue of *Memory* to focus a spotlight on the functional approach to studying AM. When we turn on the high beams what do we see down the road: what issues and concerns have been raised by this collection of papers? I outline a few of these below:

(1) Function is a concept that is based on individual needs being determined by contextual press. Nelson argues that the uses to which memory is put, particularly the extent to which the *individual* memory system must serve certain functions as opposed to relying on larger cultural memory narratives (myths and norms) to guide behaviour, depends on the cultural and historical context of a given society. This offers the possibility for research that addresses cross-cultural comparisons of how and what functions are served by AM. At the same time it begs the theoretical question: is one, or more, function of AM universal (e.g., guiding future behaviour; see Pillemer, 2003 this issue)?

(2) Even within a single culture, such as Western industrialised societies, individual-level and contextual variables still matter. The basic issue, as related to the question in point 1, is whether some functions of AM are innate, and others are

learned. Of course the more sophisticated views of nature and nurture do not concern one or the other, but issues of co-construction (Li, 2002). In this case, the call is for further research (such as that by Pasupathi, and Fivush et al.) that demonstrates individual difference variations (e.g., gender, age, personality) in the use of AM to serve self, social, and directive functions.

(3) Beyond individual differences, continued focus on social contextual variables will be crucial to understanding moderating influences on how memory serves its functions. These include such things as the length and quality of the relationship in which memory sharing occurs, and the interaction between the listener and speaker. The lifespan developmental phase of the individual, or individuals in an interaction, may also guide the ways memory is used and the uses it is put to (see Alea & Bluck, 2003 this issue). Of course, social contextual variables are of primary concern in the cases in which memory sharing occurs. Another central question to be investigated is how private remembering differs from memory sharing in serving centrally important functions such as, for example, self-continuity.

(4) The mechanisms (i.e., emotion regulation) by which functions are served also offers a ground for continued research. In addition to examining the role of emotion in how AM functions, this could include the role of memory characteristics (e.g., perceived temporal distance; Wilson & Ross, 2003 this issue), or phenomenology (e.g., first versus third person perspective, vividness, level of detail).

(5) I have also alluded to the issue of how many functions of AM there are: is three the magic number? Of course determining a number is in some ways unimportant. What is important is to continue to test hypotheses that build areas of support, or fail to support, the existing theoretical functions: self, social, and directive. Thinking about the number of functions does, however, push us to ask some conceptual questions that might guide future research. What is the overlap in how memories serve certain functions in particular situations? Do some memories provoke conflict by serving a certain function while challenging another? For example, there may be limits to how self-enhancing one's memory can be before it becomes incredible, and thereby seen as ingenuous, in social situations. Self-enhancement could thereby defeat intimacy development.

(6) Finally, as we talk of something having a function being a "match" between the individual

and his or her environment, we might also want to put more emphasis on that environment. One way to do that is suggested by Webster's contribution (2003, this issue). That is, he talks about the functional use of reminiscence as a type of movement towards growth and development, and also as a reactive stance towards loss or negative circumstance. I think this work suggests that researchers investigate the situations, or triggers, in the environment that prompt an individual (whether consciously or not) to call memory, instead of or as well as other resources, to their aid.

CONCLUSION

The body of work presented in this special issue of *Memory*, as well as other research by these and many additional investigators, demonstrates the utility of taking a functional approach. The findings presented here lend support to continued investigation of self, social, and directive functions of AM and offer a variety of methodologies for doing such work in both laboratory and natural settings. The theoretical work presented in the special issue offers us the opportunity to keep our empirical research on AM grounded not only in data but in the context of the individual (e.g., socio-emotional context), and sometimes the cultural-historical, context. In addition, looking across these papers offers us a glimpse of the direction in which this literature is headed. I, for one, am looking forward to travelling the road ahead.

REFERENCES

Alea, N., & Bluck, S. (2003). Why are you telling me that? A conceptual model of the social function of autobiographical memory. *Memory, 11*, 165–178.

Baddeley, A. (1987). But what the hell is it for? In M.M. Gruneberg, P.E. Morris, & R.N. Sykes (Eds.), *Practical aspects of memory: Current research and issues* (pp. 3–18). Chichester, UK: Wiley.

Barclay, C.R. (1996). Autobiographical remembering: Narrative constraints on objectified selves. In D.C. Rubin (Ed.), *Remembering our past: Studies in autobiographical memory* (pp. 94–125). Cambridge: Cambridge University Press.

Birren, J.E., & Deutchman, D.E. (1991). *Guiding autobiography groups for older adults: Exploring the fabric of life.* Baltimore: Johns Hopkins University Press.

Bluck, S., & Alea, N. (2002). Exploring the functions of autobiographical memory: Why do I remember the autumn? In J.D. Webster & B.K. Haight (Eds.), *Critical advances in reminiscence: From theory to application.* New York: Springer.

Bluck, S., & Habermas, T. (2001).The life story schema. *Motivation and Emotion, 24*, 121–147.

Bluck, S., & Levine, L.J. (1998). Reminiscence as autobiographical memory: A catalyst for reminiscence theory development. *Ageing and Society, 18*, 185–208.

Brewer, W.F. (1986). What is autobiographical memory? In D.C. Rubin (Ed.), *Autobiographical memory* (pp. 25–49). Cambridge: Cambridge University Press.

Bruce, D. (1989). Functional explanations of memory. In L. W. Poon, D. C. Rubin, & B. A. Wilson (Eds.), *Everyday cognition in adulthood and late life* (pp. 44-58). Cambridge: Cambridge University Press.

Butler, R.N. (1963). The life review: An interpretation of reminiscence in old age. *Psychiatry, Journal for the Study of Inter-personal Processes, 26*, 65–76.

Clark, L.F., Collins, J.E., & Henry, S.M. (1994). Biasing effects of retrospective reports on current self-assessments. In N. Schwarz & S. Sudman (Eds.), *Autobiographical memory and the validity of retrospective reports* (pp. 291–304). New York: Springer-Verlag.

Cohen, G. (1989). *Memory in the real world.* Hove, UK: Lawrence Erlbaum Associates Ltd.

Cohen, G. (1998). The effects of aging on autobiographical memory. In C.P. Thompson, D.J. Hermann, D. Bruce, J.D. Read, D.G. Payne, & M.P. Toglia (Eds.), *Autobiographical memory: Theoretical and applied perspectives* (pp. 105–123). Mahwah, NJ: Lawrence Erlbaum Associates Inc.

Conway, M.A. (1996). Autobiographical knowledge and autobiographical memories. In D.C. Rubin (Ed.), *Remembering our past: Studies in autobiographical memory* (pp. 67–93). Cambridge: Cambridge University Press.

Conway, M.A., & Pleydell-Pearce, C.W. (2000). The construction of autobiographical memories in the self-memory system. *Psychological Review.*

Fitzgerald, J.M. (1996). Intersecting meanings of reminiscence in adult development and aging. In D.C. Rubin (Ed.), *Remembering our past: Studies in autobiographical memory* (pp. 360–383). Cambridge: Cambridge University Press.

Fivush, R. (1998). The functions of event memory: Some comments on Nelson and Barsalou. In U. Neisser & E. Winograd (Eds.), *Remembering reconsidered: Ecological and traditional approaches to the study of memory* (pp. 277–282). Cambridge: Cambridge University Press.

Fivush, R., Berlin, L.J., & Cassidy, J. (2003). Functions of parent-child reminiscing about emotionally negative events. *Memory, 11*, 179–192.

Fivush, R., Haden, C., & Reese, E. (1996). Remembering, recounting and reminiscing: The development of memory in a social context. In D. Rubin (Ed.), *Remembering our past: Studies in autobiographical memory* (pp. 341–359). Cambridge: Cambridge University Press.

Greenwald, A. (1980). The totalitarian ego: Fabrication and revision of personal history. *American Psychologist, 35*, 603–618.

Habermas, T., & Bluck, S. (2000). Getting a life: The emergence of the life story in adolescence. *Psychological Bulletin, 126,* 748–769.

Hyman, I.E., & Faries, J.M. (1992). The functions of autobiographical memory. In M.A. Conway, D.C. Rubin, H. Spinnler, & W.A. Wagenaar (Eds.), *Theoretical perspectives on autobiographical memory* (pp. 207–221). Dordrecht, The Netherlands: Kluwer Academic Publishers.

Janoff-Bulman, R., & Thomas, C.E. (1989). Toward an understanding of self-defeating responses following victimization. In R. Curtis (Ed.), *Self-defeating behaviors: Experimental research and practical implications* (pp. 215–234). New York: Plenum.

Lewin, K. (1926). Untersuchungen zur Handlungs- und Affektpsychologie: I. Vorbemerkyngen über die psychischen Kräfte und Energien und über die Struktur der Seele. *Psychologische Forschung, 7,* 294–329.

Li, S.-C. (in press). Biocultural orchestration of developmental plasticity across levels: The interplay of biology and culture in shaping the mind and behavior across the lifespan. *Psychological Bulletin.*

Lockhart, R.S. (1989). Consciousness and the function of remembered episodes. In H.L. Roediger & F.I.M. Craik (Eds.), *Varieties of memory and consciousness* (pp. 423–430). Hillsdale, NJ: Lawrence Erlbaum Associates Inc.

McAdams, D. (1985). *Power and intimacy.* New York: Guilford Press.

McAdams, D. (1996). Personality, modernity, and the storied self: A contemporary framework for studying persons. *Psychological Inquiry, 7,* 295–321.

McCabe, A., Capron, T., & Peterson, C. (1991). The voice of experience: The recall of early childhood and adolescent memories by young adults. In C.P.A. McCabe (Ed.), *Developing narrative structure* (pp. 137–173). Hillsdale, NJ: Lawrence Erlbaum Associates Inc.

Neisser, U. (1978). Memory: What are the important questions? In M.M. Gruneberg, P.E. Morris, & R.N. Sykes (Eds.), *Practical aspects of memory* (pp. 3–19). London: Academic Press.

Neisser, U. (1986). Nested structure in autobiographical memory. In D.C. Rubin (Ed.), *Autobiographical memory* (pp. 71–81). Cambridge: Cambridge University Press.

Neisser, U. (1988). Five kinds of self-knowledge. *Philosophical Psychology, 1,* 35–59.

Nelson, K. (1993). The psychological and social origins of autobiographical memory. *Psychological Science, 4,* 7–14.

Nelson, K. (2003). Self and social functions: Individual autobiographical memory and collective narrative. *Memory, 11,* 125–136.

Neugarten, B.L. (1979). Time, age and the life cycle. *American Journal of Psychiatry, 136,* 887–894.

Pasupathi, M. (2001). The social construction of the personal past and its implications for adult development. *Psychological Bulletin, 127,* 651–672.

Pasupathi, M. (2003). Emotion regulation during social remembering: Differences between emotions elicited during an event and emotions elicited when talking about it. *Memory, 11,* 151–163.

Pasupathi, M., Stallworth, L.M., & Murdoch, K. (1998). How what we tell becomes what we know: Listener effects on speaker's long-term memory for events. *Discourse Processes, 26,* 1–25.

Pillemer, D.B. (1992). Remembering personal circumstances: A functional analysis. In E. Winograd & U. Neisser (Eds.), *Affect and accuracy in recall: Studies of "flashbulb" memories* [*Emory symposia in cognition* 4th ed., pp. 236–264]. New York: Cambridge University Press.

Pillemer, D.B. (1998). *Momentous events, vivid memories.* Cambridge, MA: Harvard University Press.

Pillemer, D.B. (2003). Directive functions of autobiographical memory: The guiding power of the specific episode. *Memory, 11,* 193–202.

Pratt, M.W., Arnold, M.L., Norris, J.E., & Filyer, R. (1999). Generativity and moral development as predictors of value socialization narratives for young persons across the adult life span: From lessons learned to stories shared. *Psychology and Aging, 14,* 414–426.

Robinson, J. (1986). Autobiographical memory: A historical prologue. In D. Rubin (Ed.), *Autobiographical memory* (pp. 19–24). Cambridge: Cambridge University Press.

Ross, M. (1989). Relation of implicit theories to construction of personal histories. *Psychological Review, 96,* 341–357.

Ross, M. (1991). *Remembering the personal past.* New York: Oxford University Press.

Staudinger, U.M., & Bluck. S. (2002). *Looking back and looking ahead: diachronous correlates of subjective well-being across the adult life span.* Manuscript submitted for publication.

Suedfeld, P., & Pennebaker, J.W. (1997). Health outcomes and cognitive aspects of recalled negative life events. *Psychosomatic Medicine, 59,* 172–177.

Walker, W.R., Vogl, R.J., & Thompson, C.P. (1997). Autobiographical memory: Unpleasantness fades faster than pleasantness over time. *Applied Cognitive Psychology, 11,* 399–413.

Webster, J.D. (1993). Construction and validation of the Reminiscence Functions Scale. *Journals of Gerontology: Psychological Sciences, 48,* 256–262.

Webster, J.D., & Cappeliez, P. (1993). Reminiscence and autobiographical memory: Complementary contexts for aging research. *Developmental Review, 13,* 54–91.

Webster, J.D. (2003). The reminiscence circumplex and autobiographical memory functions. *Memory, 11,* 203–215.

Wilson, A.E., & Ross, M. (2003). The identity function of autobiographical memory: Time is on our side. *Memory, 11,* 137–149.

MEMORY, 2003, *11* (2), 125–136

Self and social functions: Individual autobiographical memory and collective narrative

Katherine Nelson

City University of New York Graduate Center, USA

The personal functions of autobiographical memory build on the basic biological functions of memory common to most mammals that, however, do not have the kind of episodic memories that compose human autobiographical memory according to present theory. The thesis here is that personal autobiographical memory is functionally and structurally related to the use of cultural myths and social narratives, and that the relative emphasis put on the self in different cultural and social contexts influences the form and function of autobiographical memory and the need for developing a uniquely personal life narrative in those contexts. Historical and cross-cultural trends revealed in psychological and literary research are invoked to support this thesis.

Why do we tell stories of ourselves to ourselves? Why do we tell them to others? These are the questions raised by the theme of this special issue of *Memory*: the function of autobiographical memory. In this article I argue that the function of self stories is related to the social and cultural milieu within which they are situated, and the alternative resources available within the milieu for understanding self and society. Based on the assumption that a unique and important characteristic of all human life is the capacity for and habit of telling stories, I am suggesting that self stories derived from autobiographical memory are one version of the stories that humans share with one another.

At the broadest level are cultural stories, shared in and retold by all members of a cultural group, such as religious and historical accounts. Within a culture, subgroups such as professions, genders, classes, or ages, construct and circulate stories of passing or enduring interest. Often this is classified as gossip. On a personal and social level people exchange stories of personal significance to the individual, family, or close associates. The general claim here is that auto-

biographical memory serves the latter social function, at the same time that it serves as a vehicle for self-expression and definition. In addition, all forms—cultural, social, and personal—can be seen to serve very general functions of extending knowledge about the social and physical world as a basis for prediction and explanation. From this perspective autobiographical memory is individuated knowledge based on self experience that may be shared with others, whereas social and cultural stories draw on broader sources of group experience and imaginative constructions.

An important claim here is that the personal and the social and cultural are both functionally and structurally related. To make this claim it is necessary to see the relation between memory as an individual function, its role in the phylogenetic scheme of adaptation, and narrative as the medium of shared memories, collective memories, and fictional creations. Focus on this relation brings out the problematic question of the role of narrative in the composition of autobiographical memory, and whether autobiographical memory exists in a raw, non-narrative form. When we examine the functions of autobiographical mem-

Requests for reprints should be sent to Katherine Nelson, 50 Riverside Drive, New York, NY 10024, USA.
Email: knelson@gc.cuny.edu

ory we do so from a particular point in human evolutionary and socio-historical time. Thus my argument takes a semi-historical form, beginning with the functions of individual memory in a cognitive evolutionary framework, through cultural uses of group memory in prehistory and historical times, to modern individualist narratives, factual and fictional, to questions about the place of autobiographical memory in the contemporary narrative space. Finally I will ask how these excursions shed light on understanding the function of autobiographical memory as it develops in early childhood.

AUTOBIOGRAPHICAL MEMORY IN EVOLUTIONARY CONTEXT

Tulving (1983) made the claim that the type of memory termed episodic is uniquely human, which raised the issue of how and why it could arise in the course of human evolution. Although this claim has been contested, it seems probable that memory for temporally sequenced events or activities—a characteristic of episodic memory—may have evolved as functional for certain kinds of knowledge: how to build a nest, for example, or how to locate and dig out termites. In the terms of evolutionary epistemology (Plotkin, 1988) basic memory functions retain information about the particular conditions of social and physical life of individuals, beyond that which can be anticipated in the genetic heritage of the species in its environmental niche. Basic memory is therefore a knowledge source that anticipates future needs; it is not about the past but about the future (Nelson, 1993a,b, 1996; Tulving & Lepage, 2000). By retaining information about both common and novel events, it provides the basis for taking action in the present and anticipating future needs. Taking account of the epistemic value of memory in its natural setting we can better appreciate the distinction that Tulving made between episodic memory and other types of declarative memory. There are two main bases for this distinction: it is temporally situated as an event in a specific point in the past, and it is about the individual self's experience (Tulving, 1983). Episodic memory in particular is characterised by *autonoesis*, re-experience of the past, as distinguished from semantic memory, or *noesis*, that is, factual memory with no accompanying sense of self-experience in a specific past. Autobiographical memory is clearly a form of episodic memory in

this sense, although not all everyday episodic memories are retained in the set of "self stories" that constitute an adult's autobiographical memory. Indeed, as my colleagues and I have shown (Hudson & Nelson, 1986; see also Linton, 1982), episodic memories that are followed by repetitions of similar events become absorbed in general scripts for "what happens", that is, they become general knowledge structures, although of a temporally organised kind.

There are two aspects of temporal structuring that characterise episodic memory; first, there is the situatedness of the event in specific past time in relation to the present. Second there is the temporal sequencing within the episode remembered. Both of these aspects rely on a conscious sense of the "extended self" (Damasio, 1999; Moore & Lemmon, 2001; Neisser, 1997). The significance of this "self in time" (Nelson, 1989, 1997) has become recognised increasingly, especially with regard to memory development. An important function of autobiographical memory is now seen as providing the sense of the continuity of the self across time from the past to the future.

With the advent of human language in the course of human evolution, temporally organised memory could be put to new uses, specifically the use of sharing knowledge across the social group. With language, individuals could pass on to other members of the group specific information about what they had experienced or observed. Individual episodic memories could be turned into episodic narratives, thereby expanding the practical knowledge base within the group, and establishing a shared memory store that could be passed on through symbolic means to later generations.

CULTURAL NARRATIVES

Memory for personally experienced episodes is not all that individuals might share with the group. What might initially have been individual thoughts about the natural world, proposing explanations for unexpected occurrences and making predictions about future events, could be shared as well, and these might borrow the narrative form used to exchange stories. Narratives situate action in time and place, introduce agents, connect events through mental and physical causal and temporal sequences moving towards a goal or outcome. Complex narratives serve as origins stories, symbolic accounts of the beginning of the earth and its inhabitants, morality tales, religious myths, epics of heroic deeds, and so on. All human cultures have narratives of these kinds that encode shared beliefs, from which they derive coherence and the group cohesiveness that has been both the glory and the bane of human existence throughout its history.

Donald (1991) argued that the primary function served by language for early *Homo sapiens* was narrative. The invention of language, in this view, was the catalyst that made all of human culture the rich tapestry that we have observed over the millennia of history and prehistory. Narratives served for the production of cultural myths that solidified social structures, and provided common ways of understanding and explaining the world. Individuals participate in these myths, and may contribute to them, but their function is primarily communal, not personal. Carrithers (1991) asserted that human societies would not be possible without the aid of narrative, which ties together not only family structures over generations, but importantly marks the generations of political hierarchies, establishing legitimacy of power. In Carrithers' view, human societies themselves would not exist without the glue that narratives make possible.

Thus I am suggesting that a particular form of temporally organised individual memory came to serve a cultural function through shared narratives, producing the mythic structures that have served as the cohesive glue of cultural groups. Personal memories, which had been encapsulated within the individual, became transformed through verbal narratives into cultural memory, incorporating a cultural belief system. An important point to note is that, like language, narrative is assumed to be a group construction, one that turns individual memories into shared conceptual systems. Societal narratives establish an inclusiveness that in turn relies on the common memories of individuals within the society. Whether religious, secular poetic, or historic in form, communal narratives tend to reflect unchanging hierarchical forms of societies, providing information for individuals of their place within the society, whether low or high, and the behaviours (and even thoughts) that are acceptable for those places. Moreover, and this point is critical, to the extent that cultural narratives provide the explanatory structure that defines individual human lives, as is characteristic of most pre-Modern societies, there is little call for individuals to seek self-definitions for their own lives. As a result there is little use for the personal function of autobiographical memory as an explanatory self story.

The thrust of this proposal is that the evolution of temporally organised memory gave rise in human culture to communal narratives that serve an adaptive function, for both the society and for the individual. The temporally organised memory that was originally encapsulated in individuals became functional within the society and thus served individuals in a different more expanded way. The memory burden for the individual is then different; it has more sources outside the person's own experience. At the same time, minor experiential variations may be ignored when life is expected to be the same in an unchanging future world, determined in advance by the communal memory. Whereas temporality and self are important components of autobiographical memory, in the communal narrative time is a salient feature while self remains hidden from view.

An implication of this view of the relation between cultural narratives and individual memory is that the stronger and more coherent a mythic societal foundation, the more integrated the social structure, and the less likely that individual variations of experience will be valued or encouraged. The psychological question then is whether such individual variations will be or can be privately harboured. Can we assume that autobiographical memory is a psychological universal with a universal function?

THE RISE OF INDIVIDUALISM IN NARRATIVE AND MEMORY

Mythically based cultures rest on a world view of the recurrence of the cycles of lives, where the future is expected to repeat the past. In Europe as recently as the 17th century, the world view in the West was of an eternal enduring reality where each individual lifespan was determined in terms of its place within the whole society (Watt, 2001/ 1957). In such frameworks, specific past happenings are of only passing interest if they do not fit the cultural moulds. Art and literature are expressions of the common narratives of the culture, not of specific individual lives. Then, given a strong mythic foundation, individuals within a society have little incentive to compose individualised pasts and project unique individual aspirations for the future.

The last three centuries of European history comprise a period during which changes in economic arrangements, with repercussions on family life, were accompanied by wide-ranging changes in world views, reflected in new forms of philosophy, literature, and art. Specifically, an emerging individualistic perspective permeated the institutions and practices of society. The philosophical individualism of both Descartes and Locke (different as their views might be) can be seen as both reflective of and contributing to this shift in world view. The emergence of individualism was a product of converging societal forces, encouraged by the emphasis on individual responsibility in Puritan and Protestant forms of Christianity. Changing economic arrangements, as the production of goods such as textiles moved out of extended households into commercial businesses located in urban areas, required that individuals establish their own social and economic place, no longer determined solely by the locale and status of one's family. As a result, the traditional extended family structure tended to disintegrate, as children left home to seek their fortunes in the burgeoning cities, where new identities, and new nuclear families were formed. (See Watt 2001/1957 for an excellent summary of these social and cultural shifts.)

The rise of both the novel and biography in the 18th century reflected this emergence of individualistic world views. Both are based on individual life stories and thus depend on real or fictional versions of autobiographical memory. The relation between the individualism of the Modern era and its expression in written forms, particularly the novel and autobiography, has been intensively discussed by scholars of 18th century history and literature. Watt (2001/1957) focused on "the rise of the novel" (in the book of that title) as a product of the social and economic changes taking place in Britain during the 18th century. In characterising the novels of Defoe, Richardson, and Fielding, Watt emphasised a new "realism" that focused on the particularities of the everyday world in the lives of individual characters with distinctive personalities, and on time sequences that mirrored those of the everyday events they reported. This realism contrasted with classic literary forms—classic drama, epic poetry—based on conventional plots and structures. New productions of the classical type, including Shakespeare's, varied the expression but not the plot of their narratives. These literary forms thus reflected a mythic view of cyclical time, presented through summaries of events, omitting detailed descriptions of scenes, which, because of

their familiarity, could be easily re-imagined by the hearers of the standard tales.

Watt (2001/1957) pointed out that the novel was the first wholly written (printed) literary genre. Prior to the 18th century literary forms were basically oral, meant to be read or recited aloud, often in groups. Novels, however, are usually read alone, thereby encouraging the individual reader's identification with its characters, "reliving" the events with them. Other printed forms, emerging at about the same time, included diaries and individualistic autobiographies. These written forms of a person's own life (ongoing or retrospective and reflective) transformed everyday personal episodic memory into a retelling of a life story that was at least sometimes meant to be shared, if not with the world at large, then with a later version of the self.

During the course of the 19th century the novel was also used to illuminate lives from perspectives and contexts beyond the middle (reading) class and the dominant male perspective. In the 19th century women became recorders of their own perspectives on lives as lived, through diaries as well as novels. For example, Jane Austen explored the marriage conventions of the English gentry, and its often deleterious effects on women's lives. Throughout the 19th century women "scribblers" comprised a large proportion of the authors of novels.

The social characteristics that Watt (2001/1957) cited as contributing to the rise of the novel in England in the first place—individualism, economic opportunity—were especially characteristic of American life, where autonomy, personal freedom, and self-reliance were part of the national psyche from the beginning (documented by de Toqueville 1945/1835). Following the example set by Dickens, who shed light on the ravages of rural and urban poverty on children as well as adults in 19th century Britain, American novelists by the end of the 19th century began to focus on the more pernicious aspects of urban life in industrial societies, especially pronounced among the large and growing immigrant populations. Novelists such as Dreiser gave voice to the intractable problems individuals with few resources faced within the capitalist American economy.

Whereas the classic literature of pre-Modern Europe envoiced the common cultural assumptions on which lives were structured, novels emerging in the 18th and 19th centuries as individualistic narratives served a similar communal function through providing descriptions of different possible life patterns. Rather than describing an eternally unchangeable life space, the new individualistic literature described the problems that life circumstances posed for the individual within a community where change and challenge were to be expected. Literature no longer reflected mythic time and a settled world; freedom and change (progress) were shown in their dark as well as light sides. Individuals were thus faced with charting their own futures in the light of their own remembered pasts.

TIME, NARRATIVE, AND MEMORY

Freeman's (1998) discussion of modes of human time attempted to put some of these societal changes in individual psychological perspective. He proposed three distinctive modes of time: mythic, historical, and narrative, where each provides a different perspective on the world. Mythic time is basically cyclical, in that the past is expected to be repeated in the present and future, and individual lives repeat those who came before. Mythic time thus incorporates meaning for both the society and the individual, and tends to pre-empt meaning of the individual life's sojourn. Historical time, in contrast, is scientific and linear, its causal sequences impersonal and determinative; thus historical time lies outside personal time and meaning. In Freeman's account, a shift from mythic to historical time was the notable development of the 18th century. Narrative time, according to this scheme, is eventful and discontinuous, structured and configured with meaning. Freeman sees narrative time as characteristic of the contemporary world, and dates its emergence as a dominant form to the social upheavals of the 19th century.

In Freeman's view narrative time—eventful, discontinuous—is an inherent characteristic of autobiographical memory. This view contrasts with my earlier proposal relating cultural narratives to individual memory, where narrative was seen as a group construction that was adaptable to individual memory functions (e.g., anticipating the future). Brockmeier (2002, p. 9) takes a more integrated view of memory and culture, stating that "there is no principal separation of what traditionally is viewed as individual or personal memory from what traditionally is viewed as social, collective or historical memory. Considering the manifold layers of the cultural fabric that weaves together individual, group and society, the

idea ... of an isolated and autonomous individual becomes meaningless."

Another temporal perspective has been put forth by social psychologists (McGrath & Kelly, 1986), who have pointed out the distinctiveness of experiential or transactional time that orders individual human lives. Transactional time refers to the cultural organisation of daily, seasonal, and societally significant events. It is based on the temporal order of "doing" activities, rather than the temporal order of "telling" about these activities. It brings together the broader cultural configuration of time in action with its individual configuration; transactional time thus organises experiential time in memory as well as in daily living. Transactional time forms the framework of autobiographical memories, which societal-level temporal orders (mythic, historical, or narrative) may each then contribute to or transform (Nelson, 1998).

It is an essential part of Watt's (2001/1957) argument on the rise of the novel that literature and the surrounding social structures and values are connected. The additional point I want to suggest is that they are organically connected, in that during periods of mythic time, the literature that constitutes the communal form of shared memory tends to exclude expressions of the individuality of time and experience; whereas with the breaking through to historic and narrative time, where change is both expected and welcomed, a vacuum of self-determination is created which may be filled with individual life narratives that use the past to project into the future.

Certainly, the temporal experience of events is not the same as narrative time. Time in the novel is very different from transactional or experiential time. Watt (2001/1957) noted that some early novelists, in particular Sterne, attempted to recreate the experience of time in the novel, but the effort inevitably failed. Similarly, personal narratives, derived from autobiographical memories, are imposed on selected experiences for purposes that are individually significant, whether they incorporate cultural meanings or not. This claim differs from Freeman's, as well as that of psychologists like Bruner (1986) who see narrative as an inherent mode of thought, contrasted to the paradigmatic mode. In the present view, in contrast, narrative form is a cultural invention, one that may be adopted by individuals in organising their own autobiographical memories. The further implications of this view are that the extent and effect of individual adoption of a particular cultural narrative form and/or content varies among cultures and historical periods, and that individuals learn the cultural forms in early childhood to greater or lesser degrees of usefulness.

A point that follows from this is that if narratives are imposed on event memories for the telling, providing the coherence and point that are the same for the listener as the teller, the teller may no longer truly "remember" the memory (Mink, 1980). In the distancing necessary to compose the narrative, the teller may find it difficult to participate fully in re-experiencing the past that Tulving claims is a prime criterion for episodic/autobiographic memory. Whereas the meaning for the individual resides in the re-experience, the imposed narrative is a way of establishing shared (not idiosyncratic) meaning. It is not necessary to agree with Mink (1980) that telling destroys the "true" experience of the memory to accept the point that narrativising it is a way of sharing meaning.

THE AUTOBIOGRAPHICAL SELF IN MEMORY AND FICTION

A different perspective is provided by Eakin's (1985) commentary on the fiction of memory, implying a close parallel between the novel and the "reinvention of the self" in autobiography, a reinvention based on the original "invention" of self in that period of early childhood now recognised as the beginning of autobiographical memory, self, and time (Nelson, 1996, 1997, 2001). The "fiction" of memory that Eakin refers to is a product of its reliance on re-construction in context, dependent on differing elicitations and circumstances. In another, cognitive, sense it can be asserted that autobiographical memory is as imaginative as is future projection of the self. Both are based on past experience re-imagined (or re-constructed) to fit the present or future circumstances, although typically we believe memory to be more mimetic with respect to "reality" and future plans to be freer of the constraints of what has already taken place. Nonetheless, these considerations begin to reveal the closeness of the connection between autobiographical memory and fiction, a connection made manifest by overtly autobiographical novelists such as Erica Jong or Philip Roth.

Eakin (1985) cites a number of autobiographers (James, 1956/1983; Kingston, 1977;

Nabokov, 1966) who remark on the emergent realisation of the self through the medium of language at about the age of 4 years. Prior to this age only an implicit self was seen to exist by these writers, whereas the reflective self in relation to others and to temporality—the continuity of self over time—is an explicit linguistic construction, or invention. Eakin (p. 192) states "that the self and language are mutually implicated in a single interdependent system of symbolic behavior." He quotes Benveniste (p. 195): "With the advent of language ... the gradual emergence of the self accelerates. It is not a question of language endowing a hitherto mute self with the capacity for self-expression, but, quite possibly of language constituting the self in its very make-up." It is striking that these quotations mirror the evolving recognition among developmental psychologists of the close connection between language practices and the emergence of autobiographical memory in early childhood, indeed at the specific age span identified by these literary sources (Fivush, 1991; Nelson, 1996).

The most dramatic evidence of the close relation of self and language comes from Helen Keller's famous autobiography (Keller, 1905/1954) in which she relates how at the age of 6 years she awakened to the power of words as her teacher (Annie) finger-spelled the word "water" into her hand while pumping water into it. She relates that following this incident she asked for and learned the "words" for everything in her immediate world, and at once came into a new sense of herself in the world around her, a sense of being a self in relation to others. That she had some inchoate memories from the years prior to this event suggests that personal memory *per se* does not depend on language, but that language has the power to make these memories explicit and to provide a wholly new sense of the self in its context.

The other autobiographers noted by Eakin emphasise that it is the relational aspects of language—the I in relation to the Other and to the continuity of the I in the past, present, and ongoing into the future—that brings out the self in its reflective and reflexive form. These ideas relate well to current psychological theories of the origin of autobiographical memory in early childhood; very similar claims made in commentary on the autobiography genre from a literary perspective are independently made in the contemporary literature on the emergence of autobiographical memory (see Nelson, 2001; Nelson & Fivush,

2000, 2002). In his most recent book Eakin (1999) lays even more stress on the inherent relational aspect of autobiography and its origins in discursive cultural practices, which aligns well with the developmental and cultural research.

AUTOBIOGRAPHICAL MEMORY AND NARRATIVE IN CONTEMPORARY CULTURES

In contemporary Euro-American societies, autobiographical memory emerges somewhere around $3\frac{1}{2}$ years of age, as shown in numerous studies of adult recall of memories from early childhood (Pillemer & White, 1989). Moreover, it is during this period of early childhood that adults typically begin to talk with children about their memories (Nelson & Fivush, 2000). Such adult talk differs in its forms and emphases, some being more elaborative and narrative-like than others (Reese & Fivush, 1993). It has been shown in a number of studies that the ways in which adults talk with their children about the past is correlated with children's later (as much as two years) memory reports in both quantity and completeness (Nelson & Fivush, 2000). Autobiographical memory also differs among people, both in its age of onset, and in the density and quality of the memories from early childhood.

Important to the present account is the fact that differences in onset, quantity, and quality also characterise individuals from different cultures. Contemporary cultural differences in autobiographical memory have been documented in a series of studies (Han, Leichtman, & Wang, 1998; Mullen, 1994; Wang, Leichtman, & Davies, 2000) showing that members of Asian societies (China, Korea, Japan) report fewer autobiographical memories, and have fewer and later memories from early childhood than do Euro-Americans. Leichtman (2001) has reported the most extreme differences among cultures. She and her colleagues studied autobiographical memories of people residing in a rural Indian farming community. Native speakers interviewed adults of both sexes and varying ages about their memories of the past, and especially of their memories of childhood. Almost all the interviewees claimed that they did not remember specific episodes from the past, and further that there was "no point" to doing so. They did report generalities of life in the past, but somewhat reluctantly and in skeletal form. They differed in these respects from urban dwellers from the same area and linguistic group, who were able to provide some specific accounts of past lives, although fewer than would be expected from a Western population.

Leichtman and her colleagues also obtained video tapes of families with young children in their homes, with the aim of analysing references to the past in conversations between adults and children, and found that, as expected, there was little talk about the past, and what there was tended to be about general or "semantic" issues, such as what homework was assigned. These findings strongly suggest, as inferred from the previous research on mother–child memory talk, that in the absence of models who provide guidance in formulating narratives about the personal past, and of societal values that give such narratives meaning, individuals do not compose life stories in the same way that we expect people in Western societies to do. A further interpretation is that the traditional society in which the rural Indian people live provides a strong sense of prescribed life roles in an unchanging world, precluding the value of reproducing individual life experiences in memory accounts.

Given the widely accepted assumptions that autobiographical memory serves both social and self functions, and given the cultural differences in memory found in cross-cultural studies, the question arises: Are these functions served in different ways in different cultures, for example in contemporary Asian societies and in Western ones? It is now accepted that the sense of self and identity differs between these two meta-cultures, with Asian individuals reporting more interpersonal identification and a closer self-identity with family and friends than do Americans, who tend to value autonomy more (Markus & Kitayama, 1991). As implied in the previous sections, the relations between individual memory and communal forms of memory, between narratives of the self, social narratives of others, and communal narratives of all kinds are keys, I believe, to understanding the source and meaning of the social and self functions of autobiographical memory.

To understand contemporary autobiographical memory, then, it is important to situate it in its cultural context, and not solely in the social and individual context of its development. It is necessary therefore to examine the constituents of contemporary American culture that heighten attention on autobiographical memory, and on the possible reasons for this attention. In doing this, however, it is important to keep in mind the multicultural composition of contemporary American society. As Mullen (1994) and Wang and Ross (2001) have documented in a number of studies, cultural differences in autobiographical memory between Chinese-Americans and Euro-Americans are found in the same directions as in comparisons of Euro-Americans with Chinese people in China, although somewhat muted in size. Characteristics of American culture, where the majority of the work on the early development and later characteristics of autobiographical memory have been carried out, are those of the "mainstream" middle-class native-born population. Similar descriptions may apply to other Western or Westernised societies and to other groups within the United States, but differences must also be recognised. There is considerable room for additional exploration of both differences and similarities in the characteristics of autobiographical memory among people of different cultures.

FROM INDIVIDUALISM TO PERSONALISM

It is often claimed that American culture and cultural values have changed little since de Toqueville's observations in the early 19th century. However, technical, economic, and social changes in American life and society over the past century imply otherwise. Given the thesis of this article that individual memory relates to cultural narratives in various ways, the characteristics of contemporary culture that may bear on our understanding of the functions of autobiographical memory bear examination. In particular, changes in these characteristics over the past 50 years have frequently been noted in the general media as well as in professional literature. Classic sociological studies of the 1950s (e.g., Riesman, 1961; Whyte, 1956) pointed out changes from the previous generations of Americans towards a more "other-directed" individual—other-directed not towards traditional family and community members, but toward peers and the institutions (corporations, governments) that related to and controlled their adult lives. Thirty years later Lasch (1979) described the "culture of narcissism" in terms that related the dense interpersonal conditions of modern life to a newly intense focus on self. These writers and others since have shared the conviction that cultural changes, reflected in cultural productions such as

literature and visual media, have had profound influences on the inhabitants of modern urban societies, perhaps especially American. Here I want to speculatively explore some of these influences and their pathways in relation to cultural differences in the functions of autobiographical memory.

In the last half of the 20th century, the child-rearing practices of the adults who grew up during and after World War II changed radically from the previous norms. Partly influenced by "Dr Spock" (Spock, 1946) former emphases on order, routine, and respect for the authority of adults in family, school, church, and community, were replaced by a child-centred emphasis on freedom of expression, flexibility of daily routines, and healthy personality development. Changes in family structure over this period have been dramatic, partly due to the sexual revolution of the 1960s and later. As the majority of women took on lifetime employment in the 1970s, the ways that families organised their households and lives changed. In addition, an unprecedented increase in unmarried parenting in all social classes, as well as of single-parent families has taken place. In comparison with generations who were children prior to the 1950s, the greatest differentiating factor may be the pervasiveness of television, music, video—and for the last 15 years computers—which now dominate so much of the time in children's lives. These changes in the way that people live of course affected the children who have grown up during this period ("baby boomers" and "Generation X", now adults in their 20s to 50s), especially in terms of their expectations of adult life and of their relation to peers and their communities.

Educational institutions, in response to pressures from trends in child-rearing, as well as political and technical change, gradually began to adjust to these changes in far-reaching ways. By the 1960s many schools had abandoned dress codes and adopted more flexible scheduling, "open" classrooms, with revised textbooks and novel curriculums designed to adapt to a multicultural and technically sophisticated population. The "radical" movements of the 1960s for racial equality, women's rights, and associated demands for political and institutional change, resulted in such educational innovations as university curricula individually constructed by each student, coeducational dorm life, and the like.

National mythology and cultural narratives that were formerly purveyed through school, community, and church gradually disappeared from view during the last half of the 20th century. Bible stories had been commonly taught in elementary schools as well as Sunday Schools, along with tales of adventure and war, such as the Knights of the Round Table, fairy tales, and the morality tales that were common in the Readers used for generations in American schools. Today, individual families are responsible for conveying society's histories, myths, and values as they view them, through their own choices of what stories their children hear, what places they visit, what TV, video, and movies they watch, what books they are encouraged to read, and what conversations they engage in. Conservative commentators in response decry the loss of traditional values common to all replaced by a multicultural plurality of values.

A summary view of these recent societal trends might be termed the "personalisation of culture", which may be particularly pervasive in the United States but is not confined to that country. Whereas individualism conveys autonomy within a common society where values are generally shared, personalism conveys "person-defined" needs and values independent of the surrounding society (sometimes changing in response to different social contexts as Gergen, 1994, argues). These generational changes have all been subject to a great deal of commentary and speculation among academics and other professionals as well as journalists. Here the question is how they might bear on the relation of cultural narratives and the self and societal functions of autobiographical memory that has been proposed in the previous sections. If self stories reflect general cultural narratives, whether purveyed in myths, novels, or in contemporary forms such as movies and television, there should be observable changes in the content, form, or function of autobiographical memory over this period. How to track such changes is the problem, and here I can only suggest some possible directions.

In contrast to the previous period of conformity to accepted models (whether derived from novels, movies, or religious tracts), everyone now must have a personal story to tell, beginning in preschool, and everyone's story must emphasise his or her unique individuality. Common culture consists, not of common knowledge of political and social affairs and expectations of personal responsibility, but of common recognition of personalities from different quarters of society, whether sports, politics, movies, music, or fashion.

Filling these needs is an increasing number of personal memoirs, biographies, and autobiographies, as well as magazine "profiles" of famous and not-so-famous people, an art form perfected in recent years. Newspapers place a "feature story hook" on the majority of news reports, beginning with a personal account of some person or family before launching into the facts of what the news is about. Even more, television news focuses much of its attention on individual stories designed to illustrate general points.

Schools have substituted a new kind of inclusiveness for the old common culture through a practice of self-expression, beginning in preschools and the early elementary years with "sharing time" or "show and tell". Prior to the institution of these traditions sometime in the post-World War II period, group activities were organised around learning projects, not individual expression. Family activities, trips, pets, and other personal experiences were not part of the school curriculum, and were not expected to be brought into the classroom. Mary's "little lamb" was a cautionary tale, not a model to be followed.

Recent developmental research on memory has focused on the ways in which parents encourage their children to engage in talk about remembered episodes (Fivush, 1991; Nelson & Fivush, 2000), concluding that children learn the narrative ways of formulating their stories about themselves, to contribute to the discourse, and to build up autobiographical memory. In the present social context where personal histories have become very important, both school and parent practices of this kind can be viewed as apprenticeship to personhood. Further, the self function and the social function of the self story converge. It is important to imagine one's past and future for one's own self-image and concept; at the same time, it is important to learn to tell the narrative in ways that interest the listener as well as the teller.

Autobiographical memory in contemporary America is thus revealed as particularly important because, in the light of the vanishing of mythic or fictional models that instruct individuals how they are to live their lives, lives must be individually composed. The individual construction of a life plan depends on the conscious continuity and integration of the self through time and with society. When there is no historical line to continue, to fill in, or to take one's place in, but rather a unique personal line to be filled, autobiographical memory must serve as a source of direction and personal strength. However, one must not only have a life, but also present it effectively to other people. Thus, the personalisation of American culture in addition means that acquiring narrative skill is important for the telling of one's unique story. These observations suggest the reasons that parents, preschools, and kindergartens might put special emphasis on encouraging children to become good at telling about their past. The hypothesis here is that this practice may be a particular manifestation of the focus on the personal that is so much a part of contemporary culture. This possibility is supported by the cross-cultural research that has revealed significant differences in the timing and quality of autobiographical memories among different national groups, consistent with attributions of different self and identity concepts in the different groups, as well as differences in parental practices of encouraging talk about the self in the past.

What is implied here is that what we are studying today in developmental research on autobiographical memory is at least partly the result of recent societal changes, and that autobiographical memory may serve more important functions to members of this culture than in any previous society. Because establishing a unique and autonomous self is more important than ever before to taking one's place in this society, autobiographical memory is more important to the individual in both its social and personal functions. It expresses the self to others and establishes peer relations, at the same time that it provides ballast for maintaining identity within a somewhat fractured community, where in the eyes of some observers (e.g., Gergen, 1994) there is no single self but rather many selves to be displayed on different occasions.

This is not to deny that children in general must be initiated into the practices of narrativising memory through experience with this as a discourse practice. Eakin's (1985) review of the autobiographies of Nabokov, Kingston, and others, has emphasised their accounts of the invention of the self through language in early childhood. But these authors did not depend on the intensive tutoring that some of our children are given. Indeed, in Kingston's case, as Eakin relates, as a female child in China she was strongly discouraged from telling stories of herself. However, she was exposed to narratives and family histories in tales told by her mother—and presumably exposure to such narratives may be sufficient for many or most children to construct

their own self-narratives. Leichtman's (2001) report of a culture in which memory narratives are downplayed and people deny interest in their past suggests the importance of the link between accessible narratives in the culture and composing narratives of the self. What is different today it seems, is not that children are learning the narrative form of autobiographical memory, but that they are being overtly encouraged both at home and in school to do so. The autobiographical tales have taken on a social significance that gives them a special resonance and importance to the child as well as the adult.

There are two important parts to this conclusion about the function of autobiographical memory and its relation to cultural narratives in the contemporary world. One is that the vanishing of common communal narratives, replaced with a cacophony of personal stories, makes it necessary for individuals to each add their own unique self story. The other is the necessity in today's world of perfecting the skill of the telling of one's personal story. I have argued that we can understand the relation of the personal and the cultural in the context of the different ways that stories of self and society have served similar self and social functions throughout human history, with a balance between the roles of individual and society shifting over time.

REFERENCES

Benveniste, E. (1971). *Problems in general linguistics*. Coral Gables: University of Miami Press. [Quoted in Eakin (1985) p. 195.]

Brockmeier, J. (2002). Introduction: Searching for cultural memory. [Special Issue on Narrative and Cultural Memory.] *Culture and Psychology, 8,* 5–14.

Bruner, J.S. (1986). *Actual minds, possible worlds*. Cambridge MA: Harvard University Press.

Carrithers, M. (1991). Narrativity: Mindreading and making societies. In A. Whiten (Ed.), *Natural theories of mind: Evolution, development and simulation of everyday mindreading* (pp. 305–318). Oxford: Basil Blackwell.

Damasio, A. (1999). *The feeling of what happens: Body and emotion in the making of consciousness*. New York: Harcourt, Inc.

de Tocqueville, A. (1945/1835). *Democracy in America*. New York: Vintage Books.

Donald, M. (1991). *Origins of the modern mind*. Cambridge MA: Harvard University Press.

Eakin, P.J. (1985). *Fictions in autobiography: Studies in the art of self-invention*. Princeton, NJ: Princeton University Press.

Eakin, P.J. (1999). *How our lives become stories: Making selves*. Ithaca, NY: Cornell University Press.

Fivush, R. (1991). The social construction of personal narratives. *Merrill-Palmer Quarterly*, *37*, 59–82.

Fivush, R., & Hamond, N.R. (1990). Autobiographical memory across the preschool years: Toward reconceptualizing childhood amnesia. In R. Fivush & J.A. Hudson (Eds.), *Knowing and remembering in young children* (pp. 223–248). New York: Cambridge University Press.

Freeman, M. (1998). Mythical time, historical time, and the narrative fabric of the self. *Narrative Inquiry*, *8*, 37–50.

Gergen, K.J. (1994). Mind, text, and society: Self-memory in social context. In U. Neisser & R. Fivush (Eds.), *The remembering self: Construction and accuracy in the self-narrative* (p. 78–104). New York: Cambridge University Press.

Han, J.J., Leichtman, M.D., & Wang, Q. (1998). Autobiographical memory in Korean, Chinese, and American children. *Developmental Psychology*, *34*, 701–713.

Hudson, J., & Nelson, K. (1986). Repeated encounters of a similar kind: Effects of familiarity on children's autobiographical memory. *Cognitive Development*, *1*, 253–271.

James, H. (1956/1983). *Henry James: Autobiography*. Princeton, NJ: Princeton University Press.

Keller, H. (1905/1954). *The story of my life*. New York: Doubleday.

Kingston, M.H. (1977). *The woman warrior: Memoirs of a girlhood among ghosts*. New York: Random House.

Lasch, C. (1979). *The culture of narcissism: American life in an age of diminishing expectations*. New York: W.W. Norton.

Leichtman, M.D. (2001). *Preschooler's memory environments and adults' recollections in India and the US*. Paper presented in the Symposium on Culture and Memory, Valencia, Spain: Third International Memory Conference.

Linton, M. (1982). Transformations of memory in everyday life. In U. Neisser (Ed.), *Memory observed: Remembering in natural contexts*. San Francisco: Freeman.

Markus, H., & Kitayama, S. (1991). Culture and the self: Implications for cognition, emotion, and motivation. *Psychological Review*, *98*, 224–253.

McGrath, J.E., & Kelly, J.R. (1986). *Time and human interaction: Toward a social psychology of time*. New York: Guilford Press.

Mink, L.O. (1980). Everyman his or her own annalist. In W.J.T. Mitchell (Ed.), *On narrative* (pp. 233–239). Chicago: The University of Chicago Press.

Moore, C., & Lemmon, K. (Eds.). (2001). *The self in time: Developmental perspectives*. Mahwah, NJ: Lawrence Erlbaum Associates Inc.

Mullen, M.K. (1994). Earliest recollections of childhood: A demographic analysis. *Cognition*, *52*, 55–79.

Nabokov, V. (1966). *Speak memory: An autobiography revisited*. New York: Putnam's.

Neisser, U. (1997). The roots of self knowledge: Perceiving self, it, and thou. In J.G. Snodgrass & R.L. Thompson (Eds.), *The self across psychology* (pp. 19–34). New York: New York Academy of Science.

Nelson, K. (1989). Monologue as the linguistic construction of self in time. In K. Nelson (Ed.), *Narratives from the crib* (pp. 284–308). Cambridge MA: Harvard University Press.

Nelson, K. (1993a). Explaining the emergence of autobiographical memory in early childhood. In A. Collins, M. Conway, S. Gathercole, & P. Morris (Eds.), *Theories of memory*. Hove, UK: Lawrence Erlbaum Associates Ltd.

Nelson, K. (1993b). The psychological and social origins of autobiographical memory. *Psychological Science*, *4*, 1–8.

Nelson, K. (1996). *Language in cognitive development: The emergence of the mediated mind*. New York: Cambridge University Press.

Nelson, K. (1997). Finding oneself in time. In J.G. Snodgrass & R. Thompson (Eds.), *The self across psychology. Annals of the New York Academy of Sciences*. New York: New York Academy of Sciences.

Nelson, K. (1998). Meaning in memory. Commentary on M. Freeman's "Mythical time, historical time, and the narrative fabric of the self". *Narrative Inquiry*, *8*, 409–419.

Nelson, K. (2001). Language and the self: From the "experiencing I" to the "continuing me". In C. Moore & K. Lemmon (Eds.), *The self in time: developmental perspectives* (pp. 15–35). Hillsdale, NJ: Lawrence Erlbaum Associates Inc.

Nelson, K., & Fivush, R. (2000). Socialization of memory. In E. Tulving & F. Craik (Eds.), *Handbook of memory*. New York: Oxford University Press.

Nelson, K., & Fivush, R. (in press). *Emergence of autobiographical memory: The social developmental theory*. Manuscript in preparation.

Pillemer, D.B., & White, S.H. (1989). Childhood events recalled by children and adults. In H.W. Reese (Ed.), *Advances in child development and behavior* (Vol. 21, pp. 297–340). New York: Academic Press.

Plotkin, H.C. (1988). An evolutionary epistemological approach to the evolution of intelligence. In H.J. Jerison & I. Jerison (Eds.), *Intelligence and evolutionary biology* (pp. 73–91). New York: Springer-Verlag.

Reese, E., & Fivush, R. (1993). Parental styles of talking about the past. *Developmental Psychology*, *29*, 596–606.

Riesman, D. (1961). *The lonely crowd: A study of the changing American character*. New Haven, CT: Yale University Press.

Schafer, R. (1980). Narration in the psychoanalytic dialogue. In W.J.T. Mitchell (Ed.), *On narrative* (pp. 15–49). Chicago: University of Chicago Press.

Spock, B. (1946). *Baby and child care*. New York: Pocket Books.

Tulving, E. (1983). *Elements of episodic memory*. New York: Oxford University Press.

Tulving, E., & Lepage, M. (2000). Where in the brain is the awareness of one's past? In D.L. Schachter & E. Scarry (Eds.), *Memory, brain, and belief* (pp. 208–228). Cambridge, MA: Harvard University Press.

Wang, Q., Leichtman, M.D., & Davies, K. (2000). Sharing memories and telling stories: American and Chinese mothers and their 3-year-olds. *Memory, 8,* 159–177.

Wang, Q. & Ross, M. (2001*). Memory representation vs memory narrative: The role of culture in remembering*. Paper presented at the International Conference on Memory, Valencia, Spain, July.

Watt, I. (2001/1957). *The rise of the novel: Studies in Defoe, Richardson and Fielding*. Berkeley, CA: University of California Press.

Whyte, W.H.Jr. (1956). *The organization man*. New York: Simon & Schuster.

MEMORY, 2003, *11* (2), 137–149

The identity function of autobiographical memory: Time is on our side

Anne E. Wilson

Psychology Department, Wilfrid Laurier University, Waterloo, ON, N2L 3C5 Canada.

Michael Ross

University of Waterloo, Canada

Autobiographical memory plays an important role in the construction of personal identity. We review evidence of the bi-directional link between memory and identity. Individuals' current self-views, beliefs, and goals influence their recollections and appraisals of former selves. In turn, people's current self-views are influenced by *what* they remember about their personal past, as well as *how* they recall earlier selves and episodes. People's reconstructed evaluations of memories, their perceived distance from past experiences, and the point of view of their recollections have implications for how the past affects the present. We focus on how people's constructions of themselves through time serve the function of creating a coherent—and largely favourable—view of their present selves and circumstances.

"We are what we eat" is a currently popular mantra. More interested in cognition than nutrition, psychologists are likely to assert, "We are what we remember" (Albert, 1977; Conway & Pleydell-Pearce, 2000; James, 1890/1950). Noting the dependence of self-identity on auto-biographical memory, William James (1890/1950) remarked that were an individual to awake one morning with all personal memories erased, he or she would essentially be a different person. Along the same lines, Schacter (1996) described a head-injury patient who lost his autobiographical memories and, as a result, his associated sense of self. Logically, autobiographical memory plays an indirect role in even the social sources of self-knowledge (e.g., reflected appraisals, social comparisons; Sedikides & Skowronski, 1995), because much of this knowledge may be stored in other people's memories of interactions with self. In the current paper we examine the links between autobiographical memory and self-identity. It may be a truism to say that self-identity depends on

autobiographical memory, but the nature and strength of the association depends on qualities of both the self-identity and the memories. Moreover the relation is reciprocal: People's recollections influence their self-views and vice versa (Figure 1). We describe motives and cognitive processes that connect self-identity to auto-biographical memory. We begin by considering the influence of current self-views and beliefs on people's reconstructions of the past. We then describe how people's motives and cognitive processes affect their reactions to their pasts, as well as the impact of their recalled pasts on current self-views.

CURRENT SELF-VIEWS INFLUENCE AUTOBIOGRAPHICAL MEMORY

The current self—with its associated characteristics, goals, and beliefs—influences how individuals recall their pasts (Bartlett, 1932; Fischhoff &

Requests for reprints should be sent to Anne E. Wilson, Psychology Department, Wilfrid Laurier University, Waterloo, ON, N2L 3C5 Canada.

 DOI:10.1080/09658210244000324

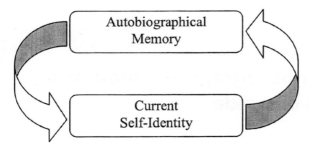

Figure 1. Bi-directional relation between autobiographical memory and current identity.

Beyth, 1975; Greenwald, 1980; Mead, 1929/64; Ross, 1989; Ross & Buehler, 1994; Singer & Salovey, 1993). Ross (1989) focused on how people reconstruct their earlier attributes and feelings. He reasoned that such recollections often involve a two-step process. Because present attributes and feelings are frequently more accessible than past ones, individuals start with current self-appraisals, such as "How do I feel about 'X' today." Next, people invoke implicit theories about the stability of their own attributes and feelings to construct a past that is similar to or different from the present. Ross (1989) reviewed a large number of studies that provided support for this analysis. For example, several researchers obtained evidence that people reconstruct their past attitude on an issue by first considering their present opinion and then evaluating whether or not they had reason to suppose that their views had shifted over time. People tend to assume that their attitudes are stable and therefore infer (sometimes incorrectly) that their prior attitudes are similar to their present views.

According to the implicit theories approach, people who believe that their attributes are stable will tend to construct a past consistent with this belief. By the same token, people who expect change (progress or decline) on a dimension will revise the past upward or downward accordingly. Conway and Ross (1984) studied participants in a study skills programme. Participants believe in the efficacy of such courses, but like most similar skills programmes Conway and Ross's was ineffective. Participants evaluated their study skills before and after participating in the skills programme. Conway and Ross reasoned that participants could maintain their belief in the value of an ineffective treatment by retrospectively amplifying their deficiencies prior to the programme. In essence participants could say to themselves: "I

may not be perfect now but I was much worse before taking the course."

At the conclusion of the study skills course, Conway and Ross asked participants to recall their pre-programme evaluations of their study skills. They were told to recall their ratings as accurately as possible and were reminded that the researcher had their prior evaluations. Course participants remembered their ratings as being worse than they had reported initially. In contrast, waiting-list control participants who did not take the course showed no systematic recall bias over the same time period. The biased recollections of individuals who took the course would support a belief that the programme improved their skills. Other research has demonstrated that when people possess a theory of decline (e.g., memory in older adults), they may retrospectively revise the past upwards, recalling themselves as better than they likely had been (e.g., McFarland, Ross, & Giltrow, 1992).

Although Ross (1989) reported research showing exaggeration of both consistency and change, the former tendency seemed much more common. Ross noted developmental evidence suggesting that people's attributes are quite stable and concluded that perhaps people simply over-generalise an often valid theory of consistency. Alternatively, consistency biases may be common because people are motivated to seek evidence from the past that implies a constant self-identity through time. James (1890/1950) claimed that a sense of personal identity requires that one perceive one's self as continuous through time. Albert (1977) concurred and suggested further that people are motivated to establish a consistent self-identity through time. According to Albert, this consistency motivation has implications for memory: People are inclined to recall pasts that are consonant with their current self-views. In other words, autobiographical memory may serve an identity function by enhancing individuals' feelings of personal consistency through time.

Our recent research indicates, however, that people do not always appear to value personal consistency; instead they often highlight shifts in their identities over time. The tendency to exaggerate personal change seems to be more widespread than Ross (1989) supposed. We next examine the role of autobiographical memory in people's perceptions of a particular kind of change in themselves, a tendency to perceive improvement over time.

THE SELF-ENHANCEMENT FUNCTION OF AUTOBIOGRAPHICAL MEMORY

In his autobiography, Arthur Koestler (1961) remarked that people are critical of their past selves: "The gauche adolescent, the foolish young man that one has been, appears so grotesque in retrospect and so detached from one's own identity that one automatically treats him with amused derision. It is a callous betrayal, yet one cannot help being a traitor to one's past" (p. 96). Our own research findings support Koestler's observation. Across various samples (e.g., university students, middle-aged individuals, celebrity interviews) and on a variety of dimensions, people reported their past selves to be inferior to their present self (Wilson & Ross, 2000, 2001a). Karney and his associates found a similar pattern in people's retrospective evaluations of their marriages (Karney & Coombs, 2000; Karney & Frye, 2002). Although marital satisfaction tends to decrease over the early years of a marriage, spouses underestimated their past contentment and often recalled it as lower than their present satisfaction. By deprecating their former satisfaction levels, individuals create the illusion of improvement even in the face of actual decline.

One explanation of such findings is that people are not actually traitors to their past selves, but merely impartial observers of former selves. Perhaps people see a past self as it really was, and view their present self too favourably. Along these lines, George Orwell (1946) recommended judging the truth of an autobiography by its unflattering content: "Autobiography is only to be trusted when it reveals something disgraceful. A man who gives a good account of himself is probably lying, since any life when viewed from the inside is simply a series of defeats" (p. 170). Karney and Frye (2002) offered a similar interpretation of their data on marital satisfaction. They suggested that spouses' retrospective evaluations of earlier stages of their marriage are more valid than their current assessments.

Social psychologists have provided considerable evidence that people in Western cultures are motivated to view their current self favourably (Baumeister, 1998; Higgins, 1996; Sedikides, 1993). It seems reasonable to suppose that people are motivated to enhance current and recent former selves, because those selves and their associated outcomes "belong to" people's present identity. In contrast, individuals may regard more psychologically remote former selves as no longer associated with their current identity—distant failures lose their power to taint and glories to flatter the present self. As a result, people can view distant selves more dispassionately, heaping scorn when it is due.

Indeed, people might think of past selves as akin to other individuals who vary in closeness to their current self. Recent selves may be comparable to intimate others and distant selves to mere acquaintances or even strangers. People tend to be blind to the faults of their intimates (Murray, Holmes, Dolderman, & Griffin, 2000), but judge distant acquaintances and strangers more severely (e.g., Taylor & Koivumaki, 1976).

Of course, criticism of others is not always valid. For example, people sometimes unfairly derogate others to enhance their own accomplishments (e.g., Tesser, 1988; Wills, 1981). Similarly, a tendency to disparage earlier selves may reflect concerns for self-enhancement rather than accuracy (Ross & Wilson, 2000; Wilson & Ross, 2001a). We suggest that people appraise the past in ways that allow them to view their current self favourably. Although dissociated from people's current self, psychologically distant selves may still serve an identity function. Conceivably, people systematically devalue their distant former selves to create the illusion that they (or their relationships) have improved over time. People find an improving trajectory to be particularly attractive and gratifying (Carver & Sheier, 1990; Frijda, 1988; Hsee, Abelson, & Salovey, 1991; Loewenstein & Prelec, 1993; Loewenstein & Thaler, 1989), partly because they adapt to their current states and so even consistently favourable circumstances become less satisfying over time (Brickman, Coates, & Janoff-Bulman, 1978). Indeed, Brickman and Campbell (1971) suggested that "perhaps the happiest adult is one who had a moderately unhappy childhood" (p. 293), because current state can best be appreciated in contrast with an inferior past. We suggest that it can be just as effective to *recall* a past as inferior, whether or not it actually was.

Examining prospective and retrospective trajectories of newlyweds' relationship satisfaction, Karney and Frye (2002) showed that the perception of improvement is linked to other indicants of relationship success. Spouses' retrospective reports of increases in relationship satisfaction predicted optimism about the relationship's future, even after controlling for any actual change in satisfaction. In contrast, absolute levels of relationship satisfaction were unrelated to expectations. By derogating earlier aspects of themselves and their relationships, people can make their current state seem superior by comparison and foster optimism about the future.

By examining conditions in which self-enhancement goals may be particularly strong, we obtained more direct evidence that disparaging the past benefits the present self (Wilson & Ross, 2000; studies 4 & 5). We manipulated people's objectives while they described themselves, encouraging participants to adopt the goal of either evaluating themselves favourably or accurately. Participants with a self-enhancement goal were more likely to include an inferior past self in their self-description than were participants with an accuracy goal. Self-enhancement motives also tend to be exacerbated by a threat to self-regard (e.g., Wills, 1981; Wood & Taylor, 1991). McFarland and Alvaro (2000) asked individuals who had experienced a personally disturbing or traumatic past event to evaluate what they were like prior to the episode. Some participants were reminded of the disturbing episode before completing the evaluation and others were not reminded. Participants who were reminded provided inferior evaluations of their earlier, pre-trauma selves. In addition, people were more critical of former selves after being reminded of severely rather than mildly disturbing experiences. This reconstruction of the past may protect current identity: By focusing on how a personally distressing event led to growth or positive outcomes for the self, individuals may minimise the negative impact of the trauma.

Can people maintain a consistent identity (Albert, 1977; James, 1890/1950; Swann & Read, 1981; Swann, Stein-Seroussi, & Giesler, 1992) while still perceiving improvement? Some researchers have argued that change over time represents a threat to self-consistency, even though it is emotionally gratifying (Keyes & Ryff, 2000). On the contrary, we propose that people can forge a personal narrative that explains and justifies change. Such narratives allow individuals to view themselves as the same person, despite change and improvement (Gergen & Gergen, 1988).

Although individuals can satisfy a desire for self-enhancement by derogating their past, they could perhaps achieve the same end by continually inflating their assessments of present self. There may be psychological advantages, however, to manipulating the past rather than the present. If people continually boosted their current selves rather than criticising their earlier selves, their present self-regard might become so inflated as to be highly inconsistent with objective indicators and difficult to maintain (Baumeister, 1989). Moreover, there are advantages to having a relatively accurate appraisal of one's present attributes. When confronted with a puddle it is useful to know how far one can jump. By derogating the past, individuals are able to create an illusion of improvement without greatly misrepresenting their present strengths and weaknesses.

APPRAISING SUBJECTIVELY RECENT VERSUS DISTANT FORMER SELVES

We have proposed that people are more inclined to criticise distant than close former selves. In our research we have operationalised closeness in terms of both actual and subjective time. As actual time increases, people become more critical of earlier selves. For example, in one study middle-aged participants (M age = 50 years) evaluated their present selves and retrospectively appraised their former selves at ages 35, 19, and 16 on a host of attributes (Wilson & Ross, 2001a). Theoretically, however, we have proposed that evaluations of former selves depend more on the subjective experience of temporal distance than on the actual passage of time. Subjective distance is often related to clock or calendar time: Yesterday typically feels closer than last month or last year. However, psychologists have long recognised that the subjective experience of time is affected by a variety of factors and is sometimes independent of actual time (e.g., Block, 1989; Brown, Rips, & Shevell, 1985; James, 1890/1950; Ross & Wilson, 2002). In our theory of temporal self-appraisal (Ross & Wilson, 2000, 2002; Wilson & Ross, 2001a), we reasoned that when people *feel* close to a past self, its successes and failures psychologically belong to the present, regardless of their actual temporal distance. To test this idea, we manipulated "apparent time" while holding actual time constant. In one study (Wilson & Ross, 2001a), university students evaluated their current self and a self of 2 months ago. In the psychologically close condition, participants were asked to "think of a point in time *in the recent past, the beginning of this term*. What were you like then?" In the psychologically distant condition, participants were instructed to "*Think all the way back to the beginning of this term*. What were you like way back then?" Even though participants were considering the identical time period, this subjective distance manipulation affected their recall of former selves. Those who were induced to regard the time period as recent recalled their former selves as being just as impressive as they were in the present, whereas those who were encouraged to see the same period as distant were significantly more critical of their former than of their current self. Additionally, we reasoned that if criticism and praise are motivated by self-enhancement concerns, then the effects of subjective distance should be strongest when participants evaluate personally significant attributes. Presumably, important dimensions have the greatest impact on overall self-regard (e.g., Crocker & Wolfe, 2001). As predicted, participants were particularly likely to praise psychologically recent and criticise distant former selves when appraising the dimension they had nominated as most important to them. The effect of temporal distance on the appraisal of past and present selves disappeared when participants evaluated themselves on their least important attribute.

FEELINGS OF SUBJECTIVE DISTANCE: PUSHING THE PAST AWAY AND PULLING IT FORWARD

In addition to influencing *what* people remember about their former selves, self-enhancement goals can affect people's subjective judgements of *when* episodes occurred. To this point we have discussed subjective distance as an independent variable: Variations in subjective distance alter appraisals of a past self or episode. In addition, subjective distance can operate as a dependent variable. Although our reconstruction of dates and times can function to organise our autobiographical memory into a chronological sequence (e.g., Thompson, Skowronski, Larsen, & Betz, 1996), our subjective experience of time does not always correspond to clock or calendar time (e.g., Ross & Wilson, 2002). We hypothesised (Ross & Wilson, 2000, 2002) that differences in the evaluative implications of past episodes affect people's feelings of the subjective distance of those events. To protect their current self-regard, people are motivated to feel farther from past failings than from achievements, even when calendar time does not differ.

For example, suppose that a woman suffers a blow to her self-esteem by performing poorly on a

job interview. She could perhaps restore her self-regard by erasing her interview from memory, but such forgetting may not be possible. The human brain is not a computer disk from which material can be erased by the tap of a key. Assume instead that our job applicant is able to distance the interview, to feel far away from it. By distancing the interview, the interviewer can render it less relevant to her current self. The poor performance belongs to an earlier and conceivably less able self. Although regarding a negative episode as distant is not the same as forgetting it, the psychological consequences may be comparable. Distancing helps individuals to put their undesirable behaviour behind them. The behaviour belongs to an "old me".

A double-edged sword, feelings of subjective distance have implications for the impact on the current self of past achievements as well as failures. As a prior success fades into the distance, its value to the current self diminishes. The achievement belongs to an earlier self. In temporal self-appraisal theory, we hypothesised that individuals can mitigate the effects of time by continuing to feel close to an episode. If an outcome feels recent, the current self can continue to claim credit for it.

Although the hypothesised asymmetry in feelings of distance could include divergent estimates of calendar time, this need not be the case. In our research, we control for actual time and examine feelings of subjective distance for past episodes that could have negative or positive implications for the current self. In one study (Ross & Wilson, 2002), we randomly assigned participants to remember the course in the previous semester in which they received either their best or worst grade. After reporting their grade, participants indicated how distant they felt from the target course on a scale with end-points labelled, "feels like yesterday" and "feels far away". The results, shown in Figure 2, evidence the predicted asymmetry: Participants felt farther from a course in which they obtained a relatively low grade, even though the actual passage of time did not differ in the two conditions. In subsequent research, we found that this asymmetry reveals both a tendency to pull favourable outcomes forward in subjective time and push inauspicious outcomes backward (Ross & Wilson, 2002), although the latter effect may be somewhat stronger. We also found that the asymmetry was obtained for personal outcomes, but not for outcomes of acquaintances. This self–other difference points to the functional

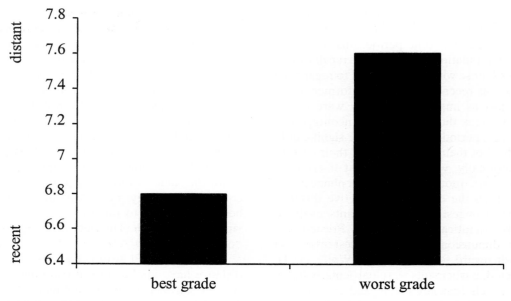

Figure 2.   Subjective distance of good and bad past grades, controlling for calendar time. Higher numbers indicate greater subjective distance, controlling for actual time. Calendar time since last academic term did not differ by grade condition.

significance of feelings of subjective distance. The asymmetry reflects a motivation to protect one's own self-regard; there exists no corresponding inclination to alter the distance of others' experiences. Arguably, shifting the subjective distance of personal events can satisfy self-enhancement goals without necessarily distorting the date or other pertinent facts about the episode.

AUTOBIOGRAPHICAL MEMORIES INFLUENCE CURRENT SELF-VIEWS

We have reviewed evidence that people's memories of their personal pasts (both *what* and *when*) are malleable and may be influenced by current self-identity and self-motives. Next, we examine the other side of the bi-directional relation between autobiographical memory and self-identity. Do people's memory revisions and distancing manoeuvres actually alter the effect of remembered outcomes on current self-regard? We tested this question directly in several studies by experimentally varying people's feelings of distance from past outcomes that differed in valence (Wilson, 2000; Wilson & Ross, 2001b). We varied subjective distance by changing representations of the *spatial* distance between two points on a time line. University students were presented with a time line that spanned many years (e.g., Birth to Today) or only the fairly

recent past (e.g., Age 16 to Today). They were instructed to locate and mark a "target" event (e.g., a good or bad past outcome in high school) on the time line. As Figure 3 illustrates, people would be induced to place a target event (in this case, their last semester of high school) much closer to "today" when the time line spanned many years than when it only included the past few years. Moreover, this manipulation altered people's reports of subjective distance from the target event: They felt psychologically closer to the events that were spatially closer to the present. Next, we assessed the impact of feeling close to or far from past episodes on participants' current evaluations. Respondents who were induced to feel close to former failures evaluated their current self less favourably than those who were persuaded to feel distant from the same failures. In contrast, participants encouraged to feel close to earlier successes appraised their current self more favourably than those who were persuaded to see the same successes as more remote.

In these experiments, the actual temporal distance of past events did not differ by condition and we controlled for actual distance in the statistical analyses. Although one might expect an equivalent pattern of results if the events differed in actual as well as subjective time (e.g., Suh, Diener, & Fujita, 1996), our studies demonstrate that subjective distance alone can moderate the impact of remembered outcomes on current self-regard.

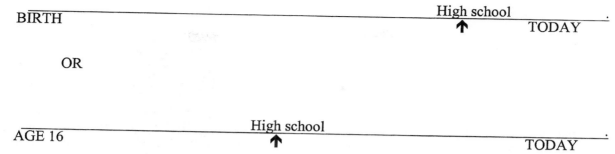

Figure 3. Time line manipulation of spatial distance. The Birth to Today time line makes high school seem subjectively more recent than the Age 16 to Today time line.

The remembered past affects people's current views of themselves, but *how* they remember matters as much as *what* they remember. The same event has a different impact, depending on whether it feels near or far.

In the course of everyday life, individuals are unlikely to encounter "time lines" that alter their experience of temporal distance. We argue, however, that there are many real-life experiences that affect feelings of subjective distance from past episodes. For example, transitions such as changing jobs, cities, or romantic partners may cause the pre-transition self to seem especially remote. In one study, Wilson and Ross (1998) asked students who had moved away from their family home to attend university to indicate how distant they felt from their 17-year-old (pre-transition) self. Half of the students were reminded of their move (by answering questions about it) whereas the remaining participants were not reminded. Students who were reminded of the move reported feeling significantly more distant from their high-school self than did the participants who were not reminded. Milestones such as birthdays, religious conversions, marriages, and even physical or material changes (e.g., getting a new haircut or car) might represent transitions to some individuals, and serve to distance earlier selves. Similarly, severely disturbing personal events may act as transitions that increase feelings of remoteness from prior selves. Feelings of temporal distance could thus contribute to the derogation of pre-trauma selves evidenced in the McFarland and Alvaro (2000) study.

Personal experiences may cause the past to feel close as well as distant. For example, revisiting a childhood haunt or attending a school reunion may pull ancient history back into the psychological present in much the same way as tasting the madeleine did for Proust (1934). Such enhanced feelings of closeness should make happy memories even more pleasurable and distressing events more disturbing.

In temporal self-appraisal theory, we focus on the self-esteem maintenance function of autobiographical memory, highlighting how people tend spontaneously to regard negative outcomes as more distant than positive episodes. People differ in the motivation to self-enhance, however, and variations in motivation should predict feelings of subjective distance. Individuals with high self-esteem are more inclined to engage in cognitive strategies that serve to maintain or enhance self-regard than are individuals with lower self-esteem (Ross & Wilson, 2002). Not surprisingly, then, people with high self-esteem are more likely than their low self-esteem counterparts to distance unflattering events and to feel close to praiseworthy episodes (Ross & Wilson, 2002). There may also be occasions, either due to individual differences or to the nature of an event, when individuals cannot help but feel psychologically close to threatening past experiences. Holman and Silver (1998) described how some people appear to become "stuck in the past", unable to put earlier traumas behind them. Similarly, Pillemer, Desrochers, and Ebanks (1998) reported that narrators sometimes spontaneously switch to the present tense when describing emotionally intense past incidents, perhaps "reliving" these earlier events whether they want to or not.

THE PSYCHOLOGICAL IMPORTANCE OF POINT OF VIEW

Nigro and Neisser (1983) reported that individuals visually recall memories from either a first-person or a third-person perspective. When adopting a first-person perspective, people perceive memories through their own eyes. When assuming a third-person perspective, individuals view their memories from the vantage point of an observer. The fundamental attribute of a third-person memory is that individuals can see themselves in the recollection.

Like subjective distance, point of view is a variable that relates to *how* people remember, rather than *what* they remember. Moreover, like subjective distance, point of view is associated with both actual temporal distance and the self-concept. Nigro and Neisser found that third-person memories tended to be older and less vivid than first-person memories. They also reported that memory perspective is malleable: participants were more likely to recall an episode from a first-person perspective when asked to focus on the *emotions* associated with an event rather than its *objective circumstances*. In an intriguing set of studies, Libby and Eibach (2002, Libby, Eibach, & Gilovich, 2002) recently related the visual perspective of autobiographical memories to the self-concept. Individuals were more likely to invoke a first-person perspective when recalling actions consistent with their current self-concept. For example, participants who were induced to feel religious (by means of a biased questionnaire) were highly likely to recall a religious memory from a first-person perspective. Participants who were encouraged to feel irreligious were significantly more likely to report that they viewed a religious memory from a third-person perspective (Libby & Eibach, 2002). In another study (Libby et al., 2002), participants were randomly assigned to recall the same episode from either a first-person or a third-person perspective. Participants who invoked a third-person perspective reported that they had changed more since the time of the episode. A third-person perspective seems to operate as a distancing mechanism, leading individuals to perceive that a past self is a different person from the current self.

Point of view can refer more generally to the degree to which individuals personalise a memory. People can think of a remembered event as occurring to themselves or they can remember the same episode as if it happened to someone else. Fergusson (1993) varied respondents' point of view in a study in which university students wrote about disturbing personal experiences. Previous work by Pennebaker and his associates (e.g., Pennebaker & Beall, 1986; Pennebaker, Colder, & Sharp, 1990; Pennebaker, Kiecolt-Glaser, & Glaser, 1988a) has indicated that writing about

disturbing events had health benefits, leading for example to fewer visits to physicians during subsequent months. However, the disclosure–health relationship has not been consistently obtained by other researchers, who have used methodologies similar to Pennebaker's (e.g., Greenberg & Stone, 1992; Murray, Lamnin, & Carver, 1989). Fergusson (1993) examined whether the benefits of disclosure would be enhanced if participants wrote in the third rather than the first person. In the third-person condition of her study, participants described their own distressing experiences, but they employed a pseudonym and the pronouns he or she. They thus wrote as if the distressing events had occurred to someone else. In the first-person condition, participants wrote about their upsetting experiences using the first-person pronoun. In the control conditions, participants wrote about trivial issues (e.g., their activities during the previous day or a description of their living accommodation) in either the third or first person.

Fergusson (1993) hypothesised that writing in the third person about negative, personally meaningful events would be especially beneficial because it circumvents people's tendencies to avoid dealing with traumatic events and, at the same time, serves a psychological distancing function that permits individuals to reframe, "work through", and ultimately leave painful experiences behind them. The research of Libby and Eibach on visual perspective suggests further that third-person narratives may be effective, in part, because they enable individuals to view negative experiences as occurring to a different self. As a result, the implication of those experiences for the current self is lessened. There are thus a variety of reasons for supposing that third-person writing could yield greater psychological and health benefits than first-person writing.

Fergusson assessed the effects of writing in a questionnaire completed 4 weeks following the final writing session. Third-person writers reported lower levels of distress associated with the events about which they wrote than did first-person writers. Third-person writers also reported a better understanding of the episodes. A subsequent examination of records obtained from the university health centre revealed additional benefits of third-person writing. Third-person writers made significantly fewer illness visits to the health centre than did first-person writers during the 50 days following the writing sessions, and marginally fewer visits than did control participants. Although the data are somewhat equivocal about the value of writing about personally disturbing events, they do suggest that third-person writing is more beneficial than first-person writing.

Clinicians working with children have noted the advantage of encouraging their patients to distance themselves psychologically from distressing experiences (Bettelheim, 1979; Fergusson, 1993; Kalter, Schaeffer, Lesowitz, Alpern, & Pickar, 1988; Mishne, 1993). Lawrence (1990) proposed the use of "third person analysis" with adults. She suggested that a patient speaking in the third person is able to adopt "a more dispassionate, detached, retrospective view of him/herself" (p. 97). Lawrence claimed that, as a result, third-person analysis yields less guilt and fewer defensive justifications. The distancing of events in third-person accounts involves reducing the psychological threat of negative experiences, not forgetting or denying their occurrence. Distancing should thus be distinguished from the dissociation or repression of traumatic episodes, which may have very different psychological implications (e.g., Schacter, 1996; Terr, 1994).

The Ross and Wilson (2002) and Libby and Eibach (2002) findings suggest novel ways of assessing the effectiveness of therapeutic procedures. Successful therapy may lead individuals to view past disturbing episodes as subjectively distant and to adopt a third-person visual perspective when remembering the events. Such effects would provide evidence that individuals have successfully put disturbing incidents behind them.

MEMORIES ALTER CURRENT AFFECT AND LIFE SATISFACTION

Memories function to regulate people's emotion and their satisfaction with different aspects of their lives. As in research on distancing and point of view, it is not *what* individuals remember but *how* they remember that determines the direction of influence. Memories often have a direct effect: People's moods and reports of life satisfaction improve when they recall pleasant personal experiences and worsen when they remember distressing personal episodes (e.g., Martin, 1990; Salovey, 1992). However, sometimes a contrast effect occurs: A pleasant memory depresses and an unpleasant memory boosts people's current mood and life satisfaction (e.g., Nolen-Hoeksema, 1987; Strack, Strack, & Gschneidinger, 1985; Tversky & Griffin, 1991; Wilson, 2000). Clark, Collins, and Henry (1994) summarised circum-

stances that influence whether direct or contrast effects occur. They proposed that direct effects arise when respondents: (1) recall *how* an event happened, (2) recall an event in vivid detail, (3) ruminate upon an event, or (4) retrieve a *recent* past episode. Conversely, contrast effects occur when people: (1) recount *why* an event occurred, (2) recall an episode sketchily or briefly, (3) fail to ruminate upon an episode (or are distracted from it), or (4) retrieve an event from the *distant* past.

Although they focus on different manipulations and measures, Clark et al. (1994) describe effects that are similar to those obtained for manipulations of subjective distance and point of view. It may be that the same basic phenomenon underlies these various processes: Past episodes directly influence current self-appraisals when the episodes are ascribed to the present self or seen as *representative* of one's current life (Strack et al., 1985). Past outcomes either have no influence or a contrasting effect when dissociated from, or seen as unrepresentative of, the present self. One can accomplish this link or separation between the past and present by varying perceptions of distance or perspective, and by altering the qualities of the memory (e.g., its vividness).

These various memory processes are likely to be interrelated. Because people typically associate a third-person perspective with older memories (Nigro & Neisser, 1983), individuals who are induced to adopt a third-person perspective might feel farther from an episode than would individuals who remember the same event from a first-person perspective. Similarly, recall of recent events is typically more vivid and less abstract than recall of distant events (Semin & Smith, 1999). As a result of this common association, people may recall vivid, detailed memories in the first person and judge them to be recent (Brown et al., 1985). Rumination and rehearsal may serve to maintain memory vividness, and thereby induce both feelings of nearness and a first-person perspective. Many people may be more inclined to revisit and rehearse positive than negative events, both privately and in conversation with others. This differential rehearsal may cause flattering memories to be better remembered over time and contribute to the discrepancy in the subjective distance of positive and negative events. People who show a heightened tendency to ruminate about unflattering events—for example, individuals who are dysphoric (Nolen-Hoeksema & Morrow, 1991)—should be less likely to distance negative episodes. In one study of the effects of rehearsal, participants who were encouraged to ruminate about a negative event felt subjectively closer to it than did those who were distracted from the event (McLellan, Wilson & Ross, 2002). In addition, ruminators experienced more unpleasant affect about the event.

Individuals think about *why* an event occurs when they seek to understand an episode (Clark et al., 1994). People generally devote more conscious problem-solving resources as well as unconscious defensive processes to making sense out of distressing as opposed to favourable events (Gilbert, Pinel, Wilson, Blumberg, & Wheatley, 1998; Taylor, 1991). In fact if making sense of events helps individuals to put episodes behind them (Silver, Boon & Stones, 1983; Taylor, 1983; Weber, Harvey & Stanley, 1987), then people may prefer *not* to make sense of positive events. T. Wilson (2002) recently reported that people sometimes favour remaining uncertain or confused about positive events. The uncertainty keeps the event "open", and promotes longer-lasting positive affect.

REMEMBERING IS OFTEN A SOCIAL ACT

We have argued that one function of autobiographical memory is to maintain a favourable view of self. However, because autobiographical memory can serve multiple functions, there exists the potential for different memory goals to conflict. We have focused on the *intrapersonal* benefits of recalling the self as continually improving, as well as regarding failings as remote and glories as close. When recalled in conversation, these same memories may also serve *interpersonal* functions (e.g., Pasupathi, 2001). Just as other types of self-enhancement can have social costs as well as benefits (e.g., Paulhus, 1998), so too may self-serving remembering. Individuals may encounter some tension between their goal of achieving a preferred view of a former self and maintaining closeness and harmony in relationships with others. Consider a past conflict between intimate partners. The transgressor may quickly attribute the misconduct to an "old me" and claim that he or she has improved since the episode (Baumeister, Stillwell, & Wotman, 1990; Cameron, Ross & Holmes, 2002). If the transgressor communicates this insight to the victim, a new conflict could ensue: Less motivated to distance the transgressor's behaviour, the victim may continue to hold the transgressor responsible for the misconduct and be less convinced of his or her metamorphosis (Baumeister et al., 1990; Cameron et al., 2002). More generally, claims of personal improvement that involve distancing past negative performances should often appear unfounded to an observer who is less motivated to distance the performer's objectionable actions. Assertions of subjective distance are especially likely to be challenged to the extent that the claims are at considerable variance with calendar time and imply major or improbable personal improvement.

In many cases, rememberers may be quite aware that their audience does not share their perceptions of change. For example, people may firmly believe that elements from their sordid pasts no longer reflect on the person they currently are, but may still keep their pasts secret because they are not confident that others will agree with their view of a changed self. Movie stars have often suppressed their embarrassing (or pornographic) early screen appearances, and President George W. Bush attempted to hide his arrest for driving under the influence even though he no longer drinks alcohol and regards himself as a changed man. Conversely, individuals who have experienced a religious conversion seem eager to describe how they have exchanged misguided and evil ways for a good and loving life (Ross & Konrath, in press). Proud and persuaded of their transformation, these individuals often don't hesitate to share it with others. They presumably suppose that they can convince others of the validity and wonder of their conversion.

Although we have emphasised the parallels between distancing and point of view, the implications of the two memory processes for social remembering are quite different. Point of view is a private experience. People typically don't tell others: "Hmm I am seeing this memory from a first(third)-person point of view." Even if they did communicate their visual perspective, they are unlikely to arouse the ire of an audience. No one else can meaningfully disagree with a rememberer's point of view. A first-person or third-person point of view cannot be right or wrong and has no direct pejorative implications.

THE UTILITY AND VERITY OF PERSONAL MEMORIES

Neisser (1988) proposed that any act of remembering lies on a continuum between "utility (using the past to accomplish some present end) and verity (using memory to recapture what really happened in the past)" (p.357). While not denying the importance of "verity", we have focused on the personal utility—or function—of memories in the current article. Identity construction is not a passive process. Individuals actively seek information that helps to confirm their desired self-views. Personal memory plays an important role in identity construction because it provides pertinent and plentiful information. Also because the past is ephemeral, there is often little concrete evidence to contradict individuals' versions of their personal histories (although accounts may be disputed when they are publicly shared). People can revise their appraisals of past selves and events, and shift the subjective distance, point of view, or way of recollecting the episodes. These revisions make it possible to use the richness of autobiographical memories, partly for their verity, but often for their utility in creating a preferred representation of self.

REFERENCES

Albert, S. (1977). Temporal comparison theory. *Psychological Review*, *84*, 485–503.

Bartlett, F.C. (1932). *Remembering: A study in experimental and social psychology*. London: Cambridge University Press.

Baumeister, R.F. (1989). The optimal margin of illusion. *Journal of Social and Clinical Psychology*, *8*, 176–189.

Baumeister, R.F. (1998). The self. In D.T. Gilbert, S.T. Fiske, and G. Lindzey (Eds.), *Handbook of social psychology* (4th edn., pp. 680–740). New York: McGraw-Hill.

Baumeister, R., Stillwell, A., & Wotman, S.R. (1990). Victim and perpetrator accounts of interpersonal conflict: Autobiographical narratives about anger. *Journal of Personality and Social Psychology*, *59*, 994–1005.

Bettelheim, B. (1979). *Surviving, and other essays*. New York: Knopf.

Block, R.A. (1989). Experiencing and remembering time: Affordances, context, and cognition. In I. Levin & D. Zakay (Eds.), *Advances in psychology: Vol. 59. Time and human cognition: A life-span perspective* (pp. 333–363). Amsterdam: North-Holland.

Brickman, P., & Campbell, D.T. (1971). Hedonic relativism and planning the good society. In M.H. Appley (Ed.), *Adaptation-level theory* (pp. 278–302). New York: Academic Press.

Brickman, P., Coates, D., & Janoff-Bulman, R. (1978). Lottery winners and accident victims: Is happiness relative? *Journal of Personality and Social Psychology*, *36*, 917–927.

Brown, N.R., Rips, L.J., & Shevell, S.K. (1985). The subjective dates of natural events in very long-term memory. *Cognitive Psychology*, *17*, 139–177.

Cameron, J.J., Ross, M., & Holmes. J.G. (2002). Loving the one you hurt: Positive effects of recounting a transgression against an intimate partner. *Journal of Experimental Social Psychology*, *38*, 307–314.

Carver C.S., & Scheier, M.F. (1990). Origins and functions of positive and negative affect: A control-process view. *Psychological Review*, *97*, 19–35.

Clark, L.F., Collins, J.E., & Henry, S.M. (1994). Biasing effects of retrospective reports on current self-assessments. In N. Schwarz & S. Sudman (Eds.), *Autobiographical memory and the validity of retrospective reports* (pp. 291–304). New York: Springer-Verlag.

Conway, M., & Ross, M. (1984). Getting what you want by revising what you had. *Journal of Personality and Social Psychology*, *47*, 738–748.

Conway, M.A., & Pleydell-Pearce, C.W. (2000). The construction of autobiographical memories in the self-memory system. *Psychological Review*, *107*, 261–288.

Crocker, J., & Wolfe, C.T. (2001). Contingencies of self-worth. *Psychological Review*, *108*, 593–623.

Fergusson, P. (1993). *Writing about traumatic events using the third person pronoun: Psychological and health effects*. Unpublished doctoral dissertation, University of Waterloo, Ontario, Canada.

Fischhoff, B., & Beyth, R. (1975). "I knew it would happen": Remembered probabilities of once-future things. *Organizational and Human Performance*, *13*, 1–16.

Frijda, N.H. (1988). The laws of emotion. *American Psychologist*, *43*, 349–358.

Gergen, K.J., & Gergen, M.M. (1988). Narrative and the self as relationship. In L. Berkowitz (Ed.), *Advances in experimental social psychology, Vol. 21: Social psychological studies of the self: Perspectives and programs* (pp. 17–56). San Diego, CA: Academic Press, Inc.

Gilbert, D.T., Pinel, E.C., Wilson, T.D., Blumberg, S.J., & Wheatley, T.P. (1998). Immune neglect: A source of durability bias in affective forcasting. *Journal of Personality & Social Psychology*, *75*, 617–638.

Greenberg, M.A., & Stone, A.A. (1992). Emotional disclosure about traumas and its relation to health: Effects of previous disclosure and trauma severity. *Journal of Personality & Social Psychology*, *63*, 75–84.

Greenwald, A.G. (1980). The totalitarian ego: Fabrication and revision of personal history. *American Psychologist*, *35*, 603–618.

Higgins, E.T. (1996). Self digest: Self-knowledge serving self-regulatory functions. *Journal of Personality and Social Psychology*, *71*, 1062–1083.

Holman, E.A., & Silver, R.C. (1998). Getting "stuck" in the past: Temporal orientation and coping with trauma. *Journal of Personality and Social Psychology*, *75*, 1146–1163.

Hsee, C.K., Abelson, R.P., & Salovey, P. (1991). The relative weighting of position and velocity in satisfaction. *Psychological Science*, *2*, 263–266.

James, W. (1950). *Principles of psychology*. New York: Dover. [Originally published in 1890.]

Kalter, N., Schaefer, M., Lesowitz, M., Alpern, D., & Pickar, J. (1988). School-based support groups for children of divorce: A model of brief intervention. In B.H. Gottlieb (Ed.), *Marshaling social support: Formats, processes, and effects* (pp. 165–185). Thousand Oaks, CA: Sage Publications, Inc.

Karney, B.R., & Coombs, R.H. (2000). Memory bias in long-term close relationships: Consistency or improvement? *Personality and Social Psychology Bulletin, 26*, 959–970.

Karney, B.R., & Frye, N.E. (2002). "But we've been getting better lately": Comparing prospective and retrospective views of relationship development. *Journal of Personality and Social Psychology, 82*, 222–238.

Keyes, C.L.M., & Ryff, C.D. (2000). Subjective change and mental health: A self-concept theory. *Social Psychology Quarterly, 63*, 264–279.

Koestler, A. (1961). *Arrow in the blue, an autobiography*. New York: Macmillan.

Lawrence, L. (1990). On the theory and application of third person analysis in the practice of psychotherapy. *The Journal of Mind and Behavior, 11*, 97–104.

Libby, L.K., & Eibach, R.P. (2002). Looking back in time: Self-concept change affects visual perspective in autobiographical memory. *Journal of Personality and Social Psychology, 82*, 167–179.

Libby, L.K., Eibach, R.P., & Gilovich, T. (2002, February). *It depends on how you look at it: Memory perspective affects perceived and actual change in the self*. Poster presented at the 3rd Annual Meeting of the Society for Personality and Social Psychology, Savannah, GA.

Loewenstein, G., & Prelec, D. (1993). Preferences over outcome sequences. *Psychological Review, 100*, 91–108.

Loewenstein, G., & Thaler, R.H. (1989). Intertemporal choice. *Journal of Economic Perspectives, 3*, 181–193.

Martin, M. (1990). On the induction of mood. *Clinical Psychology Review, 10*, 669–697.

McFarland, C., & Alvaro, C. (2000). The impact of motivation on temporal comparisons: Coping with traumatic events by perceiving personal growth. *Journal of Personality and Social Psychology, 79*, 327–343.

McFarland, C., Ross, M., & Giltrow, M. (1992). Biased recollections in older adults: The role of implicit theories of aging. *Journal of Personality and Social Psychology, 62*, 837–850.

McLellan, L., Wilson, A.E., & Ross, M. (2002). *To dwell or distract: The effects of rumination versus distraction on subjective distance from negative events*. Unpublished thesis, Wilfrid Laurier University, Canada.

Mead, G.H. (1929/1964). *Selected writings*. Indianapolis: Bobbs-Merrill.

Mishne, J.M. (1993). *The evolution and application of clinical theory: Perspectives from four psychologies*. New York: The Free Press.

Murray, E.J., Lamnin, A.D., & Carver, C.S. (1989) Emotional expression in written essays and psychotherapy. *Journal of Social & Clinical Psychology, 8*, 414–429.

Murray, S.L., Holmes, J.G., Dolderman, D., & Griffin, D.W. (2000). What the motivated mind sees: Comparing friends' perspectives to married partners' views of each other. *Journal of Experimental Social Psychology, 36*, 600–620.

Neisser, U. (1988). What is ordinary memory the memory of? In U. Neisser & E. Winograd (Eds.), *Remembering reconsidered: Ecological and traditional approaches to the study of memory. Emory symposia in cognition, 2* (pp. 356–373). New York: Cambridge University Press.

Nigro, G., & Neisser, U. (1983). Point of view in personal memories. *Cognitive Psychology, 15*, 467–482.

Nolen-Hoeksema, S. (1987). Sex differences in unipolar depression: Evidence and theory. *Psychological Bulletin, 101*, 259–282.

Nolen-Hoeksema, S., & Morrow, J. (1991). A prospective study of depression and posttraumatic stress symptoms after a natural disaster: The 1989 Loma Prieta earthquake. *Journal of Personality and Social Psychology, 61*, 115–121.

Orwell, G. (1946). Benefit of clergy: Some notes on Salvador Dali. In G. Orwell (Ed.), *Dickens, Dali & others: Studies in popular culture*. Cornwall, NY: The Cornwall Press.

Pasupathi, M. (2001). The social construction of the personal past and its implications for adult development. *Psychological Bulletin, 127*, 651–672.

Paulhus, D.L. (1998). Interpersonal and intrapsychic adaptiveness of trait self-enhancement: A mixed blessing? *Journal of Personality & Social Psychology, 74*, 1197–1208.

Pennebaker, J.W., & Beall, S.K. (1986). Confronting a traumatic event: Toward an understanding of inhibition and disease. *Journal of Abnormal Psychology, 95*, 274–281.

Pennebaker, J.W., Colder, M., & Sharp, L.K. (1990). Accelerating the coping process. *Journal of Personality & Social Psychology, 58*, 528–537.

Pennebaker, J.W., Kiecolt-Glaser, J.K., & Glaser, R. (1988). Disclosure of traumas and immune function: Health implications for psychotherapy. *Journal of Consulting & Clinical Psychology, 56*, 239–245.

Pillemer, D.B., Desrochers, A.B., & Ebanks, C.M. (1998). Remembering the past in the present: Verb tense shifts in autobiographical memory narratives. In C.P. Thompson, D.J. Herrmann, D. Bruce, J.D. Read, D.G. Payne, & M.P. Toglia (Eds.), *Autobiographical memory: Theoretical and applied perspectives.* (pp. 145–162). Mahwah, NJ: Lawrence Erlbaum Associates Inc.

Proust, M. (1934). *Remembrance of things past*. New York: Random House.

Ross, M. (1989). The relation of implicit theories to the construction of personal histories. *Psychological Review, 96*, 341–357.

Ross M., & Buehler, R. (1994). Creative remembering. In U. Neisser & R. Fivush (Eds.), *The remembering self* (pp. 205–235). New York: Cambridge University Press.

Ross, M., & Konrath, S. H. (in press). Synergies. *Psychological Inquiry*.

Ross, M., & Wilson, A.E. (2000). Constructing and appraising past selves. In D.L. Schacter & E. Scarry (Eds.), *Memory, brain, and belief* (pp. 231–258). Cambridge, MA: Harvard University Press.

Ross, M., & Wilson, A.E. (2002). It feels like yesterday: Self-esteem, valence of personal past experiences, and judgments of subjective distance. *Journal of Personality and Social Psychology, 82*, 792–803.

Salovey, P. (1992). Mood-induced self-focused attention. *Journal of Personality & Social Psychology, 62*, 699–707.

Schacter, D.L. (1996). *Searching for memory: The brain, the mind, and the past.* New York: Basicbooks, Inc.

Sedikides, C. (1993). Assessment, enhancement, and verification determinants of the self-evaluation process. *Journal of Personality and Social Psychology, 65*, 317–338.

Sedikides, C., & Skowronski, J.J. (1995). On the sources of self-knowledge: The perceived primacy of self-reflection. *Journal of Social and Clinical Psychology, 14*, 244–270.

Semin, G.R., & Smith, E.R. (1999). Revisiting the past and back to the future: Memory systems and the linguistic representation of social events. *Journal of Personality & Social Psychology, 76*, 877–892.

Silver, R.L., Boon, C., & Stones, M.H. (1983). Searching for meaning in misfortune: Making sense of incest. *Journal of Social Issues, 39*, 81–101.

Singer, J.A., & Salovey, P. (1993). *The remembered self: Emotion and memory in personality.* Toronto: Maxwell Macmillan International.

Strack, F., Strack, N., & Gschneidinger, E. (1985). Happiness and reminiscing: The role of time perspective, affect, and mode of thinking. *Journal of Personality and Social Psychology, 49*, 1460–1469.

Suh, E., Diener, E., & Fujita F. (1996). Events and subjective well-being: Only recent events matter. *Journal of personality and Social Psychology, 70*, 1091–1102.

Swann, W.B., Read, S.J. (1981). Acquiring self-knowledge: The search for feedback that fits. *Journal of Personality and Social Psychology, 41*, 1119–1128.

Swann, W.B., Stein-Seroussi, A., & Giesler, R.B. (1992). Why people self-verify. *Journal of Personality & Social Psychology, 62*, 392–401.

Taylor, S.E. (1983). Adjustment to threatening events: A theory of cognitive adaptation. *American Psychologist, 38*, 1161–1173.

Taylor, S.E. (1991). Asymmetrical effects of positive and negative events: The mobilization-minimization hypothesis. *Psychological Bulletin, 110*, 67–85.

Taylor, S.E., & Koivumaki, J.H. (1976). The perception of self and others: Acquaintanceship, affect, and actor-observer differences. *Journal of Personality and Social Psychology, 33*, 403–408.

Terr, L.C. (1994). *Unchained memories.* New York: Basic Books.

Tesser, A. (1988). Toward a self-evaluation maintenance model of social behavior. In L. Berkowitz (Ed.), *Advances in experimental social psychology, Vol. 21* (pp. 181–227). New York: Academic Press.

Thompson, C.P., Skowronski, J.J., Larsen, S.F., & Betz, A. (1996). *Autobiographical memory: Remembering what and remembering when.* Mahwah, NJ: Lawrence Erlbaum Associates Inc.

Tversky, A., & Griffin, D. (1991). On the dynamics of hedonic experience: Endowment and contrast in judgments of well-being. In F. Strack, N. Schwarz, & M. Argyle (Eds.), *Subjective well-being* (pp. 108–118). London: Pergamon Press.

Weber, A.L., Harvey, J.H., & Stanley, M.A. (1987). The nature and motivations of accounts for failed relationships. In R. Burnett & P. McGhee (Eds.), *Accounting for relationships: Explanation, representation and knowledge* (pp. 114–133). New York: Methuen.

Wills, T.A. (1981). Downward comparison principles in social psychology. *Psychological Bulletin, 90*, 245–271.

Wilson, A.E. (2000). *How do people's perceptions of their former selves affect their current self-appraisals?* Unpublished doctoral dissertation, University of Waterloo, Canada.

Wilson, A.E., & Ross, M. (1998). [*Life transitions and subjective distance.*] Unpublished raw data.

Wilson, A.E., & Ross, M. (2000). The frequency of temporal-self and social comparisons in people's personal appraisals. *Journal of Personality and Social Psychology, 78*, 928–942.

Wilson, A.E., & Ross, M. (2001a). From chump to champ: People's appraisals of their earlier and current selves. *Journal of Personality and Social Psychology, 80*, 572–584.

Wilson, A.E., & Ross, M. (2001b, February). *How do perceptions of former selves affect current self-appraisals?* Paper presented at the Society for Personality and Social Psychology Convention, San Antonio, TX

Wilson, T. (2002). *Self knowledge and the pleasures of uncertainty.* Keynote address at the 3rd Annual Meeting of the Society for Personality and Social Psychology, Savannah, GA.

Wood, J.V., & Taylor, K.L. (1991). Serving self-relevant goals through social comparison. In J. Suls & T.A. Wills, (Eds.), *Social comparison: Contemporary theory and research* (pp. 23–49). Hillsdale, NJ: Lawrence Erlbaum Associates Inc.

MEMORY, 2003, 11 (2), 151–163

Emotion regulation during social remembering: Differences between emotions elicited during an event and emotions elicited when talking about it

M. Pasupathi

University of Utah, USA

This paper examines emotion regulation as a function of autobiographical remembering in social contexts. Two studies (n = 38 and 123, respectively) are presented that provide evidence that autobiographical remembering in social settings can result in changes in the emotions associated with an experience. However, the results also suggest that whether changes occur depends on features of the recall context, including the gender of participants, and the responses of their listeners. Across both studies, men showed greater emotional benefits from talking about events than women. Moreover, greater listener agreement was associated with greater benefits for emotion. The results are discussed in terms of functions of autobiographical remembering, gender, social support, and emotion regulation.

INTRODUCTION

Our past connects us with others, tells us who we are, and informs us about what we ought to do in the future. These functions of autobiographical memory are typically labelled social, self-related, and directive (Bluck & Alea, 2002; Cohen, 1998; Pillemer, 1998). In practice, functions co-occur and overlap (Cohen, 1998), and these broad classifications are likely composed of various "subfunctions", which may be important to examine in their own right (Webster, 1993, 1997; Webster & McCall, 1999; Wong & Watt, 1991). The present paper examines how conversational remembering may serve emotion regulatory functions, and how the "success" of conversational remembering for emotion regulation depends in part on the social context.

Autobiographical remembering and emotion regulation

Emotion regulation is typically defined as efforts to alter the ongoing experience and expression of emotion (Gross, 2001). Constructive aspects of memory (Conway & Pleydell-Pearce, 2000; Schacter, 1996) permit people to choose memories to regulate their emotions, and to recall memories in ways that enhance positive and diminish negative emotion, suggesting that remembering may be an ideal tool for emotion regulation. Surprisingly, emotion regulation *per se* does not appear frequently in the literature on functions of autobiographical memory (Bluck & Alea, 2002; Webster & McCall, 1999; Wong & Watt, 1991). However, taxonomies of functions of autobiographical remembering include specific functions that are emotion-regulatory. For example,

Requests for reprints should be sent to Monisha Pasupathi, PhD, Department of Psychology, University of Utah, 390 S. 1530 E. BEH-S 502, Salt Lake City, UT 84112, USA.

Data collection for these studies was supported by a University Research Grant from the University of Utah and a Proposal Initiative Grant from the College of Social and Behavioral Sciences at the University of Utah awarded to the author. Thanks are due to Susan Bluck, Jeff Webster, Sarah Lucas, and Frank Drews for comments on earlier drafts. Amy Coombs, Gina Erickson, Casey Parry, and David Shaw provided assistance in data collection and management.

http://www.tandf.co.uk/journals/pp/09658211.html

DOI:10.1080/09658210244000333

Webster (1993; Webster & McCall, 1999) proposed that memory functions to reduce boredom and also to revive bitterness, both of which represent uses of memory to regulate emotion. Wong and Watt (1991) proposed escapist and obsessive styles of remembering, which, respectively, consist of focusing on past glories (presumably to enhance positive emotion in the present), or of ruminating about past difficulties or problems (again, in the service of resolving such difficulties, albeit perhaps with little success). Baumeister and Newman (1994) argue for remembering as constructing meaning, including affectively evaluating experiences. All such functions influence whether one feels positive or negative about the past, in the present.

Ironically, emotion regulation may be relatively absent from the literature because of its pervasiveness. Recalling past positive experiences bolsters self-esteem and elicits positive affect; remembering "how we met" can strengthen and deepen a relationship, but also induce positive emotion, and recalling past successes to cope with a current failure can likewise lead to positive emotion. In short, remembering may regulate emotion regardless of, or in conjunction with, other functions of autobiographical memory.

Other work suggests that people can and do use memory to regulate emotion. First, remembering past experiences tends to reinstate the emotions associated with that experience, as indicated by the use of memory as an emotion induction (Levenson, Carstensen, Friesen, & Ekman, 1991). In other studies, participants are induced to feel positive or negative and are then asked to recall past experiences (Josephson, Singer, & Salovey, 1996; Parrott & Sabini, 1990). Typically, participants experiencing negative emotions recall negative events. However, in some cases, mood-*in*congruent recall is observed. For example, if participants in negative moods are asked to recall two experiences, the second recalled experience is sometimes positive. Participants acknowledge "trying to feel better" when asked about the reason for choosing that second experience (Josephson et al., 1996). A recent review (Gross, 1998) suggests various ways in which remembering can be used to regulate emotion. For example, in solitary reminiscing, the selection of positive memories can be viewed as a strategy for inducing or maintaining positive emotions—what Gross terms "situation selection". Memory may also be employed in cognitive reframing and reappraisal, both processes shown to regulate emotional responding (Park & Folkman, 1997; Vaillant, 1995).

An alternative way to examine the use of memory in emotion regulation is to explore remembering among groups known to prioritise emotional regulation, such as older adults (Carstensen, Isaacowitz, & Charles, 1999). Relative to younger adults, older adults show positive and self-justifying biases in recall (Charles, Mather, & Carstensen, 2002; Mather & Johnson, 2000), recall past emotions as more positive and less negative (Levine, Resnick, & Higgens, 1993), and report greater positive emotion when engaged in personal reminiscing, though not when engaged in other social activities (Pasupathi & Carstensen, 2002). Existing evidence suggests that older adults regulate emotions through remembering both by selectively focusing on positive events, and highlighting positive features of the events being recalled (Pasupathi & Carstensen, 2002; Pasupathi, Henry, & Carstensen, in press). Again, remembering serves to regulate emotion.

A different tactic is to focus on characteristics of memories for experiences with emotional consequences, and such work also suggests connections between memory and emotion regulation via self-protection and self-enhancement. People recalling instances in which they hurt others do so in ways that preserve their self-regard (Baumeister, Stilman, & Wotman, 1990). People also over-attribute successes to themselves, and externalise failures (Greenwald, 1980). In fact, memory for the particular emotions experienced at an event tends to fade over time, and reconstruction of those emotions depends on current goals (Levine & Bluck, 2002).

The special case of remembering in conversation

Much remembering occurs in conversation, to audiences (Hirst, Manier, & Apetroaia, 1997; Pasupathi, 2001; Rimé, Finkenauer, Luminet, Zech, & Phillipot, 1998; Rimé, Phillipot, Boca, & Mesquita, 1992). Audiences contribute to remembering in a variety of ways—by showing interest and agreement with the rememberer (Bavelas, Coates, & Johnson, 2000; Pasupathi, 2001; Pasupathi, Stallworth, & Murdoch, 1998), by adding details or making corrections (Hirst et al., 1997; Manier, Pinner, & Hirst, 1996), and by helping people reconstrue or come to terms with difficult experiences (Murray & Segal, 1994).

Retelling particular events in conversational settings is often done for self, social, and directive purposes (Hyman & Faries, 1992; Norrick, 1997; Pasupathi, Lucas, & Coombs, 2002). Still, conversations also involve other functions. Parents remember with their children in part to instruct children about appropriate ways of recalling personal events (Edwards & Middleton, 1988; Fivush & Haden, 1997; Han, Leichtman, & Wang, 1998; Nelson, 1991; Reese & Brown, 2000), and couples appear to remember in part to regulate shared knowledge systems (Pasupathi et al., 2002). Often, these studies do not (or cannot) address emotion regulation.

Rimé and colleagues (1998, 1992) have investigated the retelling of emotional experiences, and shown that people recall emotional events to others with astonishing frequency and universality. Nearly all highly emotional experiences are disclosed to others, often soon after the event. This is true across culture, gender, and even specific types of emotional experiences (Rimé et al., 1998). Rimé and colleagues have argued that disclosure of emotional events may aid emotional recovery, but their own work reveals some complexities. For example, events that have previously been talked about do not differ from those that have not been shared in the intensity of the emotions they *currently* evoke (Finkenauer & Rimé, 1998). Further, variations in the focus of talk about past experiences does not influence the intensity of emotions later evoked by those experiences (Zech, 2000). Such findings highlight the importance of considering specific factors involved in disclosure—the extent of emotional expression, and the responses of the audience (Rimé, Herbette, & Corsini, in press). Disclosure alone does not appear to result in improved emotions regarding an experience.

The broader literature on disclosure has primarily focused on writing about negative or traumatic events, with a few studies comparing writing to talking. The immediate effects of either writing or talking about events are a re-experiencing of negative emotion, followed by improved emotions over repeated disclosures (Murray, Lamnin, & Carver, 1989; Murray & Segal, 1994; Pennebaker & Seagal, 1999; Smyth, 1998). Talking to a person may be more beneficial than writing, provided the person is supportive (Harvey, Orbuch, Chwalisz, & Garwood, 1991; Kelly, Coenen, & Johnston, 1995; Murray et al., 1989). Interestingly, although women report more frequently talking about experiences to regulate emotion than men (Sor-

enson, Russell, Harkness, & Harvey, 1993), men show larger benefits from disclosure than women (primarily in studies of written disclosure, Smyth, 1998). So, disclosing autobiographical events is emotionally beneficial, but the existing literature primarily addresses either written disclosures, or disclosures to therapists, and focuses on traumatic events. The present studies extend this literature to examine the conversational disclosure of everyday events.

The studies reported here examine whether autobiographical remembering in conversation might alter the emotions associated with an event in emotionally beneficial ways. They do so by evaluating differences between the emotions elicited *initially* by an event, and the emotions elicited *when that event is recalled in conversation*.

STUDY 1

The goal of Study 1 was to examine whether emotions elicited by the original event and the emotions elicited by retelling it differed systematically in ways that might be attributed to emotion regulatory functions. Study 1 also examined whether the gender of the participant and telling events in order to "feel better" were associated with differences in emotion from the initial experience to the retelling.

Method

Participants

A total of 38 students from the introductory psychology pool at the University of Utah took part for course credit. They ranged in age from 17 to 38, $M(SD) = 19.8(3.4)$. The majority of participants were female (65%), and European-American (76%).

Procedure

Participants were asked to think of a recent experience that they had recounted to other people. They provided a written recall of the experience, and reported their emotional reactions *to the initial event*. Participants reported a wide range of events, including sexual abuse and bereavement, but the majority of events were everyday emotional experiences such as minor traffic violations or receiving praise from a professor. Approximately 45% of events elicited more positive than negative emotion, with the remaining events showing the reverse. Participants were also asked to describe the retelling situation, to report their emotional reactions *during the retelling*, and to characterize their main two goals for talking about the event. Order of reporting (event first, retelling first) did not impact any of the results reported here.

Measures

Emotions. Participants rated the emotions elicited by the event and the emotions elicited by retelling that event along 19 emotions (see Carstensen et al., 2000). Endorsement of eight positive (happiness, joy, contentment, excitement, pride, accomplishment, interest, and amusement) and eleven negative (anger, sadness, fear, disgust, guilt, embarrassment, shame, anxiety, irritation, frustration, and boredom) emotions were made on a 7-point Likert scale (1 = not at all, 7 = the most ever). Participants' emotion ratings for the initial event and the retelling were averaged separately across positive and negative emotion words to provide indices of positive emotions elicited by the event (α = .90), negative emotion elicited by the event (α = .87), positive emotions experienced at retelling (α = .90), and negative emotions experienced at retelling (α = .91).

Motives for retelling. Participants were asked to check their two most important goals for retelling the event from a list, which included items like "entertain the others", "give an example", and "to feel better or different". Participants who reported wanting to feel better as among their top two reasons for reporting the event were classified as having held explicit emotion-regulation goals. Ten individuals reported such goals (two men and eight women). Because men were unlikely to report this goal, analyses of gender and retelling motivation were conducted separately.

Results and Discussion

The major hypothesis of the study was that emotions during the retelling of experiences would be more positive and less negative than the emotions initially elicited by an experience. Analyses are reported separately for positive and negative emotions.

Positive emotions. Positive emotions were analysed in two general linear models with occasion (initial event versus retelling) as a within-subject factor, and either participant gender or motives for retelling (emotion regulation or other) as between-subjects factors. The model including gender revealed no effects of occasion, gender, or their interaction (all $Fs < 2.0$, $ps > .15$). The model including motives for retelling revealed no effects of occasion, motive, or their interaction on the positive emotions elicited by the event or the retelling ($Fs < 1$, ps = n.s.). Thus, positive emotions were largely stable across the initial event and the retelling, and this stability did not vary as a function of participant gender or emotion-regulation goals.

Negative emotion. Negative emotions were analysed in two general linear models with occasion (initial event versus retelling) as a within-subject factor, and either participant gender or motives for retelling (emotion regulation or other) as between subjects factors. The model including gender revealed a main effect of occasion, $F(1, 36) = 18.7$, $p < .01$, $MSE = .43$, a main effect of gender, $F(1, 36) = 4.3$, $p < .05$, $MSE = 3.5$, and an interaction of the two factors, $F(1, 36) = 3.0$, $p < .02$, $MSE = .43$. The initial event was reported as eliciting significantly more negative emotion, $M(SD) = 3.0(1.5)$, than was the retelling, $M(SD) = 2.3(1.5)$. Men reported significantly less negative emotion across both occasions, $M(SD) = 1.9 (0.9)$ than did women, $M(SD) = 2.9(1.5)$, but the gender by occasion interaction complicates this effect. As shown in Figure 1, men and women did not differ significantly in the emotions they reported during the initial event, $t(36) = 1.0$, p = n.s. However, men reported significantly less negative emotion during retelling, $t(36) = 3.0$, $p < .01$. The model including motives for retelling revealed a significant effect of occasion, $F(1, 36) = 9.3$, $p < .01$, $MSE = .52$, consistent with that already reported. The effect of motive only tended towards significance, $F(1, 36) = 3.3$, $p < .08$, $MSE = 3.6$, with endorsement of explicit emotion-regulatory goals associated with greater negative emotion, $M(SD) = 3.2(1.6)$ than no endorsement of such goals $M(SD) = 2.7(1.5)$. There were no interactions of occasion and motive, $F < 1$.

The findings show that emotions are less negative when retelling events than when experiencing them, and that people do report retelling events in order to alter their emotions. Retelling experiences in conversation was not associated with decreases in positive emotion, as might be expected if emotions are viewed as fading over

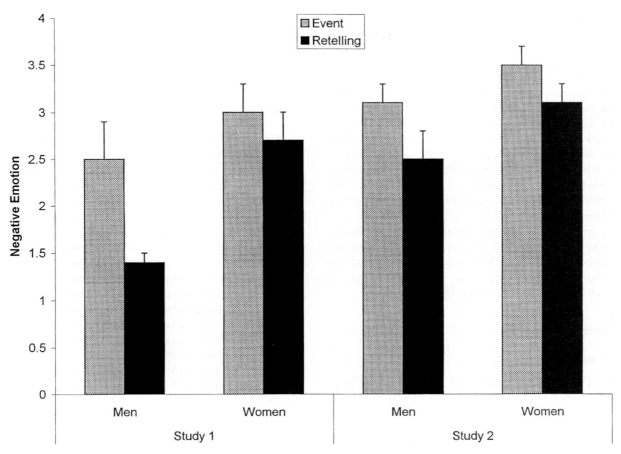

Figure 1.   Gender differences in emotion from the event to the retelling across Study 1 and Study 2.

time. These results support the notion that remembering in conversational contexts can serve emotional-regulatory functions. Consistent with findings for written disclosure (Smyth, 1998), men experienced talking about the past as less emotionally negative than did women. Finally, there was a "disconnect" between retelling events for emotion-regulatory goals and decreases in negative emotions reported during retelling situations, because having the goal of feeling better was not associated with differential changes in emotion across the two situations.

This initial study had several limitations. The small and homogeneous sample limits generalisability, and does not permit examination of potential interactions between gender and retelling motives. In studies of written disclosure, student samples show greater effects on psychological variables than other populations, so the study may overestimate differences between retelling and the initial event (Smyth, 1998). Further, there is little information provided by Study

1 participants about the nature of the events or the characteristics of their listeners' behaviour during the retelling situation. Study 2 attempts to address these issues by including a larger and more varied sample, and assessing (retrospectively) characteristics of the listener(s) behavior during retelling.

STUDY 2

Study 2 replicates the results of Study 1 with a larger, adult lifespan sample. People of different ages are equally likely to recall the past (Rimé et al., 1998; Staudinger, 1989; Webster, 1994), but may do so for different reasons (Pasupathi & Carstensen, 2002; Webster & McCall, 1999). Moreover, because there is good evidence that people remember a disproportionate number of events from young adulthood (Rubin & Schulkind, 1997), participants in Study 2 were asked to recall events without any recency constraint.

Participants were also asked to rate the applicability of emotion-regulatory goals on a Likert-type scale, to provide a more sensitive measure of explicitly held goals.

In addition to these changes, Study 2 also asked participants to characterise the responsiveness and agreeableness of their listeners. These facets of listener behaviour have been shown to be distinct (Dickinson & Givon, 1995; Pasupathi, Carstensen, Levenson, & Gottman, 1999), and to influence the amount of detail and fluency of conversational remembering (Bavelas et al., 2000; Dickinson & Givon, 1995; Pasupathi et al., 1998). However, responsive listening is also the hallmark of good clinical practice (Murray et al., 1989), and most of us feel good when others agree with our version of events. Thus, these aspects of listener behaviour may impact the emotions associated with conversational remembering.

Method

Participants

A total of 123 individuals ranging in age from 18 to 89 years, $M(SD) = 42.9(19.1)$, participated. Of these, 64% were female. The sample was not highly educated: 66% had not completed a bachelor's degree, 17% had done so, and 17% had done post-baccalaureate training—44% were single, 20% married, 24% divorced, and 8% were widowed. The majority (79%) were European-American, and the largest representation of any other ethnic group were Native Americans (7%). Individuals were compensated at 10$ per hour of study time. Age did not interact with any variables of interest, and is not considered further. Some participants are missing data for one or two questionnaires, thus, the sample size varies by analysis; missing data were not replaced.[1]

Procedure

Individuals took part in the study either at the laboratory or in residential communities. They completed a questionnaire asking about a past event that they had talked about with others. Participants were assigned to three event-type conditions: interpersonal experiences, competence experiences, or no specific instructions. These instructional conditions did not influence emotion ratings, ratings of listener behaviour, or ratings of motivations, and are not considered further.

The questionnaire asked participants to first describe the past experience. For the majority of participants (71%), the events reported had occurred within the last 2 years, and more negative (57%) than positive events (43%) were described. Participants rated how they felt *during the event* along the same 19 emotions employed in Study 1, and answered other questions not relevant for the present study. Participants were then asked to describe the *first time* they talked about the event (in pilot testing, this proved more memorable for participants). They were asked a number of questions about this occasion. Participants were asked to rate the extent of eye contact, backchannel responses (uh-huh's, mm-mmm's), facial expressions, and questions of the listener, and the degree to which the listener agreed with their version of events. They also rated the extent to which they retold the event in order to "feel better" on a 7-point Likert-type scale (1 = not at all, 7 = absolutely), and rated their emotional experience *during retelling*, again, using the same 19 emotion terms employed in Study 1.

Measures

Emotions. Participants rated the emotions elicited by the event and the emotions elicited by retelling that event for the same measure used in Study 1. Emotion ratings were averaged separately across positive and negative emotions and across contexts to provide indices of positive emotions elicited by the event ($\alpha = .92$), negative emotion elicited by the event ($\alpha = .87$), positive emotions while retelling ($\alpha = .92$), and negative emotions while retelling ($\alpha = .89$).

Emotion-regulation motives. Participants rated the extent to which they retold the event "in order to feel better" on a Likert-type scale (1 = not applicable, 7 = highly applicable).

Event characteristics. Participants rated the importance of the event and the extent to which the event revealed something important about them on 7-point Likert-type scales (1 = not at all, 7 = very). These ratings serve to rule out potential confounds between variables like listener

---

[1] Some data from part of this sample have been submitted for publication elsewhere (Pasupathi & Carstensen, 2002). However, that paper examines age differences in emotion, and does not address listener effects, which have not been previously examined.

responsiveness, and features of the events themselves.

Listener behaviour. The listener was rated along 11 Likert-type scales assessing aspects of feelings towards the listener, the listener's responsiveness, and the extent to which the listener agreed with the presented version of events (1 = very little, 7 = extensively). A principal components factor analysis with oblimin rotation was used to reduce the number of items. Three factors with eigenvalues greater than 1, accounting for a total of 63% of the variance, were identified: Responsiveness (35% of the total variance, items included "Listener asked questions" and "Listener gave verbal feedback"); Mutual Liking (18% of the total variance, items included "I liked the listener" and "I felt the listener liked me"); and Agreement (10% of the total variance, items included "The listener seemed to agree with my version of events"). Average scores for responsiveness (α = .78) and agreement (α = .53) were computed by averaging items with their highest loading on each factor. For theoretical reasons, mutual liking was not included in the present study.[2]

Results and discussion

The major hypothesis, as in Study 1, was that emotions at retelling would be more positive and less negative than the emotions initially elicited by the event. In addition, the effects of gender and emotion-regulatory motives observed in Study 1 were expected to replicate. Finally, Study 2 permits evaluation of the effects of listener behaviour on emotion during retelling. As in Study 1, positive and negative emotion were analysed separately. Follow-up analyses involving continuous variables are done with correlations. All analyses included the event's importance and self-revealing nature as covariates.

Positive emotion. For positive emotion, a general linear model was used, with occasion (initial event versus retelling) as a within-subject

factor, gender as a categorical between-subjects factor, and listener responsiveness, listener agreeableness, and emotion regulation motives as *continuous* between-subjects factors. Interactions between occasion and all between-subjects factors were tested, but interactions among between-subjects factors were not included due to lack of significance.[3]

The results revealed a significant main effect of listener agreement, $F(1, 109) = 7.5, p < .01, MSE = 5.3$, a significant main effect of emotion-regulation motives, $F(1, 106) = 12.1, p < .01, MSE = 5.3$, and a significant main effect of gender, $F(1, 106) = 6.6, p < .05, MSE = 5.3$. Averaged across retelling and initial event, positive emotion was significantly correlated with both listener agreement ($r = .21, p < .03$) and with the goal of feeling better ($r = -.27, p < .01$), and men reported more positive emotion overall, $M(SD) = 3.9(1.8)$, than did women, $M(SD) = 3.3(1.9)$. These findings suggest that men probably told more positive events than did women, that telling positive events was associated with greater listener agreement, and that the goal of feeling better was associated with telling less positive events. Both covariates (event importance, $F(1, 106) = 11.2, p < .01, MSE = 5.3$; self-revealing nature of the event, $F(1, 106) = 5.8, p < .05, MSE = 5.3$) had main effects, with more important and self-revealing events associated with greater positive emotion (rs = .33 and .28, respectively, ps < .01).

In addition to these main effects, an interaction of listener agreement with occasion, $F(1, 109) = 11.9, p < .01, MSE = .53$, was observed. To make sense of this effect, listener agreement was correlated with *the difference* in positive emotion across occasions (event—retelling). Difference scores less than zero reflect increases in positive emotion relative to the initial event, and those greater than zero reflect decreases. The resulting correlation was significant and negative ($r = -.29, p < .01$). As shown in Figure 2, the more agreement expressed by the listener, the more likely the difference score was to be less than zero, meaning retelling involved *greater* positive emotion than the initial event.

Negative emotion. For negative emotion, a general linear model was used, with occasion (initial event versus retelling) as a within-subject

---

[2] The oblimin and varimax rotations produced similar solutions; interfactor correlations for the oblimin solution were moderate (above .30), thus the oblimin solution was retained. Mutual liking has not been theoretically evaluated and includes both long-term relationship quality and conversational responding. Including mutual liking does not change any of the reported results.

---

[3] Separate evaluations of such interactions revealed that none attained statistical significance.

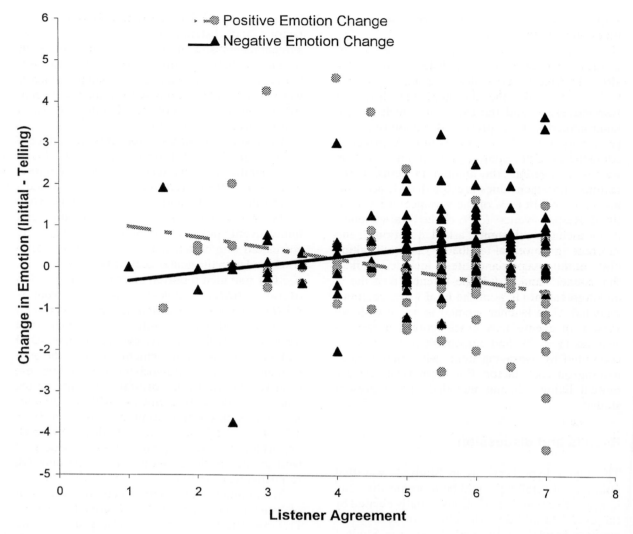

Figure 2.   Relationships between listener agreement and differences in positive and negative emotion from the event to the retelling, Study 2.

factor, gender as a categorical between-subjects factor, and listener responsiveness, listener agreeableness, and emotion regulation motives as *continuous* between-subjects factors. Interactions between occasion and all between-subjects factors were tested, but interactions among between-subjects factors were not included.

This analysis revealed main effects for listener responsiveness, $F(1, 106) = 8.3, p < .01, MSE = 3.9$, listener agreement, $F(1, 106) = 20.3, p < .01, MSE = 3.9$, the goal of feeling better, $F(1, 106) = 38.4, p < .01, MSE = 3.9$, and gender, $F(1, 106) = 5.0, p < .05, MSE = 3.9$ on overall negative emotion. Overall negative emotion (averaged across the initial event and retelling occasion) *tended* to be greater with more responsive listening ($r = .16, p <$

.10). Negative emotion was significantly greater when participants reported telling about the event in order to feel better ($r = .53, p < .001$). Finally, negative emotion was significantly lower when listeners agreed with the participant ($r = -.28, p < .01$). Men reported on average less negative emotion, $M(SD) = 2.8(1.5)$, than did women, $M(SD) = 3.3(1.6)$.

These main effects were complicated by three interactions: an occasion by listener agreement interaction, $F(1, 106) = 11.3, p < .01, MSE = .43$; an occasion by goal of feeling better interaction, $F(1, 106) = 5.6, p < .05, MSE = .43$, and an occasion by gender interaction, $F(1, 106) = 5.8, p < .05, MSE = .43$. Next, each of these interactions is considered in turn. Listener agreement was positively associated with reductions in negative emotion from the initial event to the retelling ($r = .25$, $p < .01$, see also Figure 2). Telling about the event to feel better was also positively associated with reductions in negative emotion, but only when controlling for listener agreement and participant gender (partial $r = .21$, $p < .03$). Finally, as shown in Figure 1, men reported less negative emotion across occasions, $M(SD)$event = 3.1(1.6); $M(SD)$tell = 2.5(1.6), than did women, $M(SD)$event = 3.5(1.6); $M(SD)$tell = 3.1(1.7), but this difference was only significant for the retelling, $t(117)$event = 1.3, $p > .15$; $t(117)$retelling = 2.0, $p < .05$.

Study 2 suggests that there are no *general* differences in emotions reported during an event, and emotions reported while retelling that event. Emotional changes appear contingent on features of the retelling context, including the listener's behaviour, the speaker's goals, and the speaker's gender. More agreeable listening was associated with declines in negative and increases in positive emotion (see Figure 2), and the goal of feeling better was also associated with greater decreases in negative emotion across time. Finally, in terms of negative emotion, men report greater decreases from the initial event to retelling than do women. These findings are consistent with Rimé's work (1995; Rimé et al., 1998) and that of others (Harvey et al., 1991; Kelly et al., 1995; Murray et al., 1989; Smyth, 1998), in suggesting that elements of the retelling context influence the degree to which remembering provides emotional benefits.

Moreover, participant gender and the goal of feeling better were associated with the types of events that are told. Men appear more likely to recount emotionally positive events than women and, consequently, to experience more positive emotions at retelling. More negative and fewer positive events are more likely to be retold in order to "feel better", because of the widespread belief that talking helps us feel better (Rimé et al., in press). However, such events may also result in the experience of relatively more negative and less positive emotion during retelling. Finally, consistent with a large literature on self-enhancing biases in memory (Baumeister et al., 1990; Greenwald, 1980), more positive events were reported to be more important and self-revealing. These findings replicate and extend those of Study 1. Next, findings from both studies are summarised and discussed in terms of their implications for functional approaches to autobiographical memory research.

GENERAL DISCUSSION

Earlier, I proposed that emotion regulation is one function of remembering in both social and non-social contexts. The present studies examined whether conversational remembering might serve emotion-regulatory functions by comparing the emotions initially elicited by an experience with those associated with talking about the experience. The findings, although not conclusive, demonstrate that talking about past experiences can modulate the emotions those experiences initially elicited in positive ways. However, that modulation is dependent on the context of talk about the past, including participant characteristics like gender and goals for talking, and on listener behaviours like agreement with the participant's view of "what happened".

Specifically, the results suggest that: (1) people do retell experiences with the goal of regulating emotion, especially when those experiences were negative; (2) there may be emotional benefits to talking about experiences regardless of the presence of any explicit goal to "feel better"; and (3) men may experience less negative emotion during retelling than do women. Study 2, additionally, suggests that talking about experiences provides greater emotional benefits when emotion-regulation motives are present and listeners agree with speakers' stories. Next, both limitations and implications of these findings are considered.

Very importantly, the retrospective and reconstructive nature of the data limit the conclusions that can be drawn. Retrospective judgements of emotion differ from those made "on-line" (Levine & Bluck, 1997; Levine & Bluck, 2002; Tsai, Levenson, & Carstensen, 2000). Retrospective judgements of this type may be made in a theory-driven way (Ross, 1989). To the extent that people believe telling others about their experiences results in emotional benefits (Rimé et al., 1998; Zech, 2000), their retrospective reports may demonstrate such benefits. However, emotional benefits in the present findings were evident for negative, rather than positive, emotions. Benefits emerged under specific contextual circumstances involving both participant and listener features, and were not limited to those who reported talking to feel better.

Additionally, the fact that the data are correlational and collected on a single occasion makes it problematic to conclude that retelling causes the observed benefits. To make such claims, future work will need to assess on-line reports of emotion during an experience and while retelling that experience. Such methods can better demonstrate whether differences in emotion across those two activities are better attributed to the retelling, or to other processes occurring between the event and the retelling.

Additional limitations of the studies include relatively homogeneous volunteer samples, self-reported perceptions of listener behaviour, and varying measures of emotion-regulatory goals (which produced variable results). The hypotheses and results in this study focused primarily on emotional benefits—wanting to feel better, and experiencing increased positive and decreased negative emotion. However, emotion regulation can be oriented towards negative (maintaining bitterness) outcomes (Gross, 1998; Webster, 1993), something for future work to address.

Implications for functional approaches to autobiographical memory

These findings have several implications for work on the functions of autobiographical remembering. First, they support devoting more attention to the interplay of autobiographical memory and emotion regulation, especially ways in which remembering can change emotions associated with a particular event. A key issue for further examination is the dynamics between fading of memory for emotions over time (Levine & Bluck, 2002), and the substantial flexibility such fading provides for using memory to regulate emotion. In fact, Levine and Bluck (under review) note that *current* appraisals of a past event are what predicts memory for the emotions elicited by that event. In talking about the past, people change their appraisals of events in response to their current goals, and their listeners (Pasupathi & Rich, 2002). Thus, conversational retelling may influence emotion via goal changes.

Other work has failed to find evidence of emotional benefits accruing following retelling (Rimé et al., 1992, 1998; Zech, 2000). In all cases, the emotion elicited by the original event serves as the baseline. In the present studies, emotions during retelling were assessed, and benefits found, while Rimé and colleagues examined the emotions elicited by thinking of the event at the time of the study, and found little change. Talking about emotional events may produce temporary, not lasting, changes in emotions, perhaps because

the goals for recall during talk differ from the goals of recall during a study, with emotional consequences.

Considering emotion regulation as a key function of autobiographical memory complicates distinctions between self, social, and directive functions (Cohen, 1998; Pasupathi et al., 2002). For example, is retelling events for emotion regulation serving only self-regulatory functions? Or is it also social in nature, because it involves eliciting empathy (Bluck & Alea, 2002), and may increase intimacy between speaker and listener? An alternative to the view of emotion regulation as a function of autobiographical memory is the idea that emotion-regulatory processes serve all three of the major proposed functions (self, social, and directive), and that emotion regulatory outcomes may differ depending on whether self-regulatory, social, or directive functions are at stake. For example, engaging in self-presentation (a self function) while remembering may lead to enhanced positive emotion and diminished negative emotion. In contrast, seeking empathy may involve expressing and experiencing more negative emotions (to elicit the audience's sympathy).

In further examining such issues, it is important to continue to examine social remembering. In solitary settings, people are free to reconstruct the past as it may best serve their goals, emotion regulation included (Josephson et al., 1996; Parrott & Sabini, 1990; Pennebaker & Seagal, 1999). However, the joint nature of remembering in social settings (Bavelas et al., 2000; Hirst et al., 1997; Manier et al., 1996; Pasupathi et al., 2002, 1998) means that listeners also contribute to emotion regulation. Given the prevalence of sharing emotional experiences in conversation (Rimé et al., 1992, 1998), the effects of listeners are important to understand.

In the present studies, men consistently appeared to experience less negative emotion when talking about experiences than did women. Retelling itself may be more positive for men than women, and this fits with an array of work on gender differences relevant to emotion regulation and remembering. For example, women report more intense emotions than do men (Fujita, Diener, & Sandvik, 1991), suffer from higher rates of affect disorders (Fujita et al., 1991; Nolen-Hoeksema, 2001), talk about their past experiences in more emotional, vivid, and elaborative ways (Davis, 1999; Fivush, 1998; Seidlitz & Diener, 1998), and report different strategies to regulate emotion than do men (Nolen-Hoeksema, 2001; Nolen-Hoeksema, Larson, & Grayson, 1999). In particular, women are more likely to report ruminating, or thinking about their negative emotions and the potential causes of those emotions. Rumination has been linked to more intense and long-lasting negative affect (Nolen-Hoeksema et al., 1999), and may also be related to differences in how men and women talk about the past. Social rumination might undermine the potential benefits of past talk for women. It is possible that women simply recall their past emotions as more intense (Fujita et al., 1991), or that women are more likely to experience disagreement from listeners. However, the present results do not support these explanations.

In Study 2, emotional benefits were also garnered by those whose listeners agreed with their version of events. This finding is consistent with a small literature on appraisal support (Thoits, 1986), or the affirmation social partners provide for an individual's view of the world. Appraisal support provides people with a sense that their perspective on events is reasonable and normal, which can be reassuring despite negative emotion associated with the experience. Even a negative experience like a betrayal may elicit positive emotion if told to an agreeable listener.

In sum, the present findings provide preliminary evidence that social remembering can provide emotional benefits by allowing individuals to re-experience their past in a more emotionally positive and less emotionally negative way. The context for social remembering, including the gender of the participant, the goals they bring to remembering, and the responses of audiences, will govern the extent to which such remembering results in emotional benefits. More broadly, these results suggest the potential enhancement to a functional perspective about autobiographical memory that arise from looking both across and within the specific contexts in which memory is frequently used.

REFERENCES

Baumeister, R.F., & Newman, L.S. (1994). How stories make sense of personal experiences: Motives that shape autobiographical narratives. *Personality and Social Psychology Bulletin, 20*, 676–690.

Baumeister, R.F., Stilman, A., & Wotman, S.R. (1990). Victim and perpetrator accounts of interpersonal conflict: Autobiographical narratives about anger. *Journal of Personality and Social Psychology, 59*, 994–1005.

Bavelas, J.B., Coates, L., & Johnson, T. (2000). Listeners as co-narrators. *Journal of Personality and Social Psychology, 79*, 941–952.

Bluck, S., & Alea, N. (2002). Exploring the functions of autobiographical memory: Why do I remember the autumn? In J.D. Webster & B.K. Haight (Eds.), *Critical advances in reminiscence work: From theory to application* (pp. 61–75). New York: Springer.

Carstensen, L.L., Isaacowitz, D.M., & Charles, S.T. (1999). Taking time seriously: A theory of socio-emotional selectivity. *American Psychologist, 54*, 165–181.

Carstensen, L.L., Pasupathi, M., Mayr, U., Nesselroade, J.R. (2000). Emotional experience in everyday life: Age differences from 18 to 94 years. *Journal of Personality and Social Psychology, 79*, 644–655.

Charles, S.T., Mather, M., & Carstensen, L.L. (2002). *Aging and memory for emotional pictures.* Manuscript in preparation, University of California at Irvine, Irvine, CA.

Cohen, G. (1998). The effects of aging on autobiographical memory. In C.P. Thompson, D.J. Herrmann, D. Bruce, J.D. Read, D.G. Payne, & M.P. Toglia (Eds.), *Autobiographical memory: Theoretical and applied perspectives* (pp. 105–124). Mahwah, NJ: Lawrence Erlbaum Associates Inc.

Conway, M.A., & Pleydell-Pearce, C.W. (2000). The construction of autobiographical memories in the self-memory system. *Psychological Review, 107*, 261–288.

Davis, P.J. (1999). Gender differences in autobiographical memory for childhood emotional experiences. *Journal of Personality and Social Psychology, 76*, 498–510.

Dickinson, C., & Givon, T. (1995). Memory and conversation: Toward an experimental paradigm. In T. Givon (Ed.), *Conversation: Cognitive, communicative, and social perspectives* (pp. 91–132). Amsterdam, The Netherlands: John Benjamins.

Edwards, D., & Middleton, D. (1988). Conversational remembering and family relationships: How children learn to remember. *Journal of Social and Personal Relationships, 5*, 3–25.

Finkenauer, C., & Rimé, B. (1998). Keeping emotional memories secret: Health and subjective well-being when emotions are not shared. *Journal of Health Psychology, 3*, 47–58.

Fivush, R. (1998). Gendered narratives: Elaboration, structure, and emotion in parent–child reminiscing across the preschool years. In C.P. Thompson, D.J. Herrmann, D. Bruce, J.D. Read, D.G. Payne, & M.P. Toglia (Eds.), *Autobiographical memory: Theoretical and applied perspectives* (pp. 79–104). Mahwah, NJ: Lawrence Erlbaum Associates Inc.

Fivush, R., & Haden, C.A. (1997). Narrating and representing experience: Preschoolers' developing autobiographical accounts. In P.W. van den Broek, P.J. Bauer, & T. Bourg (Eds.), *Developmental spans in event comprehension and representation* (pp. 169–198). Mahwah: Lawrence Erlbaum Associates Inc.

Fujita, F., Diener, E., & Sandvik, E. (1991). Gender differences in negative affect and well-being: The case for emotional intensity. *Journal of Personality and Social Psychology, 61*, 427–434.

Greenwald, A.G. (1980). The totalitarian ego: Fabrication and revision of personal history. *American Psychologist, 35*, 603–618.

Gross, J.J. (1998). The emerging field of emotion regulation: An integrative review. *Review of General Psychology, 2*, 271–299.

Gross, J.J. (2001). Emotion regulation in adulthood: Timing is everything. *Current Directions in Psychological Science, 10*, 214–219.

Han, J.J., Leichtman, M.D., & Wang, Q. (1998). Autobiographical memory in Korean, Chinese, and American Children. *Developmental Psychology, 34*, 701–713.

Harvey, J.H., Orbuch, T.L., Chwalisz, K.D., & Garwood, G. (1991). Coping with sexual assault: The roles of account-making and confiding. *Journal of Traumatic Stress, 4*, 515–531.

Hirst, W., Manier, D., & Apetroaia, I. (1997). The social construction of the remembered self: Family recounting. In J.G. Snodgrass & R.C. Thompson (Eds.), *The self across psychology* (pp. 163–188). New York: New York Academy of Sciences.

Hyman, I.E., & Faries, J.M. (1992). The functions of autobiographical memory. In M.A. Conway, D.C. Rubin, H. Spinnler, & W.A. Wagenaar (Eds.), *Theoretical perspectives on autobiographical memory* (pp. 207–221). Dordrecht, The Netherlands: Kluwer Academic Publishers.

Josephson, B.R., Singer, J.A., & Salovey, P. (1996). Mood regulation and memory: Repairing sad moods with happy memories. *Cognition and Emotion, 10*, 437–444.

Kelly, A.E., Coenen, M.E., & Johnston, B.L. (1995). Confidants' feedback and traumatic life events. *Journal of Traumatic Stress, 8*, 161–169.

Levenson, R.W., Carstensen, L.L., Friesen, W.V., & Ekman, P. (1991). Emotion, physiology, and expression in old age. *Psychology and Aging, 6*, 28–35.

Levine, J.M., Resnick, L.B., & Higgens, E.T. (1993). Social foundations of cognition. *Annual Review of Psychology, 44*, 585–612.

Levine, L.J., & Bluck, S. (1997). Experienced and remembered emotional intensity in older adults. *Psychology and Aging, 12*, 514–523.

Levine, L.J., & Bluck, S. (2002). *How emotions and memories fade.* Manuscript submitted for publication.

Manier, D., Pinner, E., & Hirst, W. (1996). Conversational remembering. In D. Hermann, C. McEvoy, C. Hertzog, A. Hertel, & M.K. Johnson (Eds.), *Basic and applied memory research, vol. 2* (pp. 269–286). Mahwah, NJ: Lawrence Erlbaum Associates Inc.

Mather, M., & Johnson, M.K. (2000). Choice-supportive source monitoring: Do our decisions seem better to us as we age? *Psychology and Aging, 15*, 596–606.

Murray, E.J., Lamnin, A.D., & Carver, C.S. (1989). Emotional expression in written essays and psychotherapy. *Journal of Social and Clinical Psychology, 8*, 414–427.

Murray, E.J., & Segal, D.L. (1994). Emotional processing in vocal and written expression of feelings about traumatic experiences. *Journal of Traumatic Stress, 7*(3), 391–405.

Nelson, K. (1991). Remembering and telling: A developmental story. *Journal of Narrative and Life History, 1*, 109–127.

Nolen-Hoeksema, S. (2001). Gender differences in depression. *Current Directions in Psychological Science, 10*, 173–176.

Nolen-Hoeksema, S., Larson, J., & Grayson, C. (1999). Explaining the gender difference in depression. *Journal of Personality and Social Psychology, 77*, 1061–1072.

Norrick, N. (1997). Twice-told tales: Collaborative narration of familiar stories. *Language in Society, 26*, 199–220.

Park, C.L., & Folkman, S. (1997). Meaning in the context of stress and coping. *Review of General Psychology, 1*, 115–144.

Parrott, W.G., & Sabini, J. (1990). Mood and memory under natural conditions: Evidence for mood incongruent recall. *Journal of Personality and Social Psychology, 59*, 321–336.

Pasupathi, M. (2001). The social construction of the personal past and its implications for adult development. *Psychological Bulletin, 127*, 651–672.

Pasupathi, M., & Carstensen, L.L. (2002). *Age and emotion during mutual reminiscing.* Manuscript submitted for publication.

Pasupathi, M., Carstensen, L.L., Levenson, R.W., & Gottman, J. M. (1999). Responsive listening in long-married couples: A psycholinguistic perspective. *Journal of Non-Verbal Behavior, 23*, 173–193.

Pasupathi, M., Henry, R., & Carstensen, L. L. (in press). Age and ethnicity differences in storytelling to young children: Emotionality, relationality, and socialization. *Psychology and Aging.*

Pasupathi, M., Lucas, S., & Coombs, A. (2002). Functions of autobiographical memory in discourse: Long-married couples talk about conflicts and pleasant topics. *Discourse Processes, 34*, 163–192.

Pasupathi, M., & Rich, B. (2002). *Social construction of memory and self in personal storytelling: Listener effects.* Manuscript in preparation, University of Utah.

Pasupathi, M., Stallworth, L.M., & Murdoch, K. (1998). How what we tell becomes what we know: Listener effects on speakers' long-term memory for events. *Discourse Processes, 26*, 1–25.

Pennebaker, J.W., & Seagal, J. (1999). Forming a story: The health benefits of narrative. *Journal of Clinical Psychology, 55*, 1243–1254.

Pillemer, D.B. (1998). *Momentous events, vivid memories: How unforgettable moments help us understand the meaning of our lives.* Cambridge, MA: Harvard University Press.

Reese, E., & Brown, N. (2000). Reminiscing and recounting in the preschool years. *Applied Cognitive Psychology, 14*, 1–17.

Rimé, B. (1995). Mental rumination, social sharing, and the recovery from emotional exposure. In J.W. Pennebaker (Ed.), *Emotions, disclosure, and health* (pp. 271–292). Washington, DC: American Psychological Association.

Rimé, B., Finkenauer, C., Luminet, O., Zech, E., & Phillipot, P. (1998). Social sharing of emotion: New evidence and new questions. *European Review of Social Psychology, 9*, 145–189.

Rimé, B., Herbette, G., & Corsini, S. (in press). The social sharing of emotion: Illusory and real benefits of talking about emotional experiences. In I. Nyklicek, L.R. Temoschok, & A.J.J.M. Vingerhoets (Eds.), *Emotional expression, well-being, and health*. London: Harwood Academic Publishers.

Rimé, B., Phillipot, P., Boca, S., & Mesquita, B. (1992). Long-lasting cognitive and social consequences of emotion: Social sharing and rumination. In W. Stroebe & M. Hewstone (Eds.), *European Review of Social Psychology* (Vol. 3, pp. 225–258). New York: John Wiley & Sons.

Ross, M. (1989). Relation of implicit theories to the construction of personal histories. *Psychological Review, 96*, 341–357.

Rubin, D.C., & Schulkind, M.D. (1997). Distribution of important and word-cued autobiographical memories in 20-, 35-, and 70-year-old adults. *Psychology and Aging, 12*, 524–535.

Schacter, D.L. (1996). *Searching for memory: The brain, the mind, and the past*. New York: Basic Books.

Seidlitz, L., & Diener, E. (1998). Sex differences in the recall of affective experiences. *Journal of Personality and Social Psychology, 74*, 262–271.

Smyth, J.M. (1998). Written emotional expression: Effect sizes, outcome types, and moderating variables. *Journal of Consulting and Clinical Psychology, 66*(1), 174–184.

Sorenson, K.A., Russell, S.M., Harkness, D.J., & Harvey, J.H. (1993). Account-making, confiding, and coping with the ending of a close relationship. *Journal of Social Behavior and Personality, 8*(1), 73–86.

Staudinger, U.M. (1989). *The study of life review: An approach to the investigation of intellectual development across the life span*. Berlin: Max-Planck-Institut für Bildungsforschung.

Thoits, P.A. (1986). Social support as coping assistance. *Journal of Consulting and Clinical Psychology, 54*, 416–423.

Tsai, J.L., Levenson, R.W., & Carstensen, L.L. (2000). Autonomic, subjective, and expressive responses to emotional films in older and younger Chinese Americans and European Americans. *Psychology and Aging, 15*, 684–693.

Vaillant, G.E. (1995). Repression in college men followed for half a century. In J.L. Singer (Ed.), *Repression and dissociation: Implications for personality theory, psychopathology, and health* (pp. 259–273). Chicago, IL: University of Chicago Press.

Webster, J.D. (1993). Construction and validation of the Reminiscence Functions Scale. *Journal of Gerontology: Psychological Sciences, 48*, P256–P262.

Webster, J.D. (1994). Predictors of reminiscence: A lifespan perspective. *Canadian Journal on Aging, 13*, 66–78.

Webster, J.D. (1997). The Reminiscence Functions Scale: A replication. *International Journal of Aging and Human Development, 44*, 137–148.

Webster, J.D., & McCall, M.E. (1999). Reminiscence functions across adulthood: A replication and extension. *Journal of Adult Development, 6*, 73–85.

Wong, P.T.P., & Watt, L.M. (1991). What types of reminiscence are associated with successful aging? *Psychology and Aging, 6*, 272–279.

Zech, E. (2000). *The impact of the communication of emotional experiences*. Unpublished Doctoral dissertation, University of Louvain, Louvain-la-Neuve, Belgium.

MEMORY, 2003, *11* (2), 165–178

Why are you telling me that? A conceptual model of the social function of autobiographical memory

Nicole Alea and Susan Bluck

University of Florida, USA

In an effort to stimulate and guide empirical work within a functional framework, this paper provides a conceptual model of the social functions of autobiographical memory (AM) across the lifespan. The model delineates the processes and variables involved when AMs are shared to serve social functions. Components of the model include: lifespan contextual influences, the qualitative characteristics of memory (emotionality and level of detail recalled), the speaker's characteristics (age, gender, and personality), the familiarity and similarity of the listener to the speaker, the level of responsiveness during the memory-sharing process, and the nature of the social relationship in which the memory sharing occurs (valence and length of the relationship). These components are shown to influence the type of social function served and/or, the extent to which social functions are served. Directions for future empirical work to substantiate the model and hypotheses derived from the model are provided.

Over two decades ago Neisser (1978) addressed the need for understanding memory from an ecological perspective. Since then, research on everyday memory has grown considerably and the study of autobiographical memory (AM) is no exception. The function of memory, or how we use memory, is a central tenet of the ecological memory approach that has been adopted at a theoretical level by AM researchers. Three functions of AM have been theorised: a self, a social, and a directive function (e.g., Cohen, 1998; Pillemer, 1992). Despite its intuitive appeal, however, the ecological approach has led to a limited amount of empirical work on the functions of AM. Three empirical studies offer preliminary evidence for the theoretical functions of AM (Bluck, Habermas, & Rubin, 2002; Hyman & Faries, 1992; Pasupathi, Lucas, & Coombs, 2002). Clearly, more research is needed on the function that personal memories play in individuals' daily lives.

We suggest that the lack of empirical research may be due, at least in part, to the need for a conceptual model that provides the level of specificity necessary for hypothesis-driven research. Currently, no models exist that conceptualises what AMs are used for in everyday life. Such a model could also identify crucial gaps in the existing literature where further research is needed to make more sophisticated model building possible. Thus, the objective of the current paper is to present a conceptual model of one category of functions of AM, the social functions, that illustrates the processes and variables involved when individuals share AMs for social purposes.

The model presented here focuses exclusively on the social functions of AM. Social functions of AM include using AM: to develop or maintain *intimacy* in relationship; to illustrate a point or give advice in order to *teach and inform* others; and to elicit *empathy* from others or provide

Requests for reprints should be sent to Nicole Alea, Institute on Aging, McCarty C, 5th Floor, PO Box 115911, University of Florida, Gainesville, FL, USA, 32611-5911. Email: nalea@ufl.edu

http://www.tandf.co.uk/journals/pp/09658211.html   DOI:10.1080/09658210244000342 empathy to others (see Table 1).[1] Although we recognise that empirical evidence exists for all three theoretical functions, and that models may eventually be needed for all functions, we begin model development with the social functions of remembering because it has been suggested that using AMs for social purposes, such as relationship maintenance and development, is their most fundamental use (e.g., Bruce, 1989; Nelson, 1993). In addition, individuals often talk about the past and share their experiences with others in order to fulfil social goals (e.g., Baumeister & Newman, 1994; Hirst & Manier, 1996; Norrick, 1997; Pasupathi et al., 2002). Thus, social functions warrant independent attention due to their potential fundamentality and to their ubiquity in everyday life.

In addition to focusing only on the social functions of AM, the model is also limited exclusively to memories that are shared with others and not memories that are only thought about. There is no doubt that AMs can be used for social functions in the absence of memory sharing. For example, individuals report thinking about past experiences they had with someone who has passed away in order to maintain intimacy with that person (Webster, 1995). How-

ever, autobiographical remembering frequently occurs in social contexts; it is often an interpersonal phenomenon (Graumann, 1986; Nelson & Fivush, 2000). Individuals share personal memories with others not present at the original event (Hyman & Faries, 1992) as well as collaborating and co-constructing memories with others present at the original event (e.g., Gould & Dixon, 1993; Edwards & Middleton, 1986; Fivush & Reese, 1992; Hirst & Manier, 1996; Norrick, 1997). In sum, the fundamental nature of social functions of AM, the frequent use of AMs for social purposes, and the often interpersonal nature of autobiographical remembering, make a conceptual model focused solely on the social functions of AM during AM sharing an appropriate starting point for model building, particularly at this early stage in the development of the literature.

In the next section, we provide a preliminary conceptual model of the social functions of AM during AM sharing. The pathways and components of the model are described, using relevant empirical work from the AM literature and related areas. This work is used to generate ideas, sometimes speculations, about the interrelations between each component and the social functions of remembering. In the final section, the model's utility is demonstrated by: (a) identifying areas for future research to substantiate the model, and (b) employing the model to generate specific research questions.

TABLE 1
Social functions of autobiographical memory

Type of function	Description
Intimacy	Initiating, maintaining, and developing relationship intimacy
Teach/Inform	Teaching and informing others; illustrating a point and giving advice
Empathy	Eliciting empathy and reassurance from others; showing empathy

This is not an exhaustive list of the types of social functions of AM but is based on suggestions in the literature (e.g., Cohen, 1998; Hyman & Faries, 1992; Pillemer, 1998; Webster, 1995).

A CONCEPTUAL MODEL OF THE SOCIAL FUNCTIONS OF AM

The conceptual model presented here is a first step at providing researchers with a schematic representation of the processes and variables involved when individuals use *personally meaningful* AMs, such as memories for specific events, life periods, and domains (Bluck & Habermas, 2001; Conway, 1996), to serve social functions across the lifespan. AMs can range in quality from trivial memories to memories that are important enough to be included in one's life story (Bluck & Habermas, 2000). Personally meaningful memories are the focus of the current model because this distinction may be especially salient when taking a functional approach. For example, personally meaningful memories are probably the type of memories used to serve central functions, such as maintaining relationships (e.g., Thorne,

---

[1] Eliciting empathy from others through AM sharing and showing empathy to others through AM sharing does not involve recounting only negative emotional events. Empathic functions, as they are defined here, involve sharing mutual feelings (positive or negative) with another in order for the person to feel the same way (positive or negative). Also, while conversational uses of AM (e.g., using AMs to make the conversation more enjoyable or to persuade the listener) are sometimes considered to be a social function of AM sharing (e.g., Pillemer, 1998; Webster, 1995), they are excluded from the current model. For the current paper, conversational uses are seen not as a social function *per se* (that is, as an outcome of AM sharing), but rather as part of the memory-sharing process.

Cutting, & Skaw, 1998).[2] The next section addresses how the social functions of autobiographical memory are influenced by the components of the model.

Pathways in the model

Although for clarity we present each component in isolation, they are in fact interrelated. Two paths lead to the social functions of AM: one from the dyadic interaction unit directly to the social functions of AM and one that is mediated by memory characteristics. As shown in the model (see Figure 1), the dyadic interaction unit as an entity can impact the social function of remembering the past. However, components and variables within this unit can also have a direct impact individually, but it is not feasible to represent each relation pictorially with individual pathways. Another pathway represented in the model suggests that social functions are not only an outcome of remembering, but that remembering can be decided upon a priori to serve a certain function. That is, an individual can decide that they want to share an AM for a particular purpose, such as developing intimacy, and share their memory accordingly. This is illustrated in the model by the broken arrow leading from the social functions of AM to the dyadic interaction unit. Empirical work manipulating the reasons why people share stories and other information supports this notion that stories change based on the intent of the teller (e.g., McGregor & Holmes, 1999; Sanitioso, Kunda, & Fong, 1990; Tversky & Marsh, 2000). Now that the pathways in the model have been clarified, components of the model are described.

Components of the model

The major components related to the processes involved when one individual shares an AM with another to serve social functions are also shown in Figure 1. These include the lifespan context in which all other components are embedded, char-

acteristics of the person sharing the AM (e.g., age, gender, personality), how familiar and similar the listener is to the speaker, and the level of dyadic responsiveness during the memory-sharing process. Speaker–listener characteristics and responsivity are nested within the speaker–listener relationship (e.g., valence and length of the relationship). Characteristics of the person's memory, such as level of detail and amount of emotion are included because they are influenced by the above person and relationship components and may also influence the extent to which social functions are served. Finally, both the type of social function served and the extent to which the function is served are shown as outcomes in the model. Note that this outcome is considered here only for the person doing the memory sharing. Future work might consider outcomes for both partners in the exchange or for the dyad (i.e., the relationship) as a unit of analysis.

Social functions of AM: Use and adaptivity

The model accounts for both the social *uses* of AM (i.e., which function is served) and the *adaptivity* of social functions (i.e., extent to which the function is served). Identifying the uses of AM has been the primary focus of empirical work (Bluck et al., 2002; Hyman & Faries, 1992; Pasupathi et al., 2002). The social uses of AM include using AMs for intimacy, teaching and informing others, and for eliciting and showing empathy (see Table 1). The other connotation of function, however, is that of an action being adaptive in serving some goal or leading to some preferred end state (Bruce, 1989; see also Bluck & Alea, 2002). When function is conceived as adaptation it refers to the extent to which the use of memory results in adaptive or maladaptive outcomes. For example, adaptively using AMs to develop intimacy in relationships means that when AMs are shared, intimacy is enhanced. A similar distinction to that made between uses and adaptivity of memory functions has been made between goals and goal achievement (e.g., Baumeister & Newman, 1994; Brandtstadter & Renner, 1990; Emmons, 1986). We prefer, for a variety of reasons, to maintain the focus on function instead of recasting it in terms of goals, though they may be closely allied concepts under some conditions.

Unlike the reminiscence tradition, which more seriously considers the adaptive value of memory (e.g., Watt & Wong, 1991), work in the AM

---

[2] There is a body of literature exploring how everyday talk, even about mundane events (e.g., "I went to the grocery store yesterday"), is important for sustaining relationships (e.g., Duck, Rutt, Hurst, & Strejc, 1991). While recognising this type of conversation as important for relationships, it is not clear whether talk about mundane events is different from talk about "truly autobiographical" or more meaningful events. Thus, personally meaningful past events are the focus of the current model.

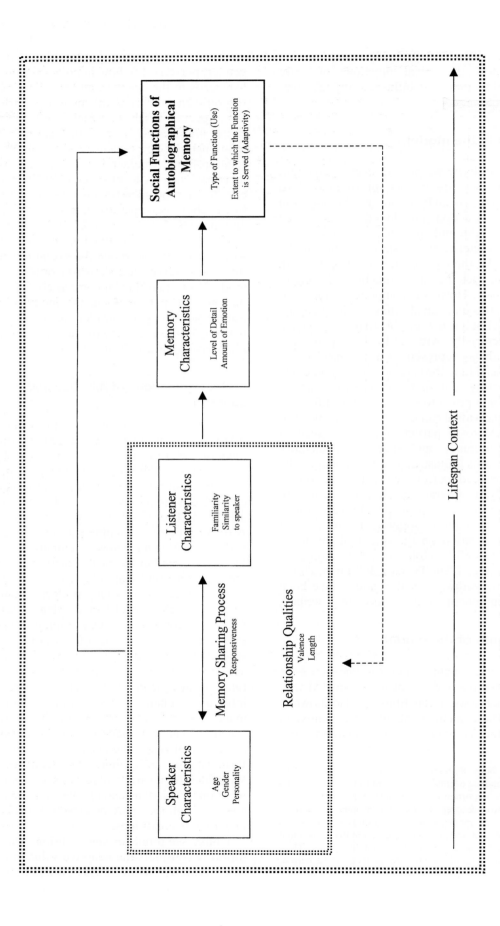

Figure 1. A conceptual model of the social functions of autobiographical memory.

literature only alludes to adaptation and does not often directly include it in research conceptualisation and design. Including the adaptive value of social functions of AM in the present model aims to stimulate work in this area. As such, the conceptual model presented here considers how memories are used, that is the different types of social functions served, as well as what factors might affect variation in how adaptively memory is employed (i.e., the extent to which the function is served). Each of the components in the model has been included because of its potential impact of which functions are served and how well. To begin, one factor that might influence the type and adaptive use of AMs that are employed for social purposes is the individual's developmental life context.

Lifespan context

The components in the model are nested in a lifespan context because such a context can directly impact how and how well AMs are used for social purposes (Wong & Watt, 1991). Researchers have only very recently incorporated a lifespan developmental approach (Baltes, Staudinger, & Lindenberger, 1999) into the study of AM (Bluck & Habermas, 2001). Taking a lifespan perspective involves understanding how changes in chronological age and an individual's life context influence the uses of AM. Conceptualising both gains and losses (Baltes, 1987) in AM across the lifespan is an integral part of understanding the function of AM. In addition, changes in developmental goals and tasks across life phases (e.g., Erikson, 1980; Havigurst, 1972) may affect how AM is used: the importance of particular social functions and the extent to which they can be adaptively served may vary across the adult lifespan. Predictable changes in, for example, social networks across the lifespan (e.g., Antonucci & Akiyama, 1995; Carstensen, 1993) can influence which social functions are most often used, and the extent to which they are adaptively employed.

For example, developmental tasks and life contexts affect the types of social functions likely to be used across the lifespan. Tasks in young adulthood revolve around developing intimacy (e.g., finding a spouse; Erikson, 1980; Havigurst, 1972), thus AMs in early adulthood are likely to be used for the social function of developing intimacy. In midlife, individuals begin to use the past for directing future goals and aspirations (Buhler, 1968) and guiding future generations (Erikson, 1980). Thus, one frequent social use of AM at this point in the lifespan may be to teach and inform others. Tasks faced in old age may concern adaptation to loss (Neugarten, 1979), including adjusting to widowhood and retirement (Havigurst, 1972). In late life using AMs for eliciting empathy from others (as well as self functions such as maintaining self continuity) may be important for managing losses. This very brief review suggests that not taking a lifespan perspective limits our understanding of the social uses of AM by assuming developmental uniformity in lifespan contexts, as well as in AM capabilities and qualities. The next section addresses the qualitative characteristics of AMs that can impact the social functions of AM.

Memory characteristics: Detail and emotion

Qualitative memory characteristics include the phenomenal qualities of remembering (Larsen, 1998). Two memory characteristics, level of detail and amount of emotion in the memory, are included here because meaningful memories are encoded with high levels of emotion and detail, or vividness (e.g., Bluck & Li, 2001; Cohen, Conway, & Maylor, 1994). Individuals have vivid memories, composed of great detail and affect, for personally meaningful events and surprising national events (e.g., flashbulb memories; Conway, 1995). Most individuals have memories of the John F. Kennedy assassination that are detailed and emotional enough to be categorised as flashbulb memories, but not for less significant events (Brown & Kulik, 1977). Similarly, specific details about conditions in a concentration camp (Wagenaar & Groeneweg, 1990) and events surrounding the *Challenger* explosion (Bohannon, 1988) are remembered well months and years later. Emotional information is often included when recalling surprising events, such as the OJ Simpson verdict announcement (e.g., Bluck, Levine, & Laulhere, 1999), and when individuals recall their most vivid personal memories (e.g., Cohen & Faulkner, 1988). How might detail and emotion relate to the social functions of AM?

Memories of specific episodes that are rich in emotion and detail communicate "meaning over and above the particular informational content of the memories, and thereby help[s] the speaker achieve important interpersonal goals" (Pillemer, 1992, p. 242). Detail and emotion influence the type of social functions served and the extent to which social functions are served. Memories that include detail are judged as more credible and persuasive by others (e.g., Bruce, 1989), thus possibly better serving the social function of teaching and informing others. Memories rich with detail and emotion also signal caring and intimacy as opposed to neutral memories, which signal emotional detachment (Tannen, 1990). The intimacy function of AM may be better served by such memories. Similarly, including details and emotional information during recall allows the listener to relate to the story being told (Schank & Abelson, 1995), thus enhancing the likelihood of an empathic function being served. In sum, memories rich with detail and emotion are common when recalling personally meaningful, emotional events, thus demonstrating their social importance. However, the extent to which AMs are detailed and emotional is partially driven by the person who is sharing the memory , that is by the speaker's characteristics.

Speaker characteristics: Age, gender, and personality

During conversational remembering, enduring qualities of the speaker clearly affect the way that events are recalled (see Pasupathi, 2001, for a review). Age, gender, and personality can affect the type of social function served and influence the qualitative characteristics of memory, thereby affecting the extent to which social functions are served.

Age. The influence of age on the frequency of remembering in order to serve social functions has been documented. Older adults are more likely than younger adults to reflect on the past in order to teach and inform others (Webster & McCall, 1999). Using the past to maintain intimacy increases steadily from age 20 to age 80 in cross-sectional work (Webster, 1995). Thus, age affects the type of social function served.

In addition to the type of social function served, age affects the extent to which social functions are served via memory characteristics. Research on age differences and similarities in qualitative characteristics of AM is equivocal. Some research finds no differences in the levels of detail of young and older adults' most vivid AMs (Cohen & Faulkner, 1988) or in the emotional quality of their memories when recalling an emotionally charged event (e.g., Bluck et al., 1999). On the other hand,

when recalling specific episodes, such as an important historical event (e.g., Cohen et al., 1994), older adults recall less detail than younger adults and are sometimes more likely than younger adults to focus on affect (e.g., Carstensen & Turk-Charles, 1994; Hashtroudi, Johnson, & Chrosniak, 1990). In general, when the event is important for the individual, age differences are attenuated (Cohen, 1998). What do these age differences imply for how social functions are served?

Since variations in amounts of detail and emotion differentially serve the social functions of memory (Pillemer, 1998), differences in the quality of older and younger adults' memories could translate into differences in the extent to which AMs can be adaptively employed for social purposes. Specifically, older adults should be just as likely to retell their AMs in ways that successfully serve social functions if there are no age differences in the characteristics of AM when remembering personally meaningful AMs (e.g., Bluck et al., 1999; Cohen & Faulkner, 1988). Older adults may better serve social functions when they recall the past with more of an affective focus than younger adults (Hashtroudi et al., 1990). Summarising, the literature shows that age affects the types of social functions that are most often employed (intimacy, teach and inform) and the extent to which shared memories may serve their intended function because of age differences and similarities in the detail and emotional characteristics of memory.

Gender. An individual's gender is related to overall frequency of reminiscence, the types of social functions served, and how well they are served. Women reminisce more often than men (e.g., Webster, 1995) and recall a greater number of personal memories, particularly of emotionally important life events (Davis, 1999). In addition to this overall tendency, women reminiscence more often than men for the social function of maintaining intimacy in relationships, but not for the social function of teaching and informing others (Webster, 1995). Women also have systematic advantages with respect to the qualitative characteristics of their AMs and thus how well their AMs may serve intended functions. When wives and husbands are asked to recall memories of specific relationship events, wives report memories that are more clear and vivid (i.e., that include more detail and emotional content; Ross & Holmberg, 1992).

If women are at an advantage with respect to the amount of detail and emotion that they remember, then they may be more able to use their AMs to serve social functions. It might also be the case that women regard the social uses of AM as particularly important and thus choose to use their memories for these reasons more often than men. This social rehearsal may be responsible for the greater levels of emotion and detail in women's AMs. Further research on gender and memory for other life events is needed.

Personality. Individuals with certain personality traits are more likely to reflect on the past to serve functions that are consistent with their personal identities. With regard to the social functions of AM, there is a positive correlation between the Big Five personality trait Extraversion and using AMs to teach and inform others. Using AMs for intimacy is unrelated to personality traits (Cully, LaVoie, & Gfeller, 2001). When constructing stories, however, individuals remember events from their past that are consistent with their personalities and motives (e.g., McAdams, Diamond, de St. Aubin, & Mansfield, 1997; Woike, Gershkovich, Piorkowski, & Polo, 1999). Specifically, generative individuals are more likely than less generative individuals to construct a life story about the sensitivity to the suffering of others and a commitment to pro-social goals (McAdams et al., 1997); they may be more likely to use AMs for teaching and informing future generations. The limited amount of work allows for tentative conclusions regarding personality and the social functions of AM. Although affect intensity is strongly related to self-defining memories (Singer & Salovey, 1996), little is known about the relation between personality characteristics and the qualitative characteristics of AM (emotion, detail), and the types of social uses of AM.

This review of the potential impact of speaker characteristics on the social functions of AM illustrates that age, gender, and personality may affect the types of functions AM is used for, and the extent to which it is served. We recognise that these conclusions are based on very few studies, thus providing an exciting area in need of further research.

Listener characteristics: Familiarity and similarity

Despite the importance of the individual speaker characteristics, speakers construct memories in conversations that take the listener into account (Grice, 1989; Pasupathi, 2001). For sim-

plicity, the current framework outlines the dyadic interaction unit; the memory-sharing process between one speaker and one listener during a single interchange. Having a listener present influences remembering in any dyadic interaction (e.g., Andersson & Roennberg, 1995; Bavelas, Coates, & Johnson, 2000). Two characteristics of the listener, their familiarity to and similarity to the speaker, have been considered in previous research.

Familiarity. Familiarity refers to how well the speaker knows the listener. Individuals share experiences from their past with family, friends, colleagues, acquaintances, strangers, and sometimes experimenters. While there are memory benefits of collaboration (e.g., Dixon & Gould, 1998), these benefits are amplified when working with familiar others versus strangers. Participants who recall episodic material with a friend remember more information than when recalling with a stranger (Andersson & Roennberg, 1995). Similar results exist for individuals remembering with their spouses (Dixon & Gould, 1998). Thus, when the goal of remembering is to produce complete memories, we recall more information (including more detail) when remembering with people we know well. This may not always be the case. People will vary the amount of information retold depending on how much they think the listener needs to know (Grice, 1989). For instance, during family remembering, when a family recounts an event they experienced together, researchers find that the person telling the story (narrator) will sometimes omit details of the event. Thus, the stories people tell are sometimes constrained by the presence of familiar listeners (e.g., family members) when they were present at the original event (Hirst & Manier, 1996). Level of familiarity seems to affect amount recalled, sometimes enhancing it and sometimes limiting it (because the person may have told the story before to someone with whom they are familiar). This amount of information or detail can, in turn, impact the extent to which social functions are served. There is no known work regarding the amount of emotion expressed in recall when remembering with known versus unknown others.

Similarity. Similarity refers to the fact that speakers and listeners can be different or similar in terms of personal characteristics such as age, gender, and personality. A small amount of research addresses the similarity between the speaker and listener when collaboratively remembering stories and disclosing personal information. Participants provide more emotional evaluations and personal reactions when retelling a story to a peer who is similar to them than when recalling for an experimenter who is dissimilar (Hyman, 1994). Likewise, individuals are more inclined to disclose personal information (including information about their past) to someone who is similar to them. Young women share more information about themselves when interacting with another young woman than when interacting with a woman who is older (Collins & Gould, 1994). The limited amount of empirical work suggests that detail and emotion, qualitative memory characteristics that heighten the extent to which social functions are served, are more likely to be included when remembering for similar others. More work is needed to substantiate this claim.

In sum, listener characteristics influence how much and what is remembered during conversations (Pasupathi, 2001). People sometimes remember more and disclose more personal information when the listener is familiar and similar. Individuals change what they tell depending on whom they are telling: sharing more emotional and personal information with a peer leads to the development of social bonds, thereby fulfilling social functions of establishing or maintaining intimate relationships (Hyman, 1994). There is no work at this point to guide speculations regarding the relation of similarity and familiarity to other social functions (e.g., teach and inform, empathy). However, work does show that sharing memories with similar and known others influences the detail and emotional quality of the memory shared and should thereby affect the extent to which functions are served.

Memory-sharing process: responsiveness

In addition to individual characteristics of speakers and listeners, qualities of the interactive memory-sharing process, such as level of responsiveness, can influence social functions of AM. Responsiveness is a two-way interaction between speakers and listeners; listeners make responses to what speakers are saying, and speakers respond in how they continue the interaction. Responsiveness can indicate attentiveness and comprehension (e.g., eye-contact), or go further by contributing to the conversation (see Pasupathi,

2001, for a review). How might levels of responsiveness influence the use of AM for social purposes?

First, responsiveness can impact the social functions of AM by affecting the type and level of personal self-disclosures (AM sharing is one kind of self-disclosure) between speakers and listeners. For example, revealing self-related information to another leads to social functions such as intimacy development and maintenance when the speaker perceives the listener as responsive (Reis & Shaver, 1988). Individuals who reveal more personal information during social interactions rate that interaction as higher in intimacy when they perceive the listener as responsive, particularly when the disclosures are emotional rather than factual (Laurenceau, Barrett, & Pietromonaco, 1998).

Second, responsive listening affects how memories are told. Speakers include less detailed information when recalling stories to uninterested or distracted listeners. Particularly, when listeners are distracted through experimental manipulations, speakers tell less dramatic and less well-organised autobiographical stories (Bavelas et al., 2000). Stories with this quality may be less likely to serve social functions of AM. Similarly, speakers with interested listeners recall more of a movie excerpt, including more elaborations, such as opinions and emotions, than those with distracted listeners or no listener (Pasupathi, Stallworth, & Murdoch, 1998). Thus, responsiveness has the potential to affect the extent to which social functions are served via the inclusion or exclusion of details and emotions during recall.

Taken together, this research suggests that responsiveness can affect one type of social function that is served (e.g., intimacy; Laurenceau et al., 1998). More work is needed to delineate the relation between responsiveness and other social functions (e.g., teach and inform, and empathy). Evidence regarding the extent to which a function is served comes from work on the quality of the memory (e.g., Bavelas et al., 2000): including more information and affect heightens the extent to which a function will be served.

Relationship qualities: Valence and length

The components reviewed so far are placed in the context of an existing relationship. Pre-existing qualities of the relationship (e.g., valence and length) between the speaker and listener are included in the model to provide the relationship context within which the memory-sharing process occurs. Two qualities of the speaker–listener relationship, valence and length, can influence the social functions of AM.

Valence. Studies of relationship satisfaction provide indirect evidence regarding the relation between the global valence of a social relationship and specific memories about that relationship. Memories are biased in the direction of current relationship satisfaction: wives who perceive their marriage as improving over time remember the past as more negative than it was (Karney & Coombs, 2000). Memories are also predictive of future satisfaction: husbands who report less expansive memories about their marriage (characterised by fewer details and feelings) are more likely to be divorced or separated years later (Buehlman, Gottman, & Katz, 1992). In the first case, memory is distorted in order to serve the function of bolstering current satisfaction (maintaining intimacy). In the second case, the qualitative characteristics of the memories (e.g., level of detail and amount of emotion) may be related to the extent to which the social function of intimacy maintenance is served. Thus far, work on the relation between valence and social functions of AM has focused on the intimacy function and the extent to which this function is served. Work on attachment style provides additional support.

An indicator of relationship valence, attachment style (see Koski & Shaver, 1997, for a review) influences the quality of personal (sometimes past) information that is shared during daily interactions. Individuals with avoidant (poor valence) attachment styles express lower levels of positive emotional information during social interactions than those with secure attachments (positive valence). Expressing fewer positive emotions leads to less intimacy in that interaction (Tidwell, Reis, & Shaver, 1996). Again, the extent to which this social function is served depends on memory characteristics: heightened emotional valence of disclosures leads to higher levels of intimacy. With the exception of intimacy, however, little is known about the extent to which social functions are served in relationships with varying valence due to the qualitative characteristics of memories.

Length. Suggestions concerning how length of relationship influences social functions of AM are drawn from research on the use of the personal past during initial introductions and research on collaborative remembering in short- and long-term marriages. Upon meeting someone, older adults are more likely than younger adults to talk spontaneously about the past (Boden & Bielby, 1983). Older stranger pairs are also more likely to incorporate personal information when recalling stories (e.g., Dixon & Gould, 1998). Thus, when there is no pre-existing relationship, older adults share more personal past information with others, possibly putting them at an advantage when using AMs to initiate relationships (e.g., an intimacy function). No conclusions can be drawn at this point regarding other social functions.

However, when a relationship already exists, how is memory sharing influenced by the duration of the existing relationship? Research on collaborative remembering finds that long-term (older) couples remember equal amounts of information (including details) from a story as do couples together for a shorter period of time. Among stranger dyads, this finding does not hold (Dixon & Gould, 1998). Couples in relationships for longer periods of time develop a "couple expertise" (Dixon & Gould, 1996) that improves memory performance (e.g., remembering more details). Thus, the length of a relationship affects the amount of information remembered, including level of detail. As conceptualised in the model, these qualitative memory characteristics (i.e., detail) and others that are similar (i.e., emotion) can impact the extent to which the social functions of remembering are served.

In sum, the valence of a relationship can influence the use of AM for intimacy maintenance, one social function of AM, by affecting what is remembered about that relationship (e.g., Buehlman et al., 1992). In addition, individuals with secure attachment styles or positive relationships interact in ways (i.e., include more emotional information) that foster social uses of memory, such as intimacy (Tidwell et al, 1996). Thus, valence influences the types of social functions that are used (e.g., intimacy) and the extent to which these functions are served via emotional characteristics of memory. Length of relationship affects the type of social function served: in initial introductions AMs are likely to be used to initiate intimacy, while for existing relationships AMs are used for maintaining intimacy. Couples who have been together longer may be expert at using AMs to serve social purposes (Dixon & Gould, 1996). Individuals in close relationships are more likely than strangers to share detailed and emotional personal memories (Pillemer, 1998), thus influencing the extent to which social functions, such as intimacy, are served. These ideas are speculations but are based on existing areas of work that provide insight into variations in the types of and extent to which social functions are served in relationships.

FUTURE DIRECTIONS AND CONCLUSION

Our major objective was to develop a conceptual model of the social functions of AM sharing across the lifespan. Modelling the critical components diagrammatically, and providing literature to link them, illustrates how AMs may be used to serve social functions in daily interactions. Future work can take two directions: (1) substantiating the model, and (2) employing the model. Both directions require empirical investigations that will advance our understanding of the social functions of AM.

Substantiating the model

Explicating the components of this model has made it evident that there are large gaps in the existing literature that need to be addressed to further substantiate the model. Among many possibilities, two major areas of work are suggested here. First, the relation between qualitative memory characteristics and the social functions of AM needs substantiating. The qualitative memory characteristics included in the model (detail and emotion) are important during autobiographical remembering and are often included when recalling meaningful events (e.g., Bohannon, 1988; Cohen et al., 1994). Related work suggests that these characteristics are relevant when using AMs for various social functions (e.g., Tannen, 1990) but there are no direct empirical investigations of these claims. It is unknown whether detail, emotion, or both are more necessary for AM to serve each particular social function. For instance, is emotion more necessary when using AMs for empathy, while detail is more important when using AMs to teach and inform others? Another unknown is the extent to which these characteristics, detail and emotion, influence the adaptive function that memory serves. Pillemer's (1998) suggestion that heightened levels of detail and emotion better serve interpersonal functions was adopted. It is unclear, however, whether or not

there is an optimal amount of detail or emotion needed to best serve a particular function. Could remembering too much detail or emotional information sometimes hinder the social functions of AM? Future work in which levels of detail and emotion in memory telling are manipulated and a variety of functional outcomes are measured will be needed to further substantiate the relations between components and functional outcomes. Such work is currently underway in our lab.

A second area in need of further development includes work on specific types of social functions. The majority of work currently available to substantiate the model focuses on one social function: intimacy. For example, literature is available to link all of the components of the model in some way to the use of AM for intimacy development and maintenance. To a lesser extent, components of the model can be linked to using the past to teach and inform others. There is almost no work addressing how model components affect the use of AM for eliciting or showing empathy. Given that social functions of AM are not limited to intimacy, future work should use multiple outcome measures to assess the relation of various components in the model to each of the various types of social functions of AM. In sum, developing a model of the social functions of AM elucidated these (and other) crucial gaps in the literature. Future directions for substantiating the model outlined here are clearly not exhaustive.

Employing the model

Despite limitations posed by current gaps in the literature, research questions can be still generated based on the existing literature as organised in the model. Two examples are provided here.

Suggestions for future work regarding the relation of speaker characteristics (e.g., age, gender, and personality) to social functions were given in a previous section. We expand upon these suggestions here by making age and gender hypotheses about using AMs to maintain intimacy in relationships. With increasing age, individuals are more likely to use AMs for intimacy maintenance. Women are also more likely to use AMs for intimacy (Webster, 1995; Webster & McCall, 1999). In addition, older adults' and women's AMs are sometimes characterised by more emotion (Carstensen & Turk-Charles, 1994; Hashtroudi et al., 1990; Ross & Holmberg, 1992). A useful question is: how do these age and gender differences and similarities in the qualitative characteristics of AM influence the extent to which the social function of intimacy is served? For instance, emotion is more relevant to using AMs for intimacy (Tannen, 1990) and thus older adults and women may be advantaged when using their AMs to serve the intimacy function. Does a single session of AM sharing (e.g., about one's spouse) increase intimacy differentially in younger and older adults, for men versus women? If so, are those age group and gender variations in intimacy as an outcome, mediated by differences in level of emotion in individuals' recalled accounts? Based on the model, a speaker characteristic hypothesis about using AMs for intimacy might be that women's AMs and older adults' AMs, which are more emotionally focused than men's and younger adults' memories, may better serve the social function of developing intimacy.

A second hypothesis can be generated based on existing work on listener characteristics (e.g., familiarity), the level of responsiveness during the memory-sharing process, and the extent to which the qualitative characteristics of AM serve a particular function, such as intimacy. Existing evidence shows that individuals are likely to share more personal details and emotions when remembering for someone that they know (Dixon & Gould, 1998) and with someone who is responsive (e.g., Bavelas et al., 2000; Pasupathi et al., 1998). Based on the relation between listener characteristics and responsiveness depicted in the model, suggestions for future hypothesis-driven work are possible. Specifically, it would be expected that sharing an AM with someone who is known (e.g., a spouse), and responsive, heightens the extent to which AMs serve an intimacy function. Sharing an AM with someone who is known but unresponsive, however, may be particularly detrimental to serving the intimacy function. While this hypothesis may be generally true, it would likely differ depending on the age of the speaker and listener. For instance, older, long-term happily married couples are more tolerant of unresponsive listening by their partner (Pasupathi, Carstensen, Levenson, & Gottman, 1999), than are younger couples. Experimentally manipulating listener familiarity (e.g., stranger or spouse) and training confederates to be more or less responsive (similar to methods used by Pasupathi et al., 1998) across different age groups would allow for a direct test of this hypothesis. In sum, these research questions have been set forth to give a snapshot of the model's utility as a catalyst for guiding future empirical work.

Conclusion

A conceptual model of the social functions of AM was developed that serves to identify existing gaps in the theoretical and empirical literature on the social functions of AM. By elucidating the variables and processes involved when AM is used to serve social functions, the model also provides a basis for hypothesis-driven research. Developing similar models of the self and directive functions of AM will be needed in order to fully explore the functional approach to the study of AM. It is hoped that this modest attempt at conceptualisation will help to translate an ecological construct with great intuitive appeal (i.e., function) in a manner that provides a catalyst for the advancement of our understanding of how, and particularly why, individuals use AMs in their everyday lives.

REFERENCES

Andersson, J., & Roennberg, J. (1995). Recall suffers from collaboration: Joint recall effects of friendship and task complexity. *Applied Cognitive Psychology*, 9, 199–211.

Antonucci, T.C. & Akiyama, H. (1995). Convoys of social relations: Family and friendships within a life span context. In R. Blieszner & V.H. Bedford, (Eds.), *Handbook of aging and the family* (pp. 355–371). Westport, CT: Greenwood Press/Greenwood Publishing Group.

Baltes, P.B. (1987). Theoretical propositions of life-span developmental psychology: On the dynamics between growth and decline. *Developmental Psychology*, 23, 611–626.

Baltes, P.B., Staudinger, U.M., & Lindenberger, U. (1999). Lifespan psychology: Theory and application to intellectual functioning. *Annual Review of Psychology*, 50, 471–507.

Baumeister, R.F., & Newman, L.S. (1994). How stories make sense of personal experiences: Motives that shape autobiographical narratives. *Personality and Social Psychology Bulletin*, 20, 676–690.

Bavelas, J.B., Coates, L., & Johnson, T. (2000). Listeners as co-narrators. *Journal of Personality & Social Psychology*, 79, 941–952.

Bluck, S., & Alea, N. (2002). Exploring the functions of autobiographical memory: Why do I remember the autumn? In J.D. Webster & B.K. Haight (Eds.), *Critical advances in reminiscence theory: From theory to application*. New York: Springer.

Bluck, S., & Habermas, T. (2000). The life story schema. *Motivation and Emotion*, 24, 121–147.

Bluck, S., & Habermas, T. (2001). Extending the study of autobiographical memory: Thinking back about life across the life span. *Review of General Psychology*, 5, 135–147.

Bluck, S., Habermas, T., & Rubin, D.C. (2002). Self-reported functions of autobiographical memory in young adults: Self-continuity, problem-solving, and development of intimacy. Manuscript in preparation.

Bluck, S., Levine, L.J. & Laulhere, T.M. (1999). Autobiographical remembering and hypermnesia: A comparison of older and younger adults. *Psychology and Aging*, 14, 671–682.

Bluck, S., & Li, K.Z.H. (2001). Predicting memory completeness and accuracy: Emotion and exposure in repeated autobiographical recall. *Applied Cognitive Psychology*, 15, 145–158.

Boden, D., & Bielby, D.D. (1983). The past as a resource: A conversational analysis of elderly talk. *Human Development*, 26, 308–319.

Bohannon, J.N. (1988). Flashbulb memories for the space shuttle disaster: A tale of two theories. *Cognition*, 29, 179–196.

Brandtstadter, J., & Renner, G. (1990). Tenacious goal pursuit and flexible goal adjustment: Explication and age-related analysis of assimilative and accommodative strategies of coping. *Psychology & Aging*, 5, 58–67.

Brown, R., & Kulik, J. (1977). Flashbulb memories. *Cognition*, 5, 73–89.

Bruce, D. (1989). Functional explanations of memory. In L.W. Poon, D.C. Rubin, & B.A. Wilson (Eds.), *Everyday cognition in adulthood and late life* (pp. 44–58). Cambridge: Cambridge University Press.

Buehlman, K.T., Gottman, J.M., & Katz, L.F. (1992). How a couple views their past predicts their future: Predicting divorce from an oral history interview. *Journal of Family Psychology*, 5, 295–318.

Buhler, C. (1968). The course of human life as a psychological problem. *Human Development*, 11, 184–200.

Carstensen, L.L. (1993). Motivation for social contact across the life span: A theory of socioemotional selectivity. In J.E. Jacobs (Ed.), *Nebraska symposium on motivation*, (pp. 209–254). Lincoln: University of Nebraska.

Carstensen, L.L., & Turk-Charles, S. (1994). The salience of emotion across the adult life span. *Psychology and Aging*, 9, 259–264.

Cohen, G. (1998). The effects of aging on autobiographical memory. In C.P. Thompson, D.J. Herrmann, D. Bruce, D.J. Read, D.G. Payne, & M.P. Toglia (Eds.), *Autobiographical memory: Theoretical and applied perspectives* (pp. 105–123). Mahwah, NJ: Lawrence Erlbaum Associates Inc.

Cohen, G., Conway, M.A., & Maylor, E.A. (1994). Flashbulb memories in older adults. *Psychology and Aging*, 9, 454–463.

Cohen, G., & Faulkner, D. (1988). Life span changes in autobiographical memory. In M.M. Gruneberg, P.E. Morris, & R.N. Sykes (Eds.), *Practical aspects of memory: Current research and issues* (Vol. 1, pp. 277–282). Chichester, UK: Wiley.

Conway, M.A. (1995). *Flashbulb memories*. Hillsdale, NJ: Lawrence Erlbaum Associates.

Conway, M.A. (1996). Autobiographical knowledge and autobiographical memories. In D.C. Rubin, (Ed.), *Remembering our past: Studies in autobiographical memory* (pp. 67–93). New York: Cambridge University Press.

Collins, C.L. & Gould, O.N. (1994). Getting to know you: How own age and other's age relate to self-disclosure. *International Journal of Aging & Human Development*, 39, 55–66.

Cully, J.A., LaVoie, D., & Gfeller, J.D. (2001). Reminiscence, personality, and psychological functioning in older adults. *The Gerontologist*, 41, 89–95.

Davis, P.J. (1999). Gender differences in autobiographical memory for childhood emotional experiences. *Journal of Personality & Social Psychology*, 76, 498–510.

Dixon, R.A., & Gould, O.N. (1996). Adults telling and retelling stories collaboratively. In P.B. Baltes & U.M. Staudinger (Eds.), *Interactive minds: Life-span perspectives on the social foundation of cognition* (pp. 221–241). Cambridge: Cambridge University Press.

Dixon, R.A., & Gould, O.N. (1998). Younger and older adults collaborating on retelling everyday stories. *Applied Developmental Science*, 2, 160–171.

Duck, S., Rutt, D.J., Hurst, M.H., Strejc, H. (1991). Some evident truths about conversations in everyday relationships. All communications are not created equal. *Human Communication Research*, 18, 228–267.

Edwards, D., & Middleton, D. (1986). Joint remembering: Constructing an account of shared experience through conversational discourse. *Discourse Processes*, 9, 423–459.

Emmons, R.A. (1986). Personal strivings: An approach to personality and subjective well-being. *Journal of Personality and Social Psychology*, 51, 1058–1068.

Erikson, E.H. (1980). *Identity and the life cycle*. New York: W.W. Norton & Company, Inc.

Fivush, R., & Reese, E. (1992). The social construction of autobiographical memory. In M.A. Conway, D.C. Rubin, & W. Wagenaar, (Eds.), *Theoretical perspectives on autobiographical memory* (pp. 1–28). Dordrecht, The Netherlands: Kluwer Academic Publishers.

Gould, O.N., & Dixon, R.A. (1993). How we spent our vacation: Collaborative storytelling by young and old adults. *Psychology and Aging*, 8, 10–17.

Graumann, C.F. (1986). Memorabilia, mementos, memoranda: Toward an ecology of memory. In F. Klix & H. Hagendorf (Eds.), *Human memory and cognitive capabilities: mechanisms and performances* (pp. 63–69). Amsterdam, North-Holland: Elsevier Science Publishers.

Grice, H.P. (1989). *Studies in the way of words*. Cambridge, MA: Harvard University Press.

Hashtroudi, S., Johnson, M.K., & Chrosniak, L.D. (1990). Aging and qualitative characteristics of memories for perceived and imagined complex events. *Psychology and Aging*, 5, 119–126.

Havigurst, R.J. (1972). *Developmental tasks and education* (3rd ed.). New York: David McKay Company, Inc.

Hirst, W., & Manier, D. (1996). Remembering as communication: A family recounts its past. In D.C. Rubin (Ed.), *Remembering our past: Studies in autobiographical memory* (pp. 271–290). New York: Cambridge University Press.

Hyman, I.E. (1994). Conversational remembering— story recall with a peer versus for an experimenter. *Applied Cognitive Psychology, 8*, 49–66.

Hyman, I.E., & Faries, J.M. (1992). The functions of autobiographical memory. In M.A. Conway, D.C. Rubin, H. Spinnler, & W.A. Wagenaar (Eds.), *Theoretical perspectives on autobiographical memory* (pp. 207–221). Dordrecht, The Netherlands: Kluwer Academic Publishers.

Karney, B.R. & Coombs, R.H. (2000). Memory bias in long-term close relationships: Consistency or improvement? *Personality & Social Psychology Bulletin, 26*, 959–970.

Koski, L.R. & Shaver, P.R. (1997). Attachment and relationship satisfaction across the lifespan. In R.J. Sternberg, & M. Hojjat (Eds.), *Satisfaction in close relationships* (pp. 26–55). New York: Guilford Press.

Larsen, S.F. (1998). What is it like to remember? On phenomenal qualities of memory. In C.P. Thompson, D.J. Hermann, D. Bruce, J.D. Read, D.G. Payne, & M. Toglia (Eds.), *Autobiographical memory: Theoretical and applied perspectives* (pp. 163–190). Mahwah, NJ: Lawrence Erlbaum Associates Inc.

Laurenceau, J., Barrett, L.F., & Pietromonaco, P.R. (1998). Intimacy as an interpersonal process: The importance of self-disclosure, partner disclosure, and perceived partner responsiveness in interpersonal exchanges. *Journal of Personality and Social Psychology, 74*, 1238–1251.

McAdams, D.P., Diamond, A., de St. Aubin, E., & Mansfield, E. (1997). Stories of commitment: The psychosocial construction of generative lives. *Journal of Personality and Social Psychology, 72*, 678–694.

McGregor, I., & Holmes, J.G. (1999). How storytelling shapes memory and impressions of relationship events over time. *Journal of Personality & Social Psychology, 76*, 403–419.

Neisser, U. (1978). Memory: What are the important questions? In M.M. Gruneberg, P.E. Morris, & R.N. Sykes (Eds.), *Practical aspects of memory* (pp. 3–19). London: Academic Press.

Nelson, K. (1993). The psychological and social origins of autobiographical memory. *Psychological Science, 4*, 7–14.

Nelson, K., & Fivush, R. (2000). Socialization of memory. In E. Tulving, & F.I.M. Craik (Eds.), *The Oxford handbook of memory* (pp. 283–295). New York: Oxford University Press.

Neugarten, B.L. (1979). Time, age, and the life cycle. *American Journal of Psychiatry, 136*, 887–894.

Norrick, N. (1997). Twice-told tales: Collaborative narration of familiar stories. *Language in Society, 26*, 199–220.

Pasupathi, M. (2001). The social construction of the personal past and its implications for adult development. *Psychological Bulletin, 127*, 651–672.

Pasupathi, M., Carstensen, L.L., Levenson, R.W., & Gottman, J.M. (1999). Responsive listening in long-married couples: A psycholinguistic perspective. *Journal of Nonverbal Behavior, 23*, 173–193.

Pasupathi, M., Lucas, S., & Coombs, A. (2002). Conversational functions of autobiographical remembering: Long-married couples talk about conflicts and pleasant topics. *Discourse Processes, 34*, 163–192.

Pasupathi, M., Stallworth, L.M. & Murdoch, K. (1998). How what we tell becomes what we know: Listener effects on speaker's long-term memory for events. *Discourse Processes, 26*, 1–25.

Pillemer, D.B. (1992). Remembering personal circumstances: A functional analysis. In E. Winograd & U. Neisser (Eds.), *Affect and accuracy in recall: Studies of "flashbulb" memories* (4th ed., pp. 236–264). New York: Cambridge University Press.

Pillemer, D. B. (1998). *Momentous events, vivid memories*. Cambridge, MA: Harvard University Press.

Reis, H.T., & Shaver, P. (1988). Intimacy as an interpersonal process. In S. Duck (Ed.), *Handbook of personal relationships* (pp. 367–389). Chichester, UK: Wiley.

Ross, M., & Holmberg, D. (1992). Are wives' memories for events in relationships more vivid than their husbands' memories? *Journal of Social & Personal Relationships, 9*, 585–604.

Sanitioso, R., Kunda, Z., & Fong, G.T. (1990). Motivated recruitment of autobiographical memories. *Journal of Personality and Social Psychology, 59*, 229–241.

Schank, R.C., & Abelson, R.P. (1995). Knowledge and memory: The real story. In R. S. Wyer Jr. (Ed.), *Advances in social cognition*, Vol. 8 (pp. 1–85). Hillsdale, NJ: Lawrence Erlbaum Associates Inc.

Singer, J.A., & Salovey, P. (1996). Motivated memory: Self-defining memories, goals, and affect regulation. In L.L. Martin & A. Tesser (Eds.), *Striving and feeling: Interactions among goals, affect, and self-regulation* (pp. 229–250). Hillsdale, NJ: Lawrence Erlbaum Associates Inc.

Tannen, D. (1990). *You just don't understand: Women and men in conversation*. New York: Ballantine.

Thorne, A., Cutting, L., & Skaw, D. (1998). Young adults' relationship memories and the life story: Examples or essential landmarks. *Narrative Inquiry, 8*, 237–268.

Tidwell, M.C.O., Reis, H.T., & Shaver, P.R. (1996). Attachment, attractiveness, and social interaction: A diary study. *Journal of Personality and Social Psychology, 4*, 729–745.

Tversky, B., & Marsh, E.J. (2000). Biased retellings of events yield biased memories. *Cognitive Psychology, 40*, 1–38.

Wagenaar, W.A. & Groeneweg, J. (1990). The memory of concentration camp survivors. *Applied Cognitive Psychology, 4*, 77-87.

Watt, L.M., & Wong, P.T.P. (1991). A taxonomy of reminiscence and therapeutic implications. *Journal of Gerontological Social Work, 16*, 37–57.

Webster, J.D., (1995). Adult age differences in reminiscence functions. In B.K. Haight & J.D. Webster (Eds.), *The art and science of reminiscing: Theory, research, methods, and applications*. Washington, DC: Taylor & Francis.

Webster, J., & McCall, M. (1999). Reminiscence functions across adulthood: A replication and extension. *Journal of Adult Development*, 6(1), 73–85.

Woike, B., Gershkovich, I., Piorkowski, R., & Polo, M. (1999). The role of motives in the content and structure of autobiographical memory. *Journal of Personality & Social Psychology*, 76, 600–612.

Wong, P.T.P., & Watt, L.M. (1991). What types of reminiscence are associated with successful aging? *Psychology and Aging*, 6, 272–279.

MEMORY, 2003, *11* (2), 179–192

Functions of parent–child reminiscing about emotionally negative events

Robyn Fivush
Emory University, GA, USA

Lisa J. Berlin
Duke University, NC, USA

Jessica McDermott Sales and Jean Mennuti-Washburn
Emory University, GA, USA

Jude Cassidy
University of Maryland, USA

Parent–child reminiscing about negative experiences influences children's developing "emotional self-concept", which comprises three interrelated functions: self-defining (this is the kind of emotional person I am), self-in-relation (this is how I express and share my emotions with others), and coping (this is how I cope with and resolve negative emotion). In this study, we examined how 70 mostly white, middle-class mothers discuss three negative experiences (fear, anger, and sadness) with their 4-year-old children. Conversations about fear elaborate on the facts of the event and emotional resolutions, thus focusing on coping. Conversations about sadness contain evaluative feedback and emotional resolutions, thus focusing on self-in-relation and coping. Finally, conversations about anger highlight the emotional state itself, thus focusing on self-definition. Mothers are also more elaborative and more evaluative with daughters than with sons, and place emotional events in a more interpersonal context with daughters than sons. Thus girls may be forming a more elaborated and more interpersonal emotional self-concept than boys.

When we talk about the past, we talk about emotions. Emotions provide a sense of meaning and personal significance to our experiences, and are a critical link between our past experiences and our current self. If much of our self-concept is defined through our autobiographical life story (e.g., Bruner, 1987; Fivush, 1988; Habermas & Bluck, 2000; MacAdams,1992; Neisser, 1988) then our emotional reactions to these experiences, as they were occurring and in the present, provide the glue that connects our past to our present and makes these experiences meaningful. It is through our subjective perspective on our past that we define ourselves in the present (Fivush, 2001).

Young children, who are just learning how to think about their past experiences, depend on adults to help them structure their representations of what occurred and to evaluate these experiences (Fivush, 1994; Nelson, 1993). More specifically, while young children can remember *what* happened, parent-guided reminiscing helps children to *organise, interpret*, and *evaluate* these experiences in ways that begin to inform children's developing sense of self (Fivush, 2001; Haden, Haine, & Fivush, 1997). Thus one of the

Requests for reprints should be sent to Robyn Fivush, Department of Psychology, Emory University, Atlanta, GA 30322, USA. Email: psyrf@emory.edu

DOI:10.1080/09658210244000351

seminal functions of parent–child reminiscing is to help young children create connections between memories of the past and current understanding of self. Given that emotional aspects of personal experience link past with present, the ways in which parents reminisce about specific kinds of emotional experiences with their young children may be a particularly important context for children's developing self-understanding (Dunn, Brown, & Beardsall, 1991; Fivush, 1993). Through understanding and evaluating specific kinds of emotional experiences, children begin to develop an "emotional self-concept"(Fivush, in press; Fivush & Buckner, in press), comprising three functions: self-defining (this is the kind of emotional person I am), self-in-relation (this is how I express and share my emotions with others), and coping (this is how I cope with and resolve negative emotion). Note that these three functions are interrelated; information relevant to any one function may also be relevant to other functions, and developments within one of these components entail developments within other components as well.

More generally, parent–child talk about emotions plays an important role in emotion socialisation (Denham, Zoller, & Couchoud, 1994; Dunn et al., 1991). Families that discuss emotional experiences in more open and integrative ways have children who develop better prosocial skills, have more positive peer relations, and show better psychological adjustment (see Halberstadt, Denham, & Dunsmore, 2001, for a review). However, this body of research does not focus on reminiscing about emotional experiences. Talking about the past differs in important ways from discussing current emotional experience (Dunn et al., 1991; Fivush, 1993), and influences the development of an emotional self-concept in at least three ways.

First, with respect to the self-defining function, parents can choose to focus their children's attention on specific past emotional experiences over others, e.g., sadness rather than anger or fear. By focusing on particular emotions, children may begin to form a concept of self as a person who experiences these specific emotions and not others, e.g., "I am a person who is sad a lot but rarely angry." Second, with respect to self-in-relation, emotions are tied closely to relationships (Campos & Barrett, 1984; Fogel, 1993). As such, the ways in which young children come to understand their emotional experiences will play a role in how they understand themselves in relation to others, and how past relationships help define current self-

concept. In reminiscing, parents may focus on the ways in which emotions emerge from and are resolved through interpersonal relationships (Fivush & Buckner, 2000; Gilligan, 1982).

Finally, with respect to coping, we all experience negative events in our lives and the way in which we make sense of these experiences may play an important role in how we come to understand and resolve aversive events (Pennebaker, 1997). Through reminiscing about negative emotional experiences, parents may help children develop a sense of self as experiencing and coping with emotions in particular ways. For example, parents may choose to focus on the emotional state itself, or the causes and consequences of particular emotional reactions, or resolutions of negative affect. Moreover, it seems quite likely that parents would discuss different kinds of emotionally negative experiences in different ways. Much of the previous research on emotion socialisation does not examine discussions of different emotions in detail, but rather groups emotions as negative or positive. From the perspective presented here, we would expect that differences in the ways in which specific negative emotions are discussed would have different consequences for children's developing emotional self-concept. Understanding and resolving events in which the child experienced fear might very well be different from understanding and resolving events in which the child experienced anger, or sadness. It is, therefore, critical that reminiscing about different emotions are examined independently in order to examine the development of coping in particular, and emotional self-concept more generally.

There have been two approaches in the literature examining parent–child reminiscing. One focuses broadly on parental style; these stylistic differences describe *how* mothers structure reminiscing and highlight differences in the *process* by which mothers introduce and evaluate new information into conversations about past events, rather than on the specific content of what is recalled. The second line of research has examined the content of parent–child reminiscing about specific emotional experiences. These studies examine *what* kind of information parents focus on when discussing specific emotional experiences and highlight the ways in which the *content* of parental reminiscing about emotional experience (e.g., emotional state, cause of emotion, resolution of emotion) may be linked to children's developing emotional self-concept.

In studies examining reminiscing style, parents are simply asked to reminisce with their preschool children, rather than focusing on specific kinds of emotional experiences. Under these conditions, parents tend to discuss highly positive emotional experiences such as family trips to amusement parks and museums, and family occasions such as weddings and holidays. Although using somewhat different terminology, several studies confirm that there are two distinct parental reminiscing styles (Engel, 1986; Fivush & Fromhoff, 1988; Hudson, 1990; Peterson & McCabe, 1992). Some parents show a highly elaborative style, discussing the past in great detail, and providing rich, vivid descriptions of what occurred. These parents also encourage their children's participation in the co-construction of the narrative to a greater extent by evaluating their children's contributions. Other parents are less elaborative, asking few and redundant questions when reminiscing with their children, and offering few evaluations of their children's contributions. Importantly, over the course of the preschool years, children of more highly elaborative parents come to tell more richly detailed stories of their own lives (Harley & Reese, 1999; Reese, Haden, & Fivush, 1993). Provocatively, some studies have also shown that parents use a more elaborative and evaluative style with girls than with boys (Reese & Fivush, 1993; Reese, Haden & Fivush, 1996; see Fivush, 1998, for a review), and by the end of the preschool years, girls are telling more richly detailed narratives of their personal experience than are boys (Buckner & Fivush, 1998).

It seems likely that more elaborative reminiscing facilitates the development of a shared history in which parents and children create a sense of togetherness through time. This shared history would further facilitate the creation and maintenance of emotional bonds and the sense of self as connected to others (Fivush, Haden & Reese, 1996; Fivush & Reese, 2002). In this way, children of more highly elaborative parents may develop a more elaborated sense of self-in-relation over time.

The second line of research has focused on gender differences in the emotional content of parent–child reminiscing (Adams, Kuebli, Boyle, & Fivush, 1995; Fivush, 1989, 1991; Fivush, Brotman, Buckner, & Goodman, 2000; Kuebli & Fivush, 1992). As adults, women express more emotion, and report experiencing and valuing emotions more than males (see Fischer, 2000, for an overview). The developmental studies confirm that parents of preschoolers are already discussing emotions differently with their daughters and sons. The findings of these studies indicate that parents talk more about emotions overall, and especially talk more about sadness, with girls than with boys, and by the end of the preschool years, girls are talking more about emotional aspects of the past, and especially sadness, than are boys (see Fivush & Buckner, 2000, for a review). In this way, girls may be socialised to have a more emotionally laden definition of self in the past, and, in particular, to have a greater definition of self as a person who experiences sadness. It may also be the case that parents work harder to help resolve negative affect with girls than with boys (Fivush, 1991). Thus girls may be learning how to both express and resolve negative affect to a greater extent than are boys in these early parent-guided conversations. Further, parents place emotions in a more interpersonal context with girls than with boys (Buckner & Fivush, 2000; Fivush, 1989). Thus girls may be developing an emotional self-concept that is more relational than boys.

In integrating the findings across these two lines of research, we argue that the functions of parent–child reminiscing are multiply determined and inextricably intertwined (see Bluck & Alea, 2002, for a theoretical discussion of the functions of autobiographical memory in general). When reminiscing with their young children, parents are simultaneously influencing the development of the child's coherent sense of self in the past and the present (self-defining), creating a shared social history which bonds them together (self-in-relation), and helping their child to interpret and evaluate their own personal experiences (coping), all of which contribute to children's developing emotional self-concept. Moreover, these functions may be differentially highlighted depending on the emotional valence of the event under discussion or the gender of the child. Negative events are a particularly interesting context to examine because in discussing negative experiences, parents may help children to understand how to cope with and resolve negative experiences, as well as how to evaluate these experiences in light of their evolving self-concept and understanding of self in relation to other. The major objective of this study is to examine parent-child reminiscing about negative emotional experiences in detail, integrating the two approaches emerging from the previous research.

More specifically, we examine both the style and the content of parent–child conversations about negative emotional experiences. Whereas previous research has demonstrated distinct parental reminiscing styles that vary on the dimension of elaborativeness, we do not yet know whether level of parental elaboration may be related to the type of emotional event being discussed. Are parents more elaborative when reminiscing about fear versus sadness versus anger? Assuming that level of elaboration is related to the functions of creating a shared history and helping children construct a more elaborated definition of self and self-in-relation, then we might predict that anger would show lower levels of elaboration than fear or sadness because anger is a less culturally acceptable emotion to express and to share with others, especially for females (Basow, 1992; Fabes & Martin, 1991). Sadness, in contrast, might show the highest level of elaboration, as sadness is an emotion that brings people together to share and resolve feelings of loss. Based on previous research, we further predict that parents will be more elaborative and more evaluative overall with girls than with boys, and especially so for sadness (Fivush & Buckner, 2000).

A second question concerns differences in the content of these conversations. Will parents differ in their focus on discussing the emotion itself, the causes of emotional experience, or resolving negative affect, depending on the type of emotional event under discussion or the gender of the child? As adults, females are more emotionally expressive than males (Fischer, 2000); therefore we predict that parents will talk more about emotions overall with girls than with boys (e.g., Fivush et al., 2000). Further, we might expect parents to resolve negative affect more with girls than with boys (Fivush, 1991). But if the content of reminiscing functions to help children interpret and evaluate their emotional life in light of their evolving concepts of self and other, how might content differ in conversations about different emotional experiences? For example, because sadness is an emotion that can link people together and anger can tear people apart, parents may focus more on talking about the emotional feeling of sadness, and focus more on the causes and resolutions of anger. However, these arguments are speculative and no strong predictions can be made.

Another aspect of content concerns the overarching theme of each conversation. What kinds of events do mothers and children select when discussing specific emotions? Given past research (Buckner & Fivush, 2000; Fivush, 1989) we predict

that mothers will place emotions in an interpersonal context to a greater extent with daughters than with sons, but how theme might differ by the specific emotion under discussion is not as clear. Anger, almost by definition, is an interpersonal emotion, but sadness and fear can be focused on either the individual's inner emotional life or on how other people are integrated into one's own emotional experience.

Finally, because we assume these conversations are bi-directional (e.g., Reese et al., 1993), we also examine what children are contributing to the discussion. More specifically, we examine children's style and content in order to place maternal style and content in perspective. Clearly, conversations are between people and therefore it is necessary to examine what both conversational partners are bringing to the conversations. This is especially important in interpreting possible gender differences; without concomitant information about what girls and boys are contributing to these conversations, it would be extremely difficult to interpret possible differences in mother's conversations with daughters versus sons. In sum, the major objective of this study is to provide a more fine-grained analysis of similarities and differences in mothers' and children's reminiscing style and content of emotion talk as a function of gender and the specific emotion being discussed.

METHODS

Participants

A total of 70 preschool-aged children (42 boys and 28 girls) and their mothers participated. The sample was predominantly Caucasian, with 97% Caucasian children and two non-Caucasian children (one was Hispanic and one was racially mixed). Most (76%) of the sample reported an annual family income of $30,000 or more. Almost all (92%) of the children's parents were married. Mothers had received an average of 16 years of education (range = 12–20 years, SD = 2.5 years). These demographics represent the population of families living in the small university town in which the study was conducted. At the time of the study, all but five children were aged between 3 years 6 months, and 4 years, with the remaining children seen shortly after their fourth birthdays. Children were of varying birth order, with most (82%) either first-born (46%) or second-born

(36%). Mothers signed fully informed consent and received $20 for their participation.

Procedure

One of six female research assistants visited all but three families in their homes. The remaining three families came to a developmental laboratory located on a university campus. Following Fivush (1991), the research assistant told the mother that a goal of the study was to examine children's memories. The mother was asked to discuss with her child three specific past events, a time that her child experienced sadness, anger, and fear. The mother was given index cards with one emotion printed on each card to remind her to ask about each emotional event ("sad", "mad", and "scared"). The cards were always given in this order. (Mothers and children were also asked to discuss a happy event first and an emotional event of their choosing last, but because our focus was on emotionally negative experiences, these conversations are not considered further in these analyses.) The experimenter encouraged the mother to structure the conversations in any way that she wanted, and to talk for as little or as much as she liked. After making sure that the mother understood the procedure, the experimenter turned on the tape recorder and stepped out of the room.

Coding

All of the mother–child conversations were transcribed verbatim and broken down into conversational utterances, defined as a subject–verb construction. Only utterances pertaining to the nominated event were examined. Both mother and child utterances were coded using the same mutually exclusive and exhaustive hierarchical coding scheme adapted from Fivush and Fromhoff (1988) and Fivush et al. (2000). Coding focused on two dimensions of talk, style and content, as defined in Table 1.

Style codes capture the way in which mothers and children introduce and evaluate new information into the conversation, and include elaborations, repetitions, and evaluations (see Table 1). Content codes determined if the utterance focused on factual aspects of the event itself or the emotion associated with the event. Emotion was further coded as focusing on attributions, causes, or resolutions (see Table 1). Finally, off-topic (e.g., talk about something happening in the present or talk of another event), place holders (such as "I don't know", "What?" "Let's see", "Think real hard") and remember prompts ("Do you remember?" or "Tell me about it") were also coded. These categories were infrequent, not theoretically relevant, and thus were not included in analyses.

TABLE 1
Style and content coding

Codes	Descriptions	Example
Style codes		
Elaborations	Any utterance that contains new details, or extends or embellishes the conversation.	"Were there swings there?" when swings have not yet been mentioned.
Evaluations	Any utterance that either confirms, negates, or questions the previous statement.	Saying "yes, that's right" or "no, we didn't see a lion".
Repetitions	Any utterance that does not contain any new information.	"We saw swings at the park" after swings have already been mentioned.
Content codes		
Factual	Any utterance that refers to actions, objects, or descriptions about the external event.	"We saw an owl" or "It was really dark that night".
Emotion	Any utterance that contains emotion words or emotion behaviours (i.e., laughing, crying).	"It was really scary" or "You laughed really hard about that, didn't you".
Attribution	Any utterance that attributes an emotional state or reaction to an individual.	"Were you scared last night?" and "I was really angry".
Cause	Any utterance that explains the cause of the emotion.	"Why were you scared?" or "You were angry because daddy didn't let you play".
Resolutions	Any utterance that attempts to resolve the negative affect experienced.	"But you know monsters aren't real" or "You could have cried but you didn't".

Two raters independently coded 20% of the transcripts and achieved 89% agreement on conversations about fear, 88% agreement on conversations about anger, and 86% agreement on conversations about sadness. After reliability was established, the remaining transcripts were divided between the two raters and coded.

A second aspect of coding for content focused on the theme of the conversation as constructed by the dyad. Note that theme is conceptualised for each conversation as a whole, and thus emerges from both mothers' and children's contributions. Through inspection of the protocols, we developed 10 thematic categories that captured the overall theme of each conversation, as defined in Table 2; these categories were then further divided into those that had an interpersonal focus and those that had an independent focus. Interpersonal themes include discussion of other people as central to the child's emotional experience whereas independent themes focused on the child's internal emotional experience. All conversations were categorised by theme by two independent coders, who achieved an overall agreement of 86% across types of emotion and themes (range from 56% to 100%).

RESULTS

The results are divided into three sections. We first discuss the style and content of maternal reminiscing depending on the type of emotional event being discussed and the gender of the child. We then turn to analyses of the style and content of children's contributions, again depending on the type of emotional event being discussed and the gender of the child. Third, we provide a descriptive analysis of the themes of the conversations for the dyads. All significant multivariate effects were followed up with appropriate univariate and post-hoc tests at the $p < .05$ level.

Style and content of maternal reminiscing

Means and standard deviations for all maternal style and content variables are displayed in Table 3 by event type. Maternal reminiscing style was examined in a 2 (gender of child) × 3 (type of emotional event: sadness, anger, and fear) × 3 (type of style utterance: elaborations, evaluations, and repetitions) MANOVA, with gender as a between-subject variable and event type and style

TABLE 2
Conversational themes and descriptions

Conversational themes	Descriptions
Interpersonal themes	
Lost relationships	Centred on the loss of an important relationship as being central to the child's emotional experience, such as not being able to play with a favourite friend.
Parental separation	Centred on episodes where the child was separated from a parent, including being left at the babysitter and a parent leaving on a business trip.
Conflict with parent	Conflict between child and parent, usually about parent not allowing the child to have a toy or perform an activity.
Conflict with peer/sibling	Fighting between child and other (not parent), usually about child fighting with their siblings over a toy.
Characters	Focused on "fictional" characters such as witches, ghosts, or monsters as being central to the child's emotional experience.
Independent themes	
Lost object/activity	Centred around lost or broken toy, or the child having to give up a desired activity.
Thunder/noise	Almost all conversations focused on lightning and thunder, but a few others were about other kinds of loud noises.
Injury	Focused on the child's minor injury or illness.
Scary activity	Activities that were identified as being scary, like rollercoaster rides or swimming in deep water.
Lack of skill	Child not yet having the skills to perform an activity, such as building a block tower or writing one's name.

TABLE 3
Means (and standard deviations) for maternal style and content variables by event type

| | Event type | | | |
	Sadness	Anger	Fear	Total
Style variables				
Elaborations	7.11 (2.92)	7.62 (4.99)	8.59 (4.23)	23.12 (10.22)
Evaluations	2.57 (2.12)	2.38 (2.04)	2.68 (2.15)	7.62 (4.42)
Repetitions	0.77 (1.08)	0.75 (1.25)	0.87 (0.98)	2.38 (2.32)
Total	10.44 (5.87)	10.75 (6.88)	12.15 (5.80)	33.12 (14.17)
Content variables				
Factual	3.26 (3.83)	3.43 (3.95)	5.03 (4.27)	11.59 (8.30)
Emotion cause	4.70 (2.54)	4.96 (3.08)	4.64 (2.85)	14.16 (5.70)
Emotion attribution	1.59 (2.84)	2.12 (2.64)	1.30 (1.69)	5.04 (4.66)
Emotion resolution	0.84 (1.60)	0.51 (1.31)	1.26 (1.98)	2.62 (3.41)
Total	10.44 (5.87)	10.75 (6.88)	12.15 (5.80)	33.12 (14.17)

as within-subject variables. There were no overall differences in amount of talk among the three types of emotional events but, as shown in Table 3, mothers used significantly more elaborations overall than evaluations, and more evaluations than repetitions, $F(2, 132) = 261.43$, $p < .001$. Furthermore, mothers talked more overall in their conversations with girls (M = 37.50, SD = 15.22) than with boys (M = 30.05, SD = 12.21), $F(1, 66) = 4.81$, $p < .05$; more specifically, mothers were more elaborative and evaluative with girls than with boys, $F(2, 132) = 2.85$, $p = .06$, but repetitions did not differ (see Figure 1). Finally, mothers were more elaborative when discussing fear than when discussing sadness or anger, $F(4, 264) = 3.08$, $p < .05$ (see Table 1).

In order to explore the content of mothers' conversations, a 2 (gender of child) × 3 (type of emotional event: sadness, anger, and fear) × 4 (content of utterance: factual, emotional attribution, emotional cause, and emotional resolution) MANOVA was conducted with gender as a between-subjects variable and event type and content as within-subject variables. Mothers talked more about the causes of emotions than about the facts of the events themselves, more about the facts than emotional attributions, and more about emotional attributions than emotional resolutions, $F(3, 192) = 62.97$, $p < .001$ (see Table 1). However, content differed depending on the type of event discussed, $F(6, 384) = 3.18$, $p < .05$. Mothers talked significantly more about the facts

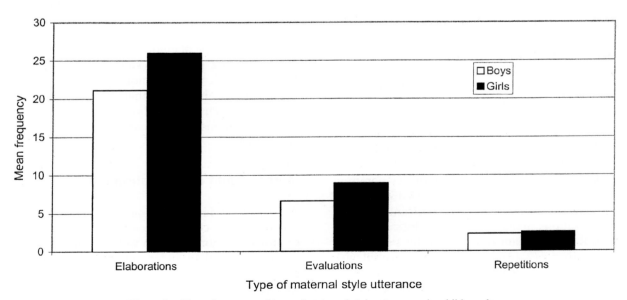

Figure 1.   Mean frequency of type of maternal style utterances by child gender.

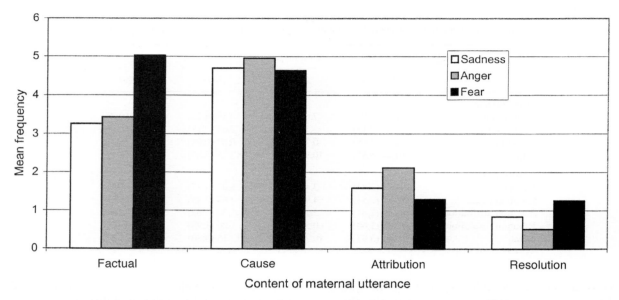

Figure 2. Mean frequency of type of maternal content utterances by type of emotional event.

of the event itself during conversations about fear than about sadness or anger. Mothers also provided more emotional resolutions during conversations about fear and sadness than about anger, but made more emotional attributions during conversations about anger than about either sadness or fear (see Figure 2). There were no differences in talk about cause across events.

Style and content of children's reminiscing

We were also interested in how children's reminiscing style and content might vary as a function of gender and emotional event type. All means and standard deviations for child style and content utterances are shown in Table 4 by event type. A 2 (gender of child) × 3 (type of emotional event: sadness, anger, and fear) × 3 (type of style utterance: elaborations, repetitions, and evaluations) MANOVA, with gender as a between-subjects variable and event type and style as within-subject variables was performed. As shown in Table 4, children produced more elaborations and evaluations than repetitions, $F(2, 132) = 99.86$, $p < .001$. Children also talked significantly more in conversations about fear than sadness, but conversations about anger did not differ significantly from either, $F(2, 132) = 4.55$, $p < .01$. Overall, girls provided more elaborations (M = 11.61, SD = 6.43) during their conversations than boys (M = 7.73, SD = 4.56), but they did not differ in number

of evaluations or repetitions, $F(2, 132) = 9.46$, $p < .001$. Finally, children provided more evaluations during conversations about fear than about sadness or anger, which did not differ significantly from each other, $F(4, 264) = 2.50$, $p < .05$.

A 2 (gender of child) × 3 (type of emotional event: sadness, anger, and fear) × 4 (type of content: factual, attribution, cause, and resolution) MANOVA on the children's utterances revealed that, overall, children were providing significantly more information about the facts of the event itself and cause of emotion than information about emotional attributions, and more about emotional attributions than resolutions, $F(3, 192) = 63.59$, $p < .001$ (see Table 4). However, this varied by type of emotional conversation, $F(6, 384) = 2.14$, $p < .05$. As shown in Table 4, children were talking significantly more about the facts in conversations about fear than about sadness or anger, and discussing emotional resolutions more in conversations about fear and sadness than about anger.

Mother–child conversational themes

As described in the coding section, each conversation was coded into one of 10 mutually exclusive categories, which were further grouped as interpersonal or independent. Note that the conversation as a whole for both mother and child was categorised. Because there were unequal numbers of boys and girls, we converted the

TABLE 4
Means (and standard deviations) for children's style and content variables by event type

| | Event type | | | |
	Sadness	Anger	Fear	Total
Style variables				
Elaborations	2.87 n(2.47)	3.16 (2.62)	3.36 (2.77)	9.32 (5.70)
Evaluations	2.53 (2.09)	2.57 (2.58)	3.51 (2.29)	8.50 (5.12)
Repetitions	0.20 (0.47)	0.17 (0.45)	0.29 (0.55)	0.66 (0.89)
Total	5.60 (3.61)	5.90 (4.40)	7.16 (4.02)	18.49 (8.57)
Content variables				
Factual	1.75 (2.23)	2.16 (3.06)	2.96 (2.81)	6.64 (4.70)
Emotion cause	2.55 (1.63)	2.71 (2.02)	2.89 (1.83)	7.88 (3.27)
Emotion attribution	0.70 (1.45)	0.96 (1.39)	0.64 (1.07)	2.23 (2.35)
Emotion resolution	0.52 (1.13)	0.23 (0.88)	0.70 (1.24)	1.46 (2.19)
Total	5.60 (3.61)	5.90 (4.40)	7.16 (4.02)	18.49 (8.57)

frequencies to the percentage of conversations falling into each of these categories by type of emotion and gender (see Table 5). Not surprisingly certain themes were more likely to be discussed in particular emotional conversations than others. For example, characters and thunder were always associated with conversations about fear, whereas conflict with peers or lost objects never were. Overall, the majority of the conversations were interpersonal across gender and events, although anger had the highest percentage of interpersonal themes, followed by sadness and then fear. Interestingly, whereas virtually every mother–daughter conversation about anger was interpersonal, 20% of mother–son conversations about anger were independent. Similarly, just over half of mother–daughter conversations about fear were interpersonal, whereas over half of mother–son conversations about fear were independent. Thus there is some suggestion that negative emotions, especially anger and fear, are placed in a more interpersonal context with girls than with boys.

Looking more specifically within themes, about a quarter of all conversations about sadness focused on a lost toy or activity for both boys and girls. Parental separation was also a frequent topic of sadness for both genders. For boys, conflicts

TABLE 5
Percentage of mother–son and mother–daughter conversations about each theme by gender and event type

| | Event type | | | | | |
| | Sadness | | Anger | | Fear | |
Themes	Sons	daughters	Sons	Daughters	Sons	Daughters
Interpersonal						
Lost relation	11	25	2	11	0	0
Parental separation	17	18	7	0	2	8
Conflict w/ parent	24	14	38	32	5	0
Conflict w/ peer	9	0	33	46	0	0
Characters	0	0	0	0	41	56
Total	60	57	80	93	45	56
Independent						
Lost object	24	25	17	4	0	0
Thunder/noise	0	0	0	0	34	16
Injury	6	14	0	4	2	0
Scary activity	4	3	0	0	16	20
Lack of skill	4	0	2	4	0	0
Total	40	43	20	7	60	44

with parents were also highly associated with sadness, whereas for girls sadness was more likely to be associated with the loss of other relationships. Not surprisingly, anger conversations focus on children's conflicts with parents as well as siblings and peers, although boys are also frequently angry about lost objects. Conversations about fear focus heavily on scary characters such as witches, monsters, and ghosts, especially so for girls. Boys are scared by loud noises more than girls, and both boys and girls experience scary activities such as rollercoasters and swimming in deep water.

One other finding deserves mention. Whereas conflict with peers or siblings was almost always associated with anger for both genders, conflicts with parents were more emotionally diverse, being discussed as sad and even sometimes fearful. Similarly, parental separation was usually sad but sometimes associated with anger and fear as well. Thus it seems that parent–child relationships are discussed in a more multidimensional way and may be more emotionally complex than relationships with peers and siblings.

Summary

Overall, mothers were more elaborative and evaluative with daughters than with sons, and more elaborative when discussing fear than sadness or anger. Similarly, girls were more elaborative than boys, and both boys and girls were more elaborative and evaluative when discussing fear than sadness or anger. Mothers generally focused on causes when discussing emotional experiences, but focused on the facts when discussing fear, emotional resolutions when discussing fear and sadness, and emotional attributions when discussing anger. Children showed a similar pattern, talking more about factual information in conversations about fear and more about resolutions in conversations about fear and sadness than anger. Conversations tended to be more interpersonal than independent across event types, especially so with girls.

DISCUSSION

In this study, we examined the style and content of mother–child reminiscing about everyday negative experiences of fear, sadness, and anger. Our results provide evidence that mothers vary in the way in which they structure conversations depending on the type of emotion being discussed

and the gender of the child. Importantly, conversations about specific emotions did not differ in overall length, so differences in the ways in which these emotional conversations were structured do not reflect willingness or interest in discussing the event, but rather reflect differences in conversational focus. As argued in the introduction, these conversations serve three interrelated functions that comprise an emotional self-concept: self-defining, self-in-relation, and coping. In order to highlight these functions, we first discuss results and specific examples for each type of emotional conversation and we then discuss more overarching results across event type.

When discussing fearful events, mothers elaborate more, and they talk more about the facts concerning the event itself than when discussing sadness or anger. Mothers also focus on resolving fear more so than anger (but not sadness, as discussed later). Children also seem to be more concerned with fearful experiences than sadness or anger. They talk more about fear overall, and they provide more evaluations and resolutions when discussing fear than when discussing sadness or anger. To illustrate, we present an excerpt from a prototypical conversation about fear (M stands for Mother and C for Child, . . . indicates some missing dialogue):

M: . . .Sometimes you're scared of shadows, right?
C: Yeah
M: At nighttime in the dark?
C: Well yeah, at night I'm scared of the nother ones
M: . . .Where are they?
C: They were [inaudible] on the wall
M: On your wall?
C: Yeah, only one
M: . . .But Mommy showed you it wasn't really a monster or anything?
C: Well, Mommy it was.
M: . . .But honey
C: Well Mommy it was just a monster shadow
M: It was the monster shadow again, you tell me, right? And that's why Mommy got you your flashlight, remember?
C: Yeah
M: So you can turn it on whenever you need to.
C: I can turn it on. I can shine it on the shadow.

As can be seen in this example, both mother and child are very concerned about discussing the reality (or nonreality) of the shadow monsters. The mother is careful to explain again that these monster shadows are not real, and also to emphasise that they have developed a way to deal with the child's fears (the flashlight) which gives the child control over the situation and the emotion. Thus these conversations are highly co-constructed with both mothers and children contributing information about what happened and how to resolve it. Mothers' focus seems to be on providing factual information about these events. Of course, this is quite likely to be developmentally sensitive. Almost all of the conversations about fear in this study focused on developmentally typical preschoolers' fears of monsters under the bed, bad dreams, or loud noises such as thunder. Although young children are obviously quite fearful of these events, mothers are certainly aware that these are not things that can really harm their children, and they elaborate on why and how these things are not real and/or not to be feared. We might expect substantial differences in mother–child conversations about fear as children grow older and their fears reflect more real-world concerns.

Parent–child conversations about truly fearful events, such as natural disasters, serious illnesses, and injuries might also look quite different. Pervious studies on parent–child conversations about a tornado (Ackil, Waters, Dropnik, Dunisch, & Bauer, 1999) and an injury resulting in emergency room treatment (Sales, Fivush, & Peterson, 2001) also show a focus on causes of the fearful event, but do not seem to find as much of a focus on resolution as we found here. For events that are traumatic, and perhaps even life-threatening, the negative affect may be more difficult to resolve. Still, our results indicate that when discussing normal childhood fears, mothers and their preschoolers focus on elaborating what happened, what caused the emotion, and what the child can do to feel better. In this way, conversations about fear seem to be focused on coping, emphasising coping and resolution of negative affect.

In contrast, in conversations about anger, mothers do not elaborate, they do not discuss the facts surrounding the event itself, nor do they resolve anger as much as they do in conversations about fear. Rather, when discussing anger, mothers focus on emotional attributions. Children also do not talk as much about anger, they do not evaluate information about anger, and they do not discuss emotional resolutions of anger to the same extent as fear or sadness, as can be seen in this excerpt:

M: …You got angry with me.
C: Cause I didn't want you to go out

M: Hmm. That made you mad. Why did that make you mad?
C: Because I wanted you to stay.
M: You did? So you were angry with me?
C: Yeah
M: …You just felt angry?
C: Yeah

Conversations about anger seem to "hang in the air". The emotion itself is discussed but the causes of the emotion are not elaborated and the negative affect is not resolved. Thus, paradoxically, although these conversations focus on attributions of emotions, mothers do not seem to be interested in helping their children to understand the factual situation surrounding anger responses nor how to deal with anger when aroused. Rather, these conversations seem to be focused on self-definitional issues, emphasising the experience of the emotion but not how it is shared with others or resolved.

Finally, sadness falls between these two extremes. Conversations about sadness are not as elaborative overall as conversations about fear, nor do mothers focus on the event itself, as they do for fear, or on emotional attributions, as they do for anger. Rather, mothers focus on evaluating and resolving sad feelings. Children also focus on resolutions, as this example illustrates:

M: How do you usually feel when we're playing at nighttime and then Mom and Dad tell you it's time to go to bed?
C: Sad.
M: Yeah, I thought so.
C: I always feel sad at bedtime.
M: …You can't stay up as late as Mom and Dad because you need to get your rest, right?
C: I want to stay up later than Brian [the child's brother].
M: …Does that make you sad when Brian talks and you're trying to sleep?
C: …I just can't get to sleep
M: Okay, we'll do that in the afternoon when it's naptime. We put Brian in before you. You want us to do that at nighttime too?
C: Yeah.
M: Okay. Well, Dad and I can think about it.

In these conversations, mothers focus on evaluating and resolving their children's experience. Note also that the conversation about anger presented earlier and this conversation are both about parental conflict, yet when this conflict is discussed in the context of anger, it is left unresolved whereas when parental conflict is discussed on the context of sadness, the mother works quite hard at understanding her child's emotional reaction and providing a resolution. Conversations about sadness accept the emotional experience as warranted and discuss ways to alleviate the negative affect. By evaluating and sharing these emotional experiences in ways that validate children's experience, mothers emphasise both self-definition and self-in-relation.

Across all three emotional conversations, mothers talk more about the causes of their children's emotions than describing the facts of the event itself, or talking about emotional attributions or resolutions. Thus a major focus of these conversations is on helping children to understand the source of their emotional experience, an aspect of coping. Further, the majority of the conversations have an interpersonal theme, suggesting that emotions are placed in the context of relationships with other people, thus contributing to children's understanding of their emotional life as related to others.

However, by focusing on the factual aspects of fearful events and resolving fearful emotions, children may be learning that the emotion of fear itself should not be as much a part of their emotional self-definition. Through explaining the "facts of the matter", mothers focus children on the non-necessity of experiencing fear; there really is nothing to be afraid of. Moreover, mothers do not provide much evaluation of their children's fear responses. Thus these conversations focus on coping (resolution) but have little self-definition or self-in-relation.

In contrast, conversations about anger focus on the emotional state itself, but provide little evaluation or resolution, in contrast to our predictions. Although anger is clearly experienced, it is not appropriate to share it with others. Through this form of reminiscing, children may be learning to keep their angry feelings to themselves, or even not to think about them at all. Thus conversations about anger focus on self-defining functions (i.e., anger is an acknowledged emotion), but have little discussion of self-in-relation (i.e., little evaluation of the experience of anger as an appropriate emotion to express and share with others) or coping (i.e., little discussion of emotional resolution).

Finally, sadness is socially shareable, as predicted, but mothers focus on evaluating their children's contributions to the conversations. Mothers pay less attention to describing and elaborating the factual aspects of sad events or to discussing the emotional state itself. Rather, mothers seem to be allowing their children to talk about sad events, and how to resolve their feelings, in a socially supportive conversational context. Thus these conversations focus on self-definition (i.e., sadness is an appropriate and validated emotional reactions), self-in-relation (i.e., sadness is very much a shared emotion), and coping (resolution). The overall pattern of results indicates that children are developing culturally appropriate emotional self-concepts about the experience and expression of specific emotions.

Mothers are also more elaborative and more evaluative overall and place emotional experience in a more interpersonal context with daughters than with sons. Similarly, although girls and boys do not differ in overall amount of talk in these conversations, girls contribute more new information to the conversation than do boys. These results confirm previous findings of gender differences in reminiscing in general (Reese et al., 1996), and reminiscing about emotions more specifically (Fivush & Buckner, 2000). Parent–daughter dyads co-construct more embellished and detailed narratives of past emotional experiences than do parent–son dyads. However, in contrast to previous studies we did not find any evidence here that mothers talked about sadness more with daughters than with sons. As this specific result has been replicated in several studies (see Fivush & Buckner, 2000, for a review), it is not clear why we did not find this difference in this study as well.

Still, the gender differences obtained in this study support previous theorising that girls are being socialised into a more embellished, emotionally laden, and interpersonal autobiographical sense of self (Fivush & Buckner, 2000, in press; Gilligan, 1982). By reminiscing in more elaborative and evaluative ways about past emotional experiences, girls may be developing a more elaborated emotional self-concept than boys. Girls may come to understand themselves as experiencing and expressing more emotion, and may see emotion as more central to their self-definition than boys. Further, emotional experience is placed in a more interpersonal context. For girls, emotions emerge from and are resolved through their interactions with others to a greater extent than for boys; thus girls emotional self-concept may be more integrated with their understanding of self-in-relation than are boys.

Last, we must acknowledge two major limitations of this study. Because we studied a homogeneous white, middle-class sample, we must be cautious about generalising too broadly. Emotion socialisation varies widely by culture (see Lutz & White, 1986, for a review) as well as by social class. For example, Miller and Sperry (1988) found that single working-class mothers living in an inner-city environment encouraged the expression of anger in their young daughters. They explicitly talked about how difficult life was and how they wanted to teach their daughters to stand up for themselves. In middle-class culture, in contrast, mothers may believe that anger expression is a detrimental trait rather than an asset. Thus the function of experiencing and expressing anger may differ depending on the larger socio-cultural context. Future research should examine the ways in which different emotional experiences are discussed in different social and cultural groups.

Further, we only examined one age group in this study. As already alluded to, the types and causes of emotions that are considered appropriate or inappropriate may change with development. Related to this is the issue of bidirectionality. We analysed mothers' and children's contributions to these conversations independently, but clearly, conversational partners are influencing each other. Further, children's individual and developmental abilities to participate in these conversations, and to comprehend emotional experience, will surely play a role in how mothers discuss these experiences with them. These are important questions for future research.

In summary, our results indicate that mother–child reminiscing about everyday emotional experiences is a rich context for the development of children's emotional self-concept. The everyday ups and downs provide the texture of our lives; our emotions provide a sense of meaning and personal significance to our daily experiences. Through participating in adult structured reminiscing about emotionally negative events, children are developing a sense of self as an emotional being, and learning how to evaluate, resolve, and share these experiences with others.

REFERENCES

Ackil, J., Waters, J., Dropnik, P., Dunisch, D., & Bauer, P. (1999). *From the eyes of the storm: Mother–child conversations about a devastating tornado.* Poster presented at the biennial meetings of the Society for Research in Child Development, Albuquerque.

Adams, S., Kuebli, J., Boyle, P., & Fivush, R. (1995). Gender differences in parent–child conversations about past emotions: A longitudinal investigation. *Sex Roles, 33,* 309–323.

Basow, S.A. (1992). *Gender stereotypes and roles.* Belmont, CA: Brooks-Cole.

Bluck, S., & Alea, N. (2002). Exploring the functions of autobiographical memory. In J.D. Webster & B.K. Haight (Eds.), *Critical advances in reminiscing work: From theory to application* (pp. 61–75). New York: Springer.

Bruner, J. (1987). Life as narrative. *Social Research, 54,* 11–32.

Buckner, J.P., & Fivush, R. (1998). Gender and self in children's autobiographical narratives. *Applied Cognitive Psychology, 12,* 407–429.

Buckner, J.P., & Fivush, R. (2000). Gendered reminiscing. *Memory, 8,* 401–412.

Campos, J.J., & Barrett, K.C. (1984). Toward a new understanding of emotions and their development. In C.E. Izard, J. Kagen, & R.B. Zajonc (Eds.), *Emotions, cognition and behavior* (pp. 229–263). New York: Cambridge University Press.

Denham, S.A., Zoller, D., & Couchoud, E.A. (1994). Socialization of preschoolers' emotion understanding. *Developmental Psychology, 30,* 928–936.

Dunn, J., Brown, J., & Beardsall, L. (1991). Family talk about feeling states and children's later understanding of others' emotions. *Developmental Psychology, 27,* 448–455.

Engel, S. (1986). *Learning to reminisce: A developmental study of how young children talk about the past.* Unpublished doctoral dissertation, City University of New York.

Fabes, R.A., & Martin, C.L. (1991). Gender and age stereotypes of emotionality. *Personality and Social Psychology Bulletin, 17,* 532–540.

Fischer, A.H. (2000). *Gender and emotion: Social psychological perspectives.* New York: Cambridge University Press.

Fivush, R. (1988). The functions of event memory: Some comments on Nelson and Barsalou. In U. Neisser & E. Winograd (Eds.), *Remembering reconsidered: Ecological and traditional approaches to memory* (pp. 277–282). New York: Cambridge University Press.

Fivush, R. (1989). Exploring sex differences in the emotional content of mother–child talk about the past. *Sex Roles, 20,* 675–691.

Fivush, R. (1991). Gender and emotion in mother–child conversations about the past. *Journal of Narrative and Life History, 1,* 325–341.

Fivush, R. (1993). Emotional content of parent–child conversations about the past. In C.A. Nelson (Ed.), *The Minnesota Symposium on Child Psychology: Memory and affect in development* (pp. 39–77). Hillsdale, NJ: Lawrence Erlbaum Associates Inc.

Fivush, R. (1994). Constructing narrative, emotion and self in parent-child conversations about the past. In U. Neisser & R. Fivush (Eds.), *The remembering self: Accuracy and construction in the life narrative* (pp. 136–157). New York: Cambridge University Press.

Fivush, R. (1998). Gendered narratives: Elaboration, structure and emotion in parent–child reminiscing across the preschool years. In C.P. Thompson, D.J. Herrmann, D. Bruce, J.D. Read, D.G. Payne, & M.P. Toglia (Eds.), *Autobiographical memory: Theoretical and applied perspectives* (pp. 79–104). Hillsdale, NJ: Lawrence Erlbaum Associates Inc.

Fivush, R. (2001). Owning experience: The development of subjective perspective in autobiographical memory. In C. Moore & K. Lemmon (Eds.), *The self in time: Developmental perspectives* (pp. 35–52). Hillsdale, NJ: Lawrence Erlbaum Associates Inc.

Fivush, R. (in press). The silenced self: Constructing self from memories spoken and unspoken. In D. Beike, J. Lampinen, & D. Behrend (Eds.), *The self and memory*. New York: Psychology Press.

Fivush, R., Brotman, M., Buckner, J.P., & Goodman, S. (2000). Gender differences in parent–child emotion narratives. *Sex Roles, 42*, 233–254.

Fivush, R., & Buckner, J.P. (2000). Gender, sadness and depression: Developmental and socio-cultural perspectives. In A.H. Fischer (Ed.), *Gender and emotion: Social Psychological perspectives* (pp. 232–253). Cambridge, UK: Cambridge University Press.

Fivush, R., & Buckner, J.P. (in press). Constructing gender and identity through autobiographical narratives. In R. Fivush & C. Haden (Eds.), *Autobiographical memory and the construction of a narrative self: Developmental and cultural perspectives*. Hillsdale, NJ: Lawrence Erlbaum Associates Inc.

Fivush, R., & Fromhoff, F. (1988). Style and structure in mother–child conversations about the past. *Discourse Processes, 11*, 337–355.

Fivush, R., Haden, C., & Reese, E. (1996). Remembering, recounting and reminiscing: The development of autobiographical memory in social context. In D. Rubin (Ed.), *Reconstructing our past: An overview of autobiographical memory* (pp. 341–359). New York: Cambridge University Press.

Fivush, R., & Reese, E. (2002). Origins of reminiscing. In J. Webster & B. Haight (Eds.), *Critical advances in reminiscence work: From theory to application* (pp. 109–122). New York: Springer.

Fogel, A. (1993). *Developing through relationships.* Chicago: University of Chicago Press.

Gilligan, C. (1982). *In a different voice: Psychological theory and women's development.* Cambridge, MA: Harvard University Press.

Habermas, T., & Bluck, S. (2000). Getting a life: The emergence of the life story in adolescence. *Psychological Bulletin, 126*, 748–769.

Haden, C., Haine, R., & Fivush, R. (1997). Developing narrative structure in parent–child conversations about the past. *Developmental Psychology, 33*, 295–307.

Halberstadt, A.G., Denham, S.A., & Dunsmore, J. (2001). Affective social competence. *Social Development, 10*, 79–119.

Harley, K., & Reese, E. (1999). Origins of autobiographical memory. *Developmental Psychology, 35*, 1338–1348.

Hudson, J.A. (1990). The emergence of autobiographic memory in mother–child conversation. In R. Fivush, & J.A. Hudson (Eds.), *Knowing and remembering in young children* (pp. 166–196). New York: Cambridge University Press.

Kuebli, J., & Fivush, R. (1992). Gender differences in parent–child conversations about past emotions. *Sex Roles, 12*, 683–698.

Lutz, C., & White, G.M. (1986). The anthropology of emotions. *Annual Review of Anthropology, 15*, 405–436.

MacAdams, D.P. (1992). Unity and purpose in human lives: The emergence of identity as a life story. In R.A. Zucker, A.I. Rabin, J. Aronoff, & S.J. Frank (Eds.), *Personality structure in the life course* (pp. 323–375). New York: Springer.

Miller, P.J., & Sperry, L.L. (1988). Early talk about the past: The origins of conversational stories of personal experience. *Journal of Child Language, 15*, 293–315.

Neisser, U. (1988). Five kinds of self-knowledge. *Philosophical Psychology, 1*, 35–59.

Nelson, K. (1993). The psychological and social origins of autobiographical memory. *Psychological Science, 1*, 1–8.

Pennebaker, J.W. (1997). *Opening up.* New York: Guilford Press.

Peterson, C., & McCabe, A. (1992). Parental styles of narrative elicitation: Effect on children's narrative structure and content. *First Language, 12*, 299–321.

Reese, E., & Fivush, R. (1993). Parental styles for talking about the past. *Developmental Psychology, 29*, 596–606.

Reese, E., Haden, C.A., & Fivush, R. (1993). Mother–child conversations about the past: Relationships of style and memory over time. *Cognitive Development, 8*, 403–430.

Reese, E., Haden, C., & Fivush, R. (1996). Mothers, father, daughters, sons: Gender differences in reminiscing. *Research on Language and Social Interaction, 29*, 27–56.

Sales, J.M., Fivush, R., & Peterson, C. (2001), *Parent–child conversations about positive and negative events.* Manuscript submitted for publication.

MEMORY, 2003, *11* (2), 193–202

Directive functions of autobiographical memory: The guiding power of the specific episode

David B. Pillemer

Wellesley College, MA, USA

Vivid memories of personal experiences provide models for present activities and contribute to successful problem solving and adaptation. The memories serve important directive functions: they inform, guide, motivate, and inspire. Yet directive functions have received less emphasis in the research literature than social or self functions. Explanations for this relative neglect are explored. Case studies and systematic research illustrate the prominence of memory directives in everyday life. Empirical studies that have compared memory functions are examined critically, reasons why directive functions may be underestimated using existing methods are discussed, and ideas for future research are outlined.

Over the past two decades, the scope of scientific research on human memory has broadened dramatically. Prior to this time, experimental research focused almost exclusively on memory structure, organisation, and accuracy. Most of this work was conducted under controlled laboratory conditions, using numbers, words, nonsense syllables, and the like as stimuli. These experiments "were not designed as a part of a grand plan to understand how people remember personal experiences" (Tulving, 1983, p. 129).

Beginning in the early 1980s, increasing numbers of researchers embraced a more naturalistic approach to the study of memory. Within this new research paradigm, target objects of recall are ongoing life events—sibling births, presidential assassinations, first dates, school experiences—rather than carefully constructed experimental materials. This shift was triggered in part by the publication of a seminal collection of studies examining memory in everyday contexts (Neisser, 1982).

As researchers began to employ more naturalistic research designs, they also broadened their focus on memory structure and accuracy to include an analysis of function, defined as the "real-world usefulness or adaptive significance of memory mechanisms" (Bruce, 1989, p. 45). Conceptual analyses and empirical studies of autobiographical memory have uncovered a diverse set of possible functions. The functions identified to date appear to cluster into three broad categories (Bluck & Alea, 2002; Cohen, 1998; Pillemer, 1992, 1998): self (intrapersonal, psychodynamic), social (interpersonal, communicative), and directive (problem solving).

Although memory functions have been divided into discrete categories, they frequently overlap in real-world circumstances (Bluck & Alea, 2002; Wong & Watt, 1991). For example, Pillemer (1998) analysed an 8-year-old's memory of being kidnapped at gunpoint (reported by Terr, 1990, pp. 5–6). The lingering memory certainly affected the child's sense of self. It also contained horrifying lessons or directives—some possibly exaggerated or irrational—about what situations are safe and what is to be avoided. Finally, the way in which the child talked about her ordeal—word choice, tone of voice, verb tense, amount of detail, repetition—undoubtedly triggered empathic and emotional responses in others, thus serving a social function.

Requests for reprints should be sent to David B. Pillemer, Department of Psychology, Wellesley College, Wellesley, MA 02482, USA. Email: dpillemer@wellesley.edu

Paul Wink provided valuable advice and access to data reanalysed for this paper.

 DOI:10.1080/09658210244000360

Although all three major types of function may be operative in many instances of recounting a salient event, questions remain about their relative prominence. Pillemer (1992, 1998, 2001) stressed the evolutionary significance and practical importance of directive functions. In contrast, many autobiographical memory researchers identified the self or social functions as central (see Bluck & Alea, 2002, for a review). For example, Nelson (1993) argued from a developmental perspective that "the initial functional significance of autobiographical memory is that of sharing memory with other people ... Memories become valued in their own right—not because they predict the future and guide present action, but because they are shareable with others and thus serve a social solidarity function" (p. 12). Additionally, a study of functions associated with particular memories found little empirical support for the directive function (Hyman & Faries, 1992).

In this paper I explore the arguments and evidence for directive functions more fully. This analysis is limited to recall of specific episodes from the personal past, what have been called "personal event memories" (Pillemer, 1998). A personal event memory represents a pinpointed event that happened at a particular time and place, and it includes the rememberer's unique circumstances at that time, with associated sensory images and feelings.

Directive functions of personal event memories have received comparatively little attention in part because general or semantic memory is seen as the primary source of direction and guidance (Pillemer, 1998). For example, Tulving commented that "knowledge of the world, by and large, is more useful to people than are personal memories" (1983, p. 52), and Neisser concurred that "many of the important things in human experience are ongoing situations rather than single events" (1985, p. 274). Behaviour is frequently governed or directed by general expectations or scripts (Abelson, 1981), which are constructed through repeated happenings. According to Nelson (1993), when it comes to "guiding present action and predicting future outcomes" ... the "most useful memory for this function is generic memory for routines that fit recurrent situations" (p. 11). But what about situations where well-established scripts do not exist or when they fail to do the job? In these instances, the directive power of specific episodes can prove to be critically important.

The thrust of the present argument is that directive functions of personal event memories are not secondary in importance to self and social functions. Rather, they are among the most basic and elemental functions served by autobiographical memory, appearing early in human history and tied closely to survival pressures. Although memory directives are linked to specific past episodes, their impact can be far-reaching and broadly applicable; these broad influences on thoughts and behaviours extend beyond the more limited definitions of "problem solving" used to operationalise "directives" in some research studies. Even in instances where autobiographical memory is clearly used in the service of problem solving, the memory operations are so common and automatic that they may not be readily identifiable via casual introspection.

Memory activities within several disparate domains will be used to illustrate the prominence of directive functions in everyday life. These examples lead to the conclusion that the power and reach of autobiographical memory directives is substantial. Then, empirical studies that speak to the relative importance of different memory functions are examined critically, reasons why directive functions may be underestimated using existing methods are discussed, and ideas for future research are offered.

TRAUMATIC EVENT MEMORIES AS DIRECTIVES

By any account, the terrorist attack on the World Trade Center in New York City qualifies as a "momentous" event (Pillemer, 1998). It happened suddenly, at a particular time and place. It triggered extraordinarily intense emotional responses: fear, sadness, and panic. For some people, it exceeded the threshold for "psychic trauma", achieved when "a sudden, unexpected, overwhelmingly intense emotional blow or a series of blows assaults the person from outside" (Terr, 1990, p. 8). According to Terr, trauma "often continues to exert a specific, ongoing influence on attitudes and behaviors" (p. 35). The tragedy's profound impact on Americans' daily activities, long-term plans, and beliefs about the world was apparent almost immediately. September 11 has been called, without exaggeration, "the day that changed America" (Thomas, 2001–2002, p. 40).

Viewing this horrific event from a vantage point months after its occurrence, how do the shared memory activities of Americans fit depictions of functions identified previously in studies of autobiographical memory? The three broad categories of function described earlier are all readily identifiable. The self function is present in the painful but spirited rethinking of what we stand for as a country, of what it means to be an "American". The social function is evident in countless retellings of the event and in the far-reaching empathy that stories of personal tragedy have engendered. The directive function was front and centre in the focal activities during the days immediately following the attack, which involved preventing additional harm and preserving the future safety of Americans. These dramatic responses were guided by memories of the unthinkable disaster, which carried violent images of danger and implied directives for how to avoid them in the future.

How could a single historical event have such a profound impact on the direction of our country's plans and activities, such that "another world began that day" (Sullivan, 2001, p. 61)? Within psychology, scripts representing predictable occurrences are commonly identified as the primary cognitive mechanisms directing behaviour. And, prior to September 11, a hypothetical "terrorist threat" script existed: "Warning about 'grand terrorism' ... and calling for 'homeland defense' has been an academic subspecialty for years. Foundation and government reports warned that it was only a matter of time before the terrorists struck America..." (Thomas, 2001–2002, p. 42). Yet it took a monumental episode, perpetuated by emotionally charged vivid memories, to trigger an urgent and vigorous response.

Following September 11, the directive power of memory was as apparent in the lives of individuals as in the broader activities of society. Extraordinary concerns for personal safety predominated. People did not fly on aeroplanes and avoided public places. To cite one example, attendance at most professional meetings for psychologists was 30–40% below expectations in the months following the attack (Hagen, 2002). It seems unlikely that these extreme reactions were prompted solely by the known "facts" of the tragedy. Many Americans witnessed the collapse of the World Trade Center towers on television, in real time as the incomprehensible events unfolded. Memories of these horrifying images and associated feelings undoubtedly contributed to the intensity and persistence of protective responses.

The directive force of personal memory was starkly apparent when major league baseball commissioner Bud Selig had to decide whether play should be postponed in the days following the attack. The decision was informed by vivid memories of personal reactions to an earlier national tragedy, the assassination of President Kennedy in 1963: "I went to a Green Bay Packer game with old Braves catcher Del Crandall ... We walked into that game and when they played the national anthem, a man standing next to us broke down and started crying. I turned to Del and said, 'What the hell are we doing here?' I thought about that this week and I thought about the San Francisco earthquake" (Shaughnessy, 2001, p. F1). Memories of reactions to September 11 will serve a similar guiding function in response to future traumas.

Additional support for the centrality of directive functions during the time interval immediately following a tragedy comes from clinical studies of people's responses to trauma. According to Herman (1992), recovery from trauma takes place in three stages. The goal of the first stage is preserving future safety: "Establishing a safe environment requires ... the development of a plan for future protection. In the aftermath of the trauma, the survivor must assess the degree of continued threat and decide what sort of precautions are necessary" (p. 164). In the second stage of recovery, the primary agenda is remembrance and mourning, and the healing mechanism is memory sharing: "the survivor tells the story of the trauma ... This work of reconstruction actually transforms the traumatic memory, so that it can be integrated into the survivor's life story" (p. 175). In the final stage of recovery, the survivor's main task is reconnection and development of a changed identity: "She has mourned the old self that the trauma destroyed; now she must develop a new self" (p. 196).

The three major categories of memory function described earlier in this paper are readily apparent in Herman's description. Social functions of memory sharing are essential to recovery in the second stage, and self functions predominate in the third stage during which a new identity is forged. Directive functions are prominent in the first stage. Initial efforts to survive are driven by vivid memories of sources of danger that must be avoided or confronted to achieve the goal of future safety. Memories of trauma often are quite specific and detailed, as are associated post-traumatic fears (Terr, 1990); powerful images of danger prompt protective psychological and behavioural responses. Successfully responding to these directives—creating a safe environment—is prerequisite to psychological recovery.

EVERYDAY EVENT MEMORIES AS DIRECTIVES

Individual and societal responses to September 11, and to traumatic events more generally, suggest that memory directives play a central role in the aftermath of disaster. Adults' recollections of more typical life episodes, salient personal events that occurred within the ongoing flow of daily activities, also frequently contain guidelines for how to act or what to believe. Pillemer (1998, 2001) identified several different directive functions of personal event memories, and provided many illustrations from memory studies, autobiographies, and media reports. The memories are not static. They come to mind repeatedly and provide guidance when encountering new life challenges. Their directive force is felt when confronting novel situations that are structurally similar to the original episode recorded in memory (Pillemer, 1998; Schank, 1980, 1990).

"Memorable messages" from powerful and respected others illustrate the persistent directive force of personal event memories (Knapp, Stohl, & Reardon, 1981; Pillemer, 1998). For example, an adolescent's memory of an interaction with her parents continued to direct social problem solving long after the initial occurrence (Pratt, Arnold, & Mackey, 2001, p. 237):

> My dad went to his high school reunion, and I didn't really want to go ... I hardly spoke a word through the entire thing ... And my mom and dad could talk to the people openly because they both knew them, and I was, like I don't know anyone and I'm just gonna sit back in a corner ... and they said, "Oh, be open, just talk with people" and so in a way they kind of taught me and they kind of showed me at the same time ... I still have trouble with it, but it showed me just talking can be easy. I don't think I'm gonna be able to forget it [the experience] for a long time. Just when I have trouble talking to people, I just have to look back on that and say, "OK, my parents can do it, I can do it ..."

Memorable messages such as this one are a common occurrence. Goldsmith and Pillemer (1988) asked college students to report vivid

memories of a statement made by a parent, and 46% of the statements provided advice or guidance. In psychotherapy, "many clients refer to statements made by their parents or teachers in the past. Actual contact with these significant others may not have occurred for many years, but their statements nevertheless play a central role in the present life of the clients" (Hermans, Kempen, & van Loon, 1992, p. 29).

The guiding power of specific memories also is illustrated by instances where a stunning moment of failure is used to provide positive motivation in future endeavours. Professional basketball star Michael Jordan's vivid memory of a stinging rejection—his failure to make the varsity team his sophomore year in high school—provided lasting inspiration (May, 1991, p. 105):

> It was embarrassing, not making that team. They posted the roster and it was there for a long, long time without my name on it. I remember being really mad, too ... Whenever I was working out and got tired and figured I ought to stop, I'd close my eyes and see that list in the locker room without my name on it, and that usually got me going again.

Similar reactions are evident among high school and college athletes who may never approach Jordan's level of prominence. For example, Harvard football captain Ryan Fitz-Gerald was motivated by memories of painful losses from the previous season. "I don't think a day goes by that I don't think about those losses," FitzGerald said. He tries to remember "how it felt after losing those awful games. I want all of us to use it as motivation so that it doesn't happen again" (Harber, 2001, p. G8).

Some lessons encapsulated in vivid memories of particular episodes are more pedestrian and experienced frequently in everyday life. A Wellesley College student learned a valuable lesson about planning following a mishap on a trip into Boston (Pillemer, 1998, p. 64):

> I remember coming home from the freshman scavenger hunt. The group of ... students I was with ... didn't have enough money to buy Senate Bus tickets in Boston to get home—We tried to take the commuter rail, but it didn't run on Saturdays ... We got on the [subway] and off at Woodland and walked home—all 6 some-odd miles ... I had popcorn and apples for dinner. Now I always check bus schedules.

Pillemer (1998) presented many additional examples and categories of lessons contained in vivid memories of pinpointed events. The directive function is as apparent in these personal episodes as in the memories of trauma presented earlier. The directives are not connected as closely to survival—preserving safety in the aftermath of crisis—but the memories are linked to future well-being through their persistent reminders of what is worth pursuing and what is to be avoided.

EMPIRICAL STUDIES OF REMINISCENCE FUNCTIONS

Given that everyday examples of directives generated by memories of specific episodes are commonplace, why have directive functions received less emphasis in the psychological research literature than social or self functions? One answer, discussed earlier, is the pervasive belief that general learning or script knowledge is the primary mechanism through which memory informs current behaviour. A second answer is that early empirical studies of memory function failed to identify directive functions as prominent. Hyman and Faries (1992) administered a questionnaire in which respondents were asked to describe memories that they had talked about frequently, and to describe circumstances in which the retellings took place. Memories were coded according to how they were used in discussion, such as self-description (to tell someone about yourself) or entertainment (to entertain others during the conversation). The coding category that resembled directive functions most closely was "problem discussion", which was defined as "telling a memory to describe a problem; often these were ongoing problems" (p. 211). Problem discussion was the focus of memory talk only infrequently. In a second study, participants described the first memory to come to mind in response to eight cue words (e.g., happy, letter). Again, problem discussion was rarely the topic of these remembrances. The authors observed that "no subject described thinking about a previous experience when trying to decide what behavior to follow in a new or similar context," and they concluded that "semantic knowledge may be more important than episodic for guiding behavior" (Hyman & Faries, 1992, p. 218).

Hyman and Faries' conclusion was qualified by an acknowledgement that the functions they identified may be highly dependent on the particular methodology used. Requests for frequently talked about memories, or for the first memories to come to mind in response to cue words, may not be the best ways to evoke memory directives. Memories that guide present behaviour are likely to come to mind when confronting current problems, but they may not be activated during casual conversation or in response to cue words presented out of context. Hyman and Faries suggested that directive functions may be more apparent in test situations that use a "problem solving context" (p. 219).

Wong and Watt (1991) examined reminiscence functions using a different methodology. Older adults were asked to describe "something of your past that is most important to you—that is something that has had the most influence on your life" (p. 275). Transcribed interviews were first divided into paragraphs, and each paragraph was assigned to a particular functional category. Six reminiscence categories were created on the basis of previously published studies and content analyses of memory reports. Wong and Watt's categories that are most closely related to the three major functional categories (self, social, directive) include, respectively, integrative (achieving a sense of self-worth and personal coherence), narrative (providing routine biographical information, recounting past events for social purposes), and instrumental (using past experiences to solve present problems). Analyses of word counts indicated that the most common function of text was narrative reminiscing, followed by integrative and instrumental reminiscing. It is important to note that these rankings refer only to the amount of text devoted to different purposes, not to the life importance of the functions. A follow-up analysis compared respondents who were judged by experts to be ageing successfully to those who were ageing less successfully. Older adults who were ageing successfully showed more instrumental and integrative reminiscence but not more narrative reminiscence. The authors explained the group differences in instrumental reminiscence as follows: "It not only provides past examples of successful solutions to present problems but may also enhance the elderly person's sense of mastery" (Wong & Watt, 1991, p. 277).

Webster (1993, 2003 this issue; Webster & McCall, 1999) developed a general method for assessing people's beliefs about how frequently they use memory to fulfil different functions. The Reminiscence Functions Scale (RFS) is not tied to particular remembered episodes; instead, respondents rate on a 6-point scale "how often they reminiscence with a particular function in mind" (1993, p. 258). The scale taps eight different factors (Webster & McCall, 1999), including three that resemble broadly defined functions commonly associated with autobiographical memory (self, social, directive): identity (using the past to "discover, clarify and crystalize important dimensions of our sense of who we are," pp. 76–77), conversation (using the past "as a means of connecting or reconnecting with others in an informal way," p. 77), and problem solving (using the past so that "past problem-solving strategies may be used again in the present," p. 77).

Webster and colleagues conducted analyses of reliability and validity, but they did not compare the factors with respect to rated frequency of use, so that their results do not bear directly on the question of the functions' relative prominence or importance. Pillemer, Wink, DiDonato, and Sanborn (in press) administered the RFS as part of a study of gender differences in autobiographical memory styles in older adults (68–79 years of age). Participants (n = 115) were assigned memory function scores by computing an average score across the individual items composing the factor. By using item averages, it was possible to make direct comparisons for the present study. Mean scores on the 6-point scale for identity (3.31, SD = 1.14), conversation (3.23, SD = .98), and problem solving (3.30, SD = .96) are nearly identical; respondents rated frequency of use as between "seldom" and "occasionally" for all three factors. Correlations between the three factors are positive, with the strongest relationship between identity and problem solving (identity and problem solving, r = .76, p < .001; identity and conversation, r = .51, p < .001; conversation and problem solving, r = .53, p < .001).

In addition to completing the RFS, participants in Pillemer et al.'s study provided lengthy personal interviews, covering such topics as parents, children, marriage, work, health, and spirituality. The narratives differed in form as well as in content. Some people tended to describe their lives in general terms, whereas others frequently punctuated their life stories with vivid descriptions of pinpointed events. To assess apparent individual differences in autobiographical memory style, interviews were coded for the occurrence of specific episodic memories within the ongoing narrative. Because the interviews differed in length, the researchers computed a measure of episodic memory density by dividing the number

of specific memories by the number of transcribed pages. A high density score indicated that the respondent provided a relatively high number of specific memories per page, and thereby told his or her life story using an episodic memory style.

Do ratings of how frequently memory is used for different functional purposes (as measured by factor scores on the RFS) predict the density of specific memories in personal narratives? Although participants' RFS ratings indicated that they use social, self, and directive functions with equal frequency, relationships with memory specificity differed across RFS factors. Correlations between episodic memory density and problem solving (r = .24, p = .009), and between memory density and identity (r = .19, p = .037) were positive and significant, whereas the correlation between memory density and conversation was not (r = .10, p = .311). People who claimed to use memory in a directive fashion—to solve current problems—or to build an identity had narratives that were more richly populated with personal event memories.

Pillemer et al. identified gender differences in memory specificity and in RFS scores: Women's narratives contained a greater number of specific memories than did men's narratives, and women also scored more highly than men on the identity and problem-solving RFS factors. For this reason, correlations between RFS scores and episodic memory density were computed for men and women separately. For men, correlations were small in magnitude and none approached statistical significance. For women, only the correlation between specific memory density and problem solving was significant, r = .34, p = .010; women who reported that they frequently used reminiscence in order to solve current problems or to learn from the past produced life narratives that were rich in specific memories. Possible reasons for gender differences in autobiographical memory are explored in depth by Pillemer et al. (in press). For the purposes of the present paper, it is noteworthy that the strongest predictor of the incidence of specific memories in women's life stories is the RFS problem-solving factor. This finding is consistent with the idea that people develop an elaborate network of personal event memories in support of directive functions.

In summary, few studies have provided data bearing directly on the importance of directive functions compared to other autobiographical memory functions, and existing data are far from conclusive. Hyman and Faries (1992) found little support for memory directives, but these authors acknowledged that asking for frequently talked about memories, or obtaining memories using cue words, may not be the best way to elicit recollections that fulfil directive functions. When scores on the RFS obtained by Pillemer et al. (in press) were examined for the current study, older adults' ratings of the frequency with which they employ social, self, and directive functions were almost identical. Another way to assess the relative importance of memory functions involves examining their relationship to independent indices of personal well-being or autobiographical style. Wong and Watt (1991) found that problem-solving and identity functions, but not narrative functions, were related to successful ageing. In the reanalysis of data from Pillemer et al. (in press), frequent use of problem-solving and identity reminiscence functions, but not conversation, was associated with highly episodic personal narratives. Overall, this analysis of the current, albeit small, scientific literature on the functions of autobiographical memory suggests that directive functions play as least as important a role as do self and social functions.

ASSESSING DIRECTIVE FUNCTIONS: CONCEPTUAL AND METHODOLOGICAL ISSUES

Examining the relative importance of different autobiographical memory functions using existing methods can be misleading. With respect to measuring frequency of use of directive functions, one issue is that definitions refer for the most part to using memory in the service of current problem solving. For example, RFS items include reminiscing "to help resolve some current difficulty", "to put current problems in perspective", and "to see how my strengths can help me solve a current problem". But this concrete, problem-oriented perspective does not capture the full range of directive functions. A vivid memory of a personal failure may provide persistent inspiration and motivation, as in the case of Michael Jordan and other athletes mentioned earlier in this paper, but the remember is not likely to define these instances as "problem solving". Similarly, the Wellesley College student whose negative experiences on a trip into Boston prompted her to "always check bus schedules" may not see this as a case of solving current problems, because the memory activity eliminates the problem.

A second issue involves the degree to which people are aware of the functional uses served by their memory activities. The RFS, for example, requires that respondents be able to estimate how frequently they "reminisce" for particular purposes. These estimates require conscious awareness, so functions that are deliberate and effortful will be featured over those that are relatively automatic. In the case of directive functions, memories are frequently triggered by a structural similarity between past and present circumstances, without purposeful mental effort or memory search activities (Pillemer, 1998). The success of episodic "remindings" requires that a memory come to mind "at just the point where that memory would be most useful for processing. This tends to be necessary when things have not gone exactly as planned" (Schank, 1980, p. 41). The memory provides a warning or a model for action based on a similar past episode.

From an evolutionary perspective, it seems unlikely that the delivery of memory directives (or indeed any autobiographical memory function) would invariably be conscious, purposeful, and deliberate. When an individual is confronted with a new situation that is problematic, confusing, or potentially dangerous, memories of past instances that resemble the current dilemma can provide guidance. Lessons contained in memories of particular episodes will be especially valuable when generalised expectations or scripts for how to respond are lacking. When a situation is threatening, there would seem to be a survival benefit for the relevant episodic directives to be delivered quickly and automatically to consciousness, without focused awareness of memory activities and time-consuming reminiscence. In their theoretical discussion of flashbulb memory, Brown and Kulik (1977) provided an example of primitive humans witnessing a serious injury to one of their group members. A vivid memory of this event—including detailed information about where and when the injury occurred—will prevent future disasters only if it comes to mind quickly when similar circumstances are encountered (Pillemer, 1984). In the present day, eyewitnesses to the destruction of the World Trade Center will have those traumatic memories come to mind involuntarily, when life circumstances trigger them. In general, memory of trauma frequently is characterised by involuntary retrieval (Brewin, 1989; McNally, 1998).

Past episodes may be triggered automatically even under less threatening circumstances. In the example presented earlier of a student who baulks when required to talk to strangers, it seems unlikely that when confronted with such situations she must search purposefully for the memorable directive provided by her parents. Rather, the message to "be open, just talk with people" is activated by situational cues. Many instances of episodic remembering share this automatic quality (Pillemer, 1998; Schank, 1980). Assessment tools that focus solely on reminiscence functions involving aware and effortful mental activity will miss these common but elusive qualities of remembering.

IDEAS FOR NEW RESEARCH

Because directive, self, and social functions of autobiographical memory are intimately connected in everyday activities, a prime topic for new research is how they interact, support, or impede each other. For example, how in the process of psychotherapy are powerful memory directives, triggered automatically by particular life circumstances, modified, transformed, and brought under conscious control through memory sharing? How does the patient's autobiographical sense of self change as a result of memory talk? Under what circumstances do the three broad types of memory function operate relatively independently, and when are they tied together most closely?

Although reminiscence functions identified by ratings of frequency of use provide useful taxonomies, other research strategies may produce more meaningful information about the relative prominence of different functions in specific circumstances. One promising research domain is parent–child talk about the past. According to the "social interaction hypothesis", children learn how to use autobiographical memory in part through conversations with their parents (Fivush, 1991; Fivush & Reese, 1992; Hudson, 1990; Nelson, 1993). Parents provide the structure and motivation for memory sharing, and thereby model functional uses of memory. Existing analyses have focused on the social solidarity functions of joint remembering (e.g., Nelson, 1993), but parent–child memory talk also reveals other functions, such as modelling the process of using memories to inform current activities (Pillemer, 1998). For example, Miller, Potts, Fung, Hoogstra, and Mintz (1990) described a conversation between an immigrant Chinese mother and her 3-

year-old son in which the parent is promoting the use of memory as a guide for behaviour. The child recounted an incident at the zoo: "Yes, in the zoo I, that slide, I didn't let the other kids play." His mother responded by drawing attention to an implied lesson: "Yes. It was your fault, wasn't it? ... Papa was mad at you ... Papa said, 'How come you didn't listen to me?' " (p. 301).

Research could address more systematically the question of which functional uses are modelled in parent–child conversations. Do parents actively attempt to teach children how to "find" a memory in order to solve a current problem? Is memory talk frequently intended to enhance the child's distinctive personal identity and autonomous sense of self? Under what circumstances do families converse about the past with no apparent purpose other than maintaining or deepening interpersonal connections?

Another potentially rich area for future study involves examining functional uses of memory across cultures, gender groups, and personality types. Research has identified cultural, gender, and personality differences in memory style: Caucasians and Asians, men and women, and depressed and non-depressed individuals differ in the structure and extensiveness of memory talk. For example, US adults frequently engage their children in elaborative memory sharing, whereas "Japanese children are not usually encouraged to narrate details of experiences that adults can and are expected to infer empathically" (Minami & McCabe, 1991, p. 577). In Mullen and Yi's (1995) cross-cultural study of parent–child discourse styles, Caucasians talked about specific past events that the child had experienced almost three times as often as did Koreans. New research could focus specifically on group differences in the functional purposes of reminiscence and memory talk. Are Caucasians more likely than Asians to encourage their children to use personal memories to construct an autonomous, independent sense of self? Are girls and women more likely than boys and men to engage in memory talk in order to build social solidarity? Some preliminary research support for cultural, gender, and personality differences in autobiographical memory styles already exists (reviewed in Pillemer, 1998; Pillemer et al., in press), but much more could be done.

The question of which type of memory function is most common, basic, or important is overly simplistic, because the adaptive value of remembering will vary across situations and individuals, and because memory functions do not operate in isolation from one another. Research strategies that focus on patterns of use and interactions between functions seem preferable to more simplistic comparisons.

REFERENCES

Abelson, R.P. (1981). Psychological status of the script concept. *American Psychologist, 36*, 715–729.

Bluck, S., & Alea, N. (2002). Exploring the functions of autobiographical memory: Why do I remember the autumn? In J.D. Webster & B.K. Haight (Eds.), *Critical advances in reminiscence: From theory to application* (pp. 61–75). New York: Springer.

Brewin, C.R. (1989). Cognitive change processes in psychotherapy. *Psychological Review, 96*, 379–394.

Brown, R., & Kulik, J. (1977). Flashbulb memories. *Cognition, 5*, 73–99.

Bruce, D. (1989). Functional explanations of memory. In L.W. Poon, D.C. Rubin, & B.A. Wilson (Eds.), *Everyday cognition in adulthood and late life* (pp. 44–58). New York: Cambridge University Press.

Cohen, G. (1998). The effects of aging on autobiographical memory. In C.P. Thompson, D.J. Herrmann, D. Bruce, J.D. Read, D.G. Payne, & M.P. Toglia (Eds.), *Autobiographical memory: Theoretical and applied perspectives* (pp. 105–123). Mahwah, NJ: Lawrence Erlbaum Associates Inc.

Fivush, R. (1991). The social construction of personal narratives. *Merrill-Palmer Quarterly, 37*, 59–81.

Fivush, R., & Reese, E. (1992). The social construction of autobiographical memory. In M.A. Conway, D.C. Rubin, H. Spinnler, & W.A. Wagenaar (Eds.), *Theoretical perspectives on autobiographical memory* (pp. 1–28). Dordrecht, The Netherlands: Kluwer Academic Publishers.

Goldsmith, L.R., & Pillemer, D.B. (1988). Memories of statements spoken in everyday contexts. *Applied Cognitive Psychology, 2*, 273–286.

Hagen, J. (2002, January). Maintaining our focus and advocacy for work with children. *Developments: Newsletter of the Society for Research in Child Development, 45*, pp. 1, 9.

Harber, P. (2001, September 1). Looking for atonement: Harvard captain uses losses as motivation. *The Boston Globe*, p. G8.

Herman, J.L. (1992). *Trauma and recovery.* New York: Basic Books.

Hermans, H.J.M., Kempen, H.J.G., & van Loon, R.J.P. (1992). The dialogical self: Beyond individualism and rationalism. *American Psychologist, 47*, 23–33.

Hudson, J.A. (1990). The emergence of autobiographical memory in mother–child conversation. In R. Fivush & J.A. Hudson (Eds.), *Knowing and remembering in young children* (pp. 166–196). New York: Cambridge University Press.

Hyman, I.E., Jr., & Faries, J.M. (1992). The functions of autobiographical memory. In M.A. Conway, D.C. Rubin, H. Spinnler, & W.A. Wagenaar (Eds.), *Theoretical perspectives on autobiographical memory* (pp. 207–221). Dordrecht, The Netherlands: Kluwer Academic Publishers.

Knapp, M.L., Stohl, C., & Reardon, K.K. (1981, Autumn). "Memorable" messages. *Journal of Communication*, 27–41.

May, P. (1991, June 11). The man who beat out Jordan. *The Boston Globe*, pp. 105, 110.

McNally, R.J. (1998). Experimental approaches to cognitive abnormality in posttraumatic stress disorder. *Clinical Psychology Review, 18*, 971–982.

Miller, P.J., Potts, R., Fung, H., Hoogstra, L., & Mintz, J. (1990). Narrative practices and the social construction of self in childhood. *American Ethnologist, 17*, 292–311.

Minami, M., & McCabe, A. (1991). *Haiku* as a discourse regulation device: A stanza analysis of Japanese children's personal narratives. *Language in Society, 20*, 577–599.

Mullen, M., & Yi, S. (1995). The cultural context of talk about the past: Implications for the development of autobiographical memory. *Cognitive Development, 10*, 407–419.

Neisser, U. (1982). *Memory observed: Remembering in natural contexts.* San Francisco: Freeman.

Neisser, U. (1985). The role of theory in the ecological study of memory: Comment on Bruce. *Journal of Experimental Psychology: General, 114*, 272–276.

Nelson, K. (1993). The psychological and social origins of autobiographical memory. *Psychological Science, 4*, 7–14.

Pillemer, D.B. (1984). Flashbulb memories of the assassination attempt on President Reagan. *Cognition, 16*, 63–80.

Pillemer, D.B. (1992). Remembering personal circumstances: A functional analysis. In E. Winograd & U. Neisser (Eds.), *Affect and accuracy in recall: Studies of "flashbulb" memories* (pp. 236–264). New York: Cambridge University Press.

Pillemer, D.B. (1998). *Momentous events, vivid memories.* Cambridge, MA: Harvard University Press.

Pillemer, D.B. (2001). Momentous events and the life story. *Review of General Psychology, 5*, 123–134.

Pillemer, D.B., Wink, P., DiDonato, T.E., & Sanborn, R.L. (in press). Gender differences in autobiographical memory styles of older adults. *Memory.*

Pratt, M.W., Arnold, M.L., & Mackey, K. (2001). Adolescents' representations of the parent voice in stories of personal turning points. In D.P. McAdams, R. Josselson, & A. Lieblich (Eds.), *Turns in the road: Narrative studies of lives in transition* (pp. 227–252). Washington, DC: American Psychological Association.

Schank, R.C. (1980). Failure-driven memory. *Cognition and Brain Theory, 4*, 41–60.

Schank, R.C. (1990). *Tell me a story: A new look at real and artificial memory.* New York: Scribners.

Shaughnessy, D. (2001, September 15). Selig looked to the past as a guide to present. *The Boston Globe*, p. F1.

Sullivan, A. (2001, September 23). This is what a day means. *The New York Times Magazine*, pp. 60–61.

Terr, L. (1990). *Too scared to cry.* New York: Basic Books.

Thomas, E. (2001–2002). The day that changed America. *Newsweek*, Dec. 31–Jan. 7 2002; double issue pp. 40–71.

Tulving, E. (1983). *Elements of episodic memory*. New York: Clarendon Press.

Webster, J.D. (1993). Construction and validation of the Reminiscence Functions Scale. *Journal of Gerontology*, *48*, 256–262.

Webster, J.D. (2003). The reminiscence circumplex and autobiographical memory functions. *Memory*, *11*, 203–215.

Webster, J.D., & McCall, M.E. (1999). Reminiscence functions across adulthood: A replication and extension. *Journal of Adult Development*, *6*, 73–85.

Wong, P.T.P., & Watt, L.M. (1991). What types of reminiscence are associated with successful aging? *Psychology and Aging*, *6*, 272–279.

MEMORY, 2003, *11* (2), 203–215

The reminiscence circumplex and autobiographical memory functions

Jeffrey Dean Webster

Langara College, Vancouver, Canada

This study investigated the potential of a circumplex model to represent the functions of both reminiscence and autobiographical memory. Participants from four pre-existing data bases (i.e., Culley, LaVoie, & Gfeller, 2001; Webster, 1997, 2002; Webster & McCall, 1999) were combined, resulting in a total of 985 participants ranging in age from 17 to 96 (*M* age = 36.63 years). A total of 392 men (39.8%) and 591 women (60.1%), with two persons not reporting their gender, completed the Reminiscence Functions Scale (RFS) as part of the original four studies. The eight RFS factors were submitted to second-order factor analysis resulting in two orthogonal dimensions (self versus social and reactive/loss-oriented versus proactive/growth-oriented) accounting for 79.57% of the variance. Further, multidimensional scaling indicated that the original eight factors could be arranged in a circular fashion such that more closely related (i.e., more highly correlated) factors were placed closer together while factors less highly related were placed further apart. Advantages of a circumplex perspective for future theory and model development are illustrated.

> Memory dies unless it's given a use
> (Michaels, 1996, p. 193).

What are the uses of memory? Due in part to a focus over the last century on the *mechanics* of memory (e.g., Bruce, 1985, 1991) we are only recently addressing this question in a systematic way (e.g., Bluck & Alea, 2002; Conway, 1990). Moreover, few psychometrically sound measures of either reminiscence, or autobiographical memory functions, exist. Consequently, there are limited means to validate empirically many of the theoretical speculations offered in the literature.

Investigations concerning the specific uses of memory in ecologically valid contexts are conducted primarily by researchers from two conceptually related yet empirically distinct subareas of memory, namely, autobiographical memory (AM) and reminiscence (REM) research. Each division provides a different lens through which to observe essentially the same phenomenon: the recall of personally experienced events from one's past. Both of these domains emphasise a functional approach to memory, that is, a concern with the adaptive advantages that personally significant memories have for coping successfully with the exigencies of everyday life.

Despite the general focus on the recall of personally significant memories from one's personal past, there are enough differences between AM and REM domains that there is very little cross-referencing between these two traditions (for an overview of the relationship between these two areas, see Webster & Cappeliez, 1993). This is unfortunate, as each area could benefit from the findings of the other (e.g., Bluck & Alea, 2002; Bluck & Levine, 1998; Fitzgerald, 1996). As one example, AM research stems from a solid theoretical and empirical tradition, the conceptual and methodological sophistication of which can serve

Requests for reprints should be sent to Jeffrey Dean Webster, Psychology Department, Langara College, 100 West 49th Avenue, Vancouver, British Columbia, Canada, V5Y 2Z6. Email: jwebster@langara.bc.ca

I greatly appreciated the constructive comments offered by Joan Anderson, Susan Bluck, Odette Gould, Michele Norman, Monisha Pasupathi, David Pillemer, and Qi Wang. I also thank Jeffrey Cully for providing his raw data.

as a model for REM research. In contrast, the psychodynamic/clinical origin of reminiscence work provides a richer phenomenological perspective, the clinical insights of which can help identify an array of memory functions not easily identified in experimental contexts that use, for example, concrete nouns as memory prompts.

This paper helps to redress the mutual lack of awareness between these two important subdomains of memory. Specifically, it addresses the question of the functions of autobiographical memory from the perspective of reminiscence. The goal is to show that a relatively comprehensive, psychometrically sound measure of reminiscence functions not only subsumes most specific functions identified in the AM literature to date but also maps onto, and extends, postulated broad dimensions (e.g., self vs social).

This report begins with a non-comprehensive, yet representative, overview of suggested autobiographical memory functions from the AM literature and then contrasts this with findings from the REM area. Subsequently, one measure from the REM domain is elaborated and the results of a second-order factor analysis using this measure are reported. The results indicate that the multidimensional space is well represented by two orthogonal dimensions and that the specific functions can be arranged in a circular fashion consistent with a circumplex (e.g., Plutchik, 1997) an approach that has proven successful in other areas of psychology.

To my knowledge, a circumplex approach to either REM or AM areas has not been previously reported. The current study, therefore, is a preliminary investigation of the heuristic utility of adopting a circumplex perspective. Consequently, the initial aim is to provide a relatively lenient and informal assessment of the possibility, rather than a stringent and formal test of the goodness of fit to data, of a circumplex approach to REM and AM research. Subsequently, implications for an AM taxonomy are illustrated.

AUTOBIOGRAPHICAL MEMORY

Conceptual classifications

A limited number of broad functions have been suggested in the AM literature and they can be usefully summarised under the general headings of self, social, and directive functions (e.g., Bluck & Alea, 2002; Pillemer, 1998). *Self* functions serve a variety of specific purposes, an important one of which is establishing and maintaining an articulated sense of identity over time (e.g., Bluck & Habermas, 2000; Brewer, 1986; Conway & Pleydell-Pearce, 2000; Eakin, 2000; Fitzgerald, 1999; Fivush, 1991; Freeman, 1993; Habermas & Bluck, 2000; Neisser, 1988; Nelson, 1993, 2000; Pillemer, 1998; Ross & Wilson, 2000). Here we retrieve memories consistent with current conceptualisations of ourselves as a particular type of person with synchronic values and goals (e.g., "I remember being a supportive husband three years ago and that reinforces my sense of being a supportive spouse today"). The main theme of self functions is to consolidate the "I".

Social functions also serve myriad purposes, such as forming and maintaining emotional bonds, establishing intimacy with significant others, and transmitting information to peers and subordinates (e.g., Cohen, 1998; Dixon & Gould, 1996; Fivush & Reese, 2002; Nelson, 2000; Pasupathi, Lucas, & Coombs, 2002). Here we retrieve memories that focus, for instance, on joint activities with family, lovers, and friends. This purpose can be accomplished privately, but is often manifested in a social context where we co-construct narratives of shared experiences both profound and pedestrian. The social function can also be more didactic, oriented towards the explicit aim of using memories to pass on valuable life lessons. The main theme of social functions is to connect with others.

Directive functions similarly have multiple uses, including drawing on past experiences to cope with current concerns, solve a problem, or prepare for future actions (e.g., Cohen, 1998; Hyman & Faries, 1992; Pillemer, 1998; Ross & Wilson, 2000; Schank, 1990). For instance, persons faced with an upcoming job interview may reminisce about a prior interview a few years ago and remember specific details concerning their preparation for that event. Hence, the focus of directive functions is on the application of schematic and event-specific knowledge to guide present and future behaviour.

Despite the provocative nature of these postulated broad dimensions, Hyman and Faires (1992) note, "... there has been little investigation of how people actually use their autobiographical memories on a daily basis" (p. 207). Their study serves as an exception and is briefly reviewed next.

Empirical taxonomies

In an initial study, Hyman and Faries (1992) solicited frequently occurring memories from 32 participants (*M* age = 29.9) and coded them for themes such as specificity, affective valence, frequency of retellings, and uses. Ten functions were derived from qualitative coding: my experience with X; what's up; reminiscing; testifying; self description; other description; entertainment; problem discussion; point illustration/advice; and day dreaming/associative thought. In this initial study, my experience with X (37%), point illustration/advice (18%), and self description (15%) were the most frequently reported functions, respectively, of autobiographical memory. Sampling and methodological limitations prompted a second study in which 19 subjects reported the first memory that came to mind when prompted by eight cue words (four object and four affect). In this second study, day dreaming/associative thought (24%), what's up (22%), and self description (17%) constituted the top three coded uses, respectively.

Hyman and Faries (1992) conclude that the self and social functions were well supported by their data, but the directive functions less so. However, they acknowledge that methodological and sampling limitations may have accounted for this pattern of findings. For instance, these results may only apply for frequently occurring memories produced by young adults. Moreover, the prompt word method may have reduced the probability of producing directive-type memories.

Despite these shortcomings, Hyman and Faries (1992) demonstrated that the broad theoretical dimensions of self, social, and directive functions postulated by theorists have some empirical validation, and further, that these broad dimensions can be differentiated into specific examples of each. It is the latter finding that provides an opportunity to link specific functions of autobiographical memory to particular outcomes which go beyond primarily cognitive processing (i.e., a focus on encoding, storage, and retrieval) such as the relationship between functions and *psychosocial* outcomes. This has been a primary focus in the REM literature to which we now turn.

REMINISCENCE

Conceptual classifications

Traditionally, research conducted within this area has been "gerocentric" (Webster, 1999) although a growing contemporary recognition of the value of a lifespan perspective is emerging. Since Butler (1963) postulated the concept of the life review, "a naturally occurring, universal mental process characterized by the progressive return to consciousness of past experiences, and, particularly, the resurgence of unresolved conflicts" (p. 66), many specific functions of reminiscence have been suggested. Paralleling the AM literature, many of these functions were theoretical conjectures, rather than validated empirical measures. Webster and Haight (1995) provide a review of this area, noting that there was a large degree of overlap among the suggested functions.

Watt and Wong (1991) described six types of reminiscence based on qualitative coding: integrative, instrumental, transmissive, escapist, obsessive, and narrative. Their results indicated that only integrative (e.g., sense of meaning and self-worth, conflict resolution and reconciliation, and self-acceptance) and instrumental (e.g., remembering past plans and goal-directed activities, coping with past difficulties, and drawing from past experiences to solve present problems) were associated with successful ageing.

Other taxonomies (e.g., Beaton, 1980; Kovach, 1995; LoGerfo, 1981; McMahon & Rhudick, 1967; Sherman, 1995) postulated approximately three broad functions (e.g., Coleman, 1974: life review, simple, and informative). For the most part, these other categories are very consistent with Watt and Wong's (1991) (see Webster & Haight, 1995, for an expanded discussion of the similarities and differences among these classifications). Again, similar to the AM area, little attention has been directed towards creating and validating psychometrically sound instruments of reminiscence functions. A brief review of such measures is presented next.

Empirical taxonomies

Approximately five paper-and-pencil measures of reminiscence uses have been investigated (e.g., Havighurst & Glasser, 1972; Merriam, 1993; Romaniuk & Romaniuk, 1981; Webster, 1993, 1997). Santor and Zuroff (1994) created an 11-

item "reminiscing about the past" scale, but it did not measure functions *per se* and so is not discussed further here.

Havighurst and Glasser (1972) introduced a 12-item measure of reminiscence uses which underwent three revisions during the course of their study although reliability and validity findings were not reported. The questionnaire was administered to three different samples of well-educated and successful older adults. Results, in part, indicated an association between high frequency of reminiscence and pleasant affect.

Romaniuk and Romaniuk (1981) created an "intuitively" generated 13-item questionnaire in which older, highly educated, and primarily female participants responded either yes, no, or not sure to each item. Factor analysis revealed self-regard/image enchancement; present problem-solving; and existential/self-understanding factors accounting collectively for 47.5% of the total variance.

Merriam (1993) combined items from both the Havighurst and Glasser scale, and the Romaniuk and Romaniuk scale, and included a few additional items for a total of 17. These items were administered to participants in the Georgia Centenarian Study of whom 70% were White and 30% Black Americans, again primarily female (67%). Factor analysis revealed therapeutic; informative; and enjoyment factors, accounting collectively for 55.8% of the total variance.

Webster (1994); Webster & McCall, 1999; Webster & Young, 1988) argued that reminiscence was best conceptualised as a lifespan phenomenon and could best be represented by a contextual metamodel (Webster, 1999, 2001). He developed a 43-item Reminiscence Functions Scale (RFS) by building on previous measures, writing additional items to reflect theoretical components omitted by earlier approaches, and by having participants generate two reasons why they reminisced and two reasons they thought other persons might reminisce. This procedure generated 115 statements which were subsequently reduced to a 54-item prototype measure. The prototype was then administered to a large (N = 710) sample of adults ranging in age from 17 to 91 from relatively diverse ethnic backgrounds (see Webster, 1993, 1997 for a full description of the development and validation of the RFS).

Results indicated that a 43-item, eight-factor measure accounted for 59.8% of the total variance and that specific factors were correlated in predicted directions (e.g., older adults scored higher

on Teach/Inform; persons high on the personality trait of Neuroticism scored higher on Bitterness Revival).

A comparison of the psychometric properties among these measures is presented in Table 1. The RFS is a valid and reliable 43-item questionnaire in which subjects indicate on a 6-point scale how often they reminisce with a particular function in mind. The items are presented as completions to the stem: "When I reminisce it is:". For example, an item following from the stem might read: "to pass the time during idle or restless hours". The RFS consists of eight factors which are briefly detailed next.

Boredom Reduction measures our propensity to reminisce when our environment is under-stimulating and we lack engagement in goal-directed activities. Death Preparation assesses the way we use our past when thoughts of our own mortality are salient. It may contribute to a sense of closure and calmness. Identity measures how we use our past in an existential manner to discover, clarify, and crystallise important dimensions of our sense of who we are. Problem Solving taps how we employ reminiscence as a constructive coping mechanism whereby the remembrance of past problem-solving strategies may be used again in the present. Conversation measures our natural inclination to invoke the past as a means of connecting or reconnecting with others in an informal way. It serves a social bonding purpose. Intimacy Maintenance measures a process whereby cognitive and emotional memorial representations of important persons in our lives are resurrected in lieu of the remembered person's physical presence. Bitterness Revival assesses the extent to

TABLE 1
Psychometric comparison of reminiscence measures

Variable	H&G	RUS	URS	RFS
N	525	91	291	1109
Age range	27	40	40	79
# of items	12	13	17	43
# of factors	Nr	3	3	8
% of variance	Nr	47.5	55.8	59.8*
Mean Alpha	Nr	.63	Nr	.84
Replicated?	No	No	No	Yes
Ethnic diversity	Low	Low	Low	High

H&G = Havighurst & Glasser's (1972) scale; RUS = Reminiscence Uses Scale (Romaniuk & Romaniuk, 1981); URS = Uses of Reminiscence Scale (Merriam, 1993); RFS = Reminiscence Functions Scale (Webster, 1993, 1997); Nr = not reported; * = Webster (1997).

which memories are used to affectively charge recalled episodes in which the reminiscer perceives themself as having been unjustly treated. It may provide a justification to maintain negative thoughts and emotions towards others. Finally, Teach/Inform measures the ways in which we use reminiscence to relay to others important information about life (e.g., a moral lesson) and/or ourselves. It is an instructional type of narrative.

It is clear from the preceding brief review that both broad dimensions (as illustrated in the AM literature) and specific functions (as identified in the REM literature) provide unique pieces to a common puzzle. One means by which these related findings might converge has recently been suggested by Bluck and Alea (2002). Specifically, they suggested that the AM self function is represented in the REM area by Watt and Wong's (1991) integrative and Webster's (1997) identity and death preparation; the AM directive function by Watt and Wong's instrumental and Webster's problem solving; and the AM social function by Watt and Wong's transmissive and narrative and Webster's teach/inform, conversation, and intimacy maintenance functions. There was no corresponding category in the AM taxonomy for either obsessive or escapist (Watt & Wong) nor bitterness revival or boredom reduction (Webster), confirming that the REM area has unique contributions to the AM perspective. Bluck and Alea (2002) provide a useful starting comparison, but again, it is theoretical conceptualisation, not empirical validation.

In contrast, the present study empirically examines possible underlying dimensions of reminiscence functions by performing a second-order factor analysis of the RFS. The goal is to represent a multidimensional space as economically as possible (i.e., with few dimensions) but with the ability to include as much differentiation as feasible (i.e., identify specific functions). One model for accomplishing this double aim is represented by circumplex perspectives. Before turning to the results therefore a brief introduction to circumplex models is warranted.

Circumplex models

As a method of data reduction and categorisation, circumplex models have been successfully used by researchers in several areas of psychology (e.g., Saucier, Ostendorf, & Peabody, 2001; Tracy &

Rounds, 1997; Wiggens & Trobst, 1997). Several well-known circumplex models exist in the literature on personality (e.g., Wiggens, 1979), emotions (e.g., Plutchik, 1997), and vocations (e.g., Holland, 1985). Plutchik (1997), p. 28; italics in original) offers the following summary:

> The circumplex is a reflection of certain types of relations or interactions. These include the idea of *similarity* and *polarity*. If the elements being considered vary in degree of similarity to one another (as do emotions, personality traits, and diagnoses) and show polarities (e.g., joy versus sorrow, dominance versus submissiveness, antisocial versus avoidant), then a circle as an analogue model may possibly be used to represent these relations.

The number of factors represented by circumplex models can vary, but when there are eight variables, as there are in the present case, the expectation is that a factor analysis will reveal ". . . four bipolar factors accounting for about half of the common variance among items" (Lorr & Strack, 1990, cited in Wiggens & Trobst, 1997).

METHOD

Participants

Participants from four pre-existing data bases (i.e., Culley et al., 2001; Webster, 1997, 2002; Webster & McCall, 1999) were combined, resulting in a total of 985 participants ranging in age from 17 to 96 (M age = 36.63 years). A total of 392 men (39.8%) and 591 women (60.1%), with two persons not reporting their gender, completed the RFS as part of one of the original four studies. Two samples were obtained in Canada and two in the United States. The average level of reported education was 13.82 years (range = 6–24).

RESULTS

Correlational analysis

Pearson Product–Moment correlations and internal consistency reliability (i.e., Cronbach Alphas) among the eight RFS factors are presented in Table 2. As can be seen from Table 2, correlations range from $r = .094, p < .01$ to $r = .736, p < .01$ ($M r = .343$). The pattern of correlations indicates that some factors are highly intercorrelated while

TABLE 2
Intercorrelation matrix and Alphas for all eight RFS factors

	1	2	3	4	5	6	7	8
1. Bitterness Revival	–							
2. Boredom Reduction	.542	–						
3. Conversation	.294	.384	–					
4. Death Preparation	.273	.292	.341	–				
5. Identity	.375	.334	.424	.369	–			
6. Intimacy Maintenance	.223	.217	.243	.400	.208	–		
7. Problem solving	.380	.405	.423	.337	.736	.181	–	
8. Teach/Inform	.110	.094	.469	.537	.321	.399	.298	–
Cronbach Alphas	.85	.86	.82	.87	.86	.83	.85	.79

All Pearson Product–Moment Correlation coefficients are significant at a $p < .01$ level.

others are not. This suggests the possible presence of a smaller number of superordinate factors, which was tested via a second-order factor analysis.

Second order factor analyses

Two-factor solution. The eight RFS factors were submitted to a Principal Components Analysis (PCA) factor procedure using SPSS-PC (v. 10) software. Criteria for factor inclusion were: (1) eigenvalues greater than 1, and (2) factor loadings > .50. Varimax rotation was used to simplify interpretation. Table 3 shows the results of the factor analysis. Two second-order factors emerged: Factor 1 (Self-focused) consists of the RFS factors of bitterness revival, boredom reduction, problem solving, and identity. These are uses that clearly centre on the self, focusing as

they do on internal concerns of, for example, consolidating a sense of "who I am" (e.g., identity) and replaying negative memories of personally painful events (e.g., bitterness revival).

Factor 2 (Social-focused) consists of teach/inform, death preparation, intimacy maintenance, and conversation. These are uses that primarily emphasise externally oriented, social functions. In fact, for three of the four second-order factors (i.e., teach/inform, conversation, and intimacy maintenance) the focus of the recall involves a specific person other than, or in addition to, oneself. Death preparation has a less obvious socially oriented function, although thoughts of our own mortality are often triggered by the deaths of significant others in our lives.

As can be seen from Table 3, the pattern of factor loadings reveals a pair of relatively strong and distinct factors which represent a "self/internal/private" versus a "social/external/public"

TABLE 3
Second-order factor loadings of the RFS for two- and four-factor solutions

First-order factor	Second-order loadings (2 factors)		Second-order loadings (4 factors)			
1. Bitterness Revival	.758		.808			
2. Boredom Reduction	.767		.848			
3. Problem solving	.750			.871		
4. Identity	.706			.885		
5. Teach/Inform		.869				.625
6. Death Preparation		.732			.690	
7. Intimacy Maintenance		.675			.864	
8. Conversation		.501				.860
% Variance	59.10		79.57			

Factor loadings < .50 are suppressed for clarity of presentation. The Teach/Inform factor loaded .593 on the second factor of the four-factor solution, but is suppressed for clarity of presentation.

dimension. This finding is consistent with speculations in the REM literature such as Havighurst and Glasser's (1972) identification of an "interpersonal" versus "intrapersonal" dimension.

Inspection of Table 2 illustrates that the intercorrelations within these second-order factors suggests some further separation may be warranted. For instance, within the "self/internal/private" category, identity is correlated very strongly with problem solving ($r = .736$) but more weakly with boredom reduction ($r = .334$). Similarly, within the "social/external/public" category, conversation is correlated strongly with teach/inform ($r = .469$) but more weakly with intimacy maintenance ($r = .243$). It seems possible that within both the self versus social category there is an additional, separable dimension. A second factor analysis was therefore conducted to test this possibility.

Four-factor solution. The eight RFS factors were submitted to a Principal Components Analysis (PCA) factor procedure using SPSS-PC (v. 10) software. Criteria for factor inclusion were the same as in the first analysis except that the numbere of factors was set a priori at four. Results can be seen in Table 3.

Four clearly distinct factors emerged, each comprising two items: (1) bitterness revival and boredom reduction; (2) problem solving and identity; (3) death preparation and intimacy maintenance; and (4) conversation and teach/inform. In conjunction with the "self versus social" dimension demonstrated earlier, a second dimension reflecting a loss-oriented, reactive pole versus a more growth-oriented, proactive pole seems evident. One method of representing these results spatially is accomplished with multidimensional scaling (MDS) techniques.

Multidimensional scaling analysis

In general, MDS seeks to graphically represent the distance between variables in an input matrix (e.g., the correlation matrix illustrated in Table 2) in one or more dimensions. The number of dimensions is determined by both statistical tests (i.e., stress and proportion of variance explained) and the interpretability of the dimensions. In the present case, because of differences among the RFS factors in terms of the number of items constituting each, RFS scores were first standardised using a Z transformation. A squared Euclidian distance matrix was used to test the goodness of fit. Results indicated that two dimensions were interpretable and provided adequate fit to the data. Specifically, stress (measured via Kruskal's stress formula; ranges from 0 to 1 with values closer to zero indicating better fit) = .17 and proportion of variance explained (as measured by the squared correlation, RSQ) = .83. These results are illustrated in Figure 1.

As can be seen in Figure 1, the MDS confirms and extends the factor-analytic results by replicating the four distinct factors and illustrating their spatial proximity to one another. In each case, the hypothesised RFS factors fell clearly into their own distinct space: Teach/Inform and Conversation define the social-proactive/growth quadrant; Identity and Problem Solving define the self-proactive/growth quadrant; Boredom Reduction and Bitterness Revival define the self-reactive/loss quadrant; and Death Preparation and Intimacy Maintenance define the social-reactive/loss quadrant.

Thus, the results of the MDS and inspection of Tables 2 and 3 illustrate all minimum criteria of a circumplex model identified by Plutchik—namely, similarity and polarity were met. By creating two orthogonal dimensions (i.e., self versus social and reactive/loss versus proactive/growth) and arranging individual RFS factors in a circular arrangement such that more similar factors are located closer together, we approach a circumplex. Figure 2 illustrates this arrangement.

As can be seen in Figure 2, adjacent factors are correlated more strongly than opposite factors, a finding required by circumplex models. For instance, bitterness revival is correlated .542 with the adjacent boredom reduction, while boredom reduction is correlated .094 with teach/inform which is located directly opposite on the circumplex. The mean adjacent correlation is .467 and the mean opposite correlation is .233.

DISCUSSION

This study has empirically tested theoretical claims from both the AM and REM literature concerning putative functions of personal memory. The results indicate that the broadly conceived self, social, and directive functions postulated in the AM literature can be modified so as to be represented as two orthogonal dimensions: self versus social and reactive/loss oriented versus proactive/growth oriented. These

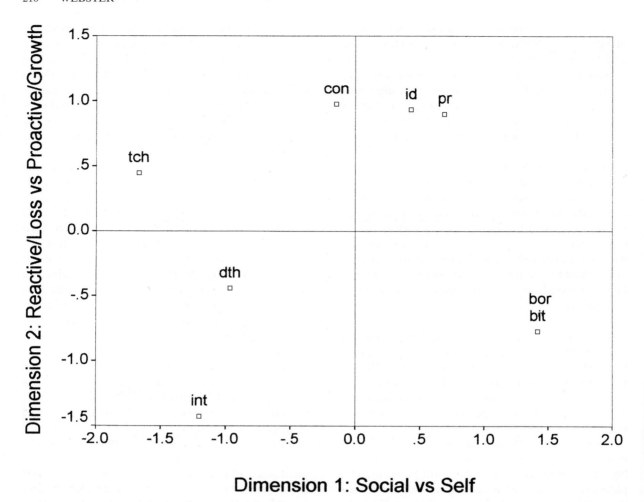

Figure 1. A two-dimensional representation of the RFS. tch = Teach/Inform; con = Conversation; id = Identity; pr = Problem Solving; dth = Death Preparation; int = Intimacy Maintenance; bor = Boredom; bit = Bitterness Revival.

two dimensions can be arranged so as to produce four quadrants (see Figure 2).

The self-reactive/loss quadrant (1) concerns memories of painful, lost opportunities (i.e., bitterness revival) and/or those triggered in reaction to understimulating environments (i.e., boredom reduction). These types of functions are clearly evident in the REM literature but not in the AM perspective (see Bluck & Alea, 2002). This finding represents a strength of the REM perspective and clearly adds a new category to the AM perspective.

In contrast, the self-proactive/growth quadrant (2) is well represented in the AM literature by both the self and directive functions. Memories from this quadrant concern crystallising a sense of self (i.e., identity) and remembering prior problem-solving strategies and successes in order to cope with current and future events (i.e., problem solving). The focus seems to be on proactively

using memories to enhance current and future functioning in terms of everyday coping and clarification, and development of a sense of who we are, and our place in the world.

Quadrant (3), the Social-proactive/growth category is also represented well in the AM literature as social functions. Memories generated from this area function to connect with other persons, establish or maintain intimate links with significant others, or pass along valuable information to partners, friends, and family (i.e., teach/inform and conversation).

Quadrant (4) the Social-reactive/loss category is less well established in the AM area, although Bluck and Alea (2002) do suggest that death preparation falls within the AM self category while intimacy maintenance is best represented by the social category. Here the functions of memory concern maintaining social connections to those

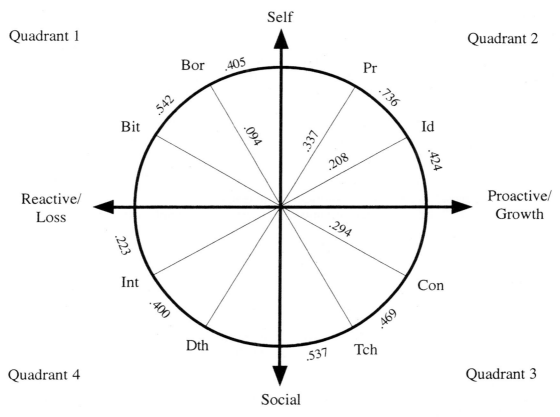

Figure 2. Dimensions, quadrants, and intercorrelations of the reminiscence circumplex.

we have lost, for instance through death or physical and/or emotional separation (i.e., intimacy maintenance) or for preparing for the ultimate loss, death (i.e., death preparation). Consequently, the focus of these memories is on other persons. This interpretation is somewhat problematic for the death preparation function and warrants further explication.

Because it involves preparing for one's own death, logically, death preparation would seem to reflect more of a self function as suggested by Bluck and Alea (2002). Indeed, inspection of items that constitute the death preparation factor (e.g., "it helps me cope with thoughts of my own mortality") suggests this could be conceptualised as a type of "existential" problem solving. In this case, death preparation resembles at some level problem solving that is an element of quadrant 2 (i.e., self-proactive/growth) with which it is correlated ($r = .337$).

Nevertheless, death has been conceived of as the ultimate separation from attachment figures (Mikulincer, Florian, & Tolmacz, 1990). Consequently, thoughts of our own death perhaps inevitably stir fears and anxieties about the rup-

turing of longtime personal bonds, and focus our memories on the family, friends, and lovers that we will miss most. In reviewing one's life in preparation for death, therefore, memories of personal connections, social relations, and intimate partnerships focus our recall on memories of others, which contributes to a social focus.

One means to partially investigate this issue is to obtain qualitative reports of persons scoring high on the death preparation and identity factors of the RFS and see whether there is in actuality a difference in memorial focus (i.e., death preparation memories revolve around significant others whereas identity memories focus on personal goals and achievement). Clearly, subsequent research is needed to clarify this point.

Advantages of a circumplex model

What advantages does conceptualising personal, episodic memories from a circumplex perspective provide? There are at least three. First, the circumplex model presented here clearly helps integrate and organise a body of extant knowledge from two related but empirically distinct research areas. The broad AM functions of self, social, and directive are retained and augmented from the REM findings but reorganised to reflect a more comprehensive and finely articulated system.

Second, the circumplex model allows greater flexibility in levels of analysis. At the broadest level, AM/REM functions can be examined at the level of a single dimension, for instance, self versus social (collapsing across the reactive/loss versus proactive/growth dimension). Questions addressed at this level might include whether there is an "expertise" effect (i.e., shorter response latencies) to "self" memory prompts relative to "social" memory prompts.

At a more specific level, one can address questions of individual differences in variables such as age, gender, personality, and culture *vis-à-vis* the four quadrants. Previous research with the RFS, for example, would suggest that older adults would score higher on the social-reactive/loss quadrant, but lower on the self-reactive/loss quadrant, relative to younger adults; African Americans would score higher on the social-proactive/growth quadrant than Caucasian Americans (Norman, Harris, & Webster, 2001); and that neurotic individuals would score higher than non-neurotic individuals on the self-reactive/loss quadrant (e.g., Cappeliez & O'Rourke, 2002).

Third, at the most specific level, the association between particular functions and specific mental health outcomes (e.g., depression, life satisfaction, happiness) could be assessed. Watt and Wong's (1991) earlier reported result of integrative (identity) and instrumental (problem-solving) reminiscence being the only correlates of life satisfaction is one example. These are only suggestions and nothing precludes assessing mental health from the broadest dimension (e.g., self versus social); rather researchers have the option to choose what they consider to be the most appropriate level.

In addition, the circumplex model presented here illustrates neglected, if not entirely missing, aspects of AM. Specifically, functions from quadrant 1 have not been the focus of AM research. This may be in part a methodological artifact or a theoretical blind spot. To illustrate, with respect to the former, in the AM tradition, participants' retrieval is cued by specific, experimenter-selected prompts (e.g., concrete nouns) which may limit the parameters of memory search. Models serve not only to organise data but also to point to omissions and areas for future research.

For instance, although both the intimacy maintenance and conversation functions have another person as a target, it is generally implicit/internal in the former while explicit/external in the latter. As Alea and Bluck (2003 this issue) illustrate, listener and relationship characteristics influence memorial processes (e.g., Pasupathi, 2002). What, then, are the consequences (e.g., vividness, affective quality, frequency of rehearsal) of simply imagining the other person (as in intimacy maintenance) rather than having the other person directly communicating with you (as in teach/inform)?

Another example, extending beyond memory, would be to see how the reminiscence circumplex maps onto other circumplex models in psychology, thus providing a bridge for interdisciplinary work. Plutchik's (1997) emotions circumplex provides one interesting point of departure where, for instance, anger and cheerfulness are seen as opposites. One could hypothesise that anger is more likely to be higher in the self-reactive/loss quadrant, and cheerfulness higher in the diametrically opposed social-proactive/growth quadrant, of the reminiscence circumplex. Such memory–emotion linkages could serve as a useful framework to investigate gender and developmental variables. For example, Fivush and Reese (2002) recently reported on a series of studies which showed that during parent–child reminiscing, emotions are focused on to a greater extent with girls than boys, and this is particularly true when the emotion under discussion is sadness.

Limitations

Limitations of the current project need to be noted. Foremost, the analysis conducted here is preliminary and meets minimal qualifications for a circumplex. More stringent criteria would involve conditions such as: opposite poles of a dimension should be close to zero, if not negatively correlated; the placement of functions around the perimeter of the circumplex should be equidistant. However, none of these is required (e.g., Putchik, 1997) and so this preliminary investigation is consistent with other results using a circumplex perspective.

Second, the placement of the functions around the circumplex was done manually, based on visual inspection of Table 2. This is obviously a preliminary and informal approach. Future research needs to employ statistical techniques which formally test for circular structure within correlation matrices, although the results of the MDS analysis provide preliminary support.

Finally, the main purpose of the present report needs to be reiterated—namely, to illustrate the feasibility of a circumplex approach in general to investigate AM and REM functions, and not to provide a stringent test of any particular model. At this very preliminary stage of model building we want to avoid reification. Labels (e.g., proactive/growth versus reactive/loss) are arbitrary and represent only initial attempts to capture the complexity of one particular data set. Moreover, in an attempt to avoid confusion, labels (e.g., social) from the AM literature were appropriated for use in the reminiscence circumplex reported here. It is certainly possible that the meaning of such terms is not isomorphic across the two literatures, and care is therefore needed when viewing the two nomenclatures as necessarily identical.

CONCLUSION

Two parallel and conceptually related domains of memory inquiry share a focus on the utility of salient, episodic recall in adaptively managing everyday life. The REM literature has traditionally emphasised the psychodynamic aspects of memory and its relation to mental health; the AM literature has historically concentrated on response latencies, organisational structures, temporal distributions, and retrieval mechanisms of autobiographical recall. As demonstrated by prior reports (e.g., Rybash & Hrubi, 1997) and this special issue of *Memory*, there is a growing realisation that cross-fertilisation from these memory cousins" can prove worthwhile.

The reminiscence circumplex, as presented in this report, represents one bridging technique with the power to integrate data not only within REM and AM traditions, but more importantly, between them. This type of synthesis broadens and strengthens each perspective. Moreover, by identifying important omissions in prior scholarship, it provides direction for future research agendas.

Subsequent work will result in refinements to, or rejection of, the reminiscence circumplex. Regardless of this, it provides an initial starting point for further collaborative work. A well articulated model of functions of REM/AM is important in its own right; facilitating the development of ecologically grounded knowledge concerning structure and process seems to be a likely and welcome byproduct of taking a functional approach.

What are the uses of memory? We are well on the way to finding out.

REFERENCES

Alea, N., & Bluck, S. (2003). Why are you telling me that? A conceptual model of the social function of autobiographical memory. *Memory*, *11*, 165–178.

Beaton, S.R. (1980). Reminiscence in old age. *Nursing Forum*, *19*, 271–283.

Bluck, S., & Alea, N. (2002). Exploring the functions of autobiographical memory: Why do I remember the autumn? In J.D. Webster & B.K. Haight (Eds.), *Critical advances in reminiscence work: From theory to application*. New York: Springer Publishing Company.

Bluck, S., & Habermas, T. (2000). The life story schema. *Motivation and Emotion*, *24*(2), 121–147.

Bluck, S., & Levine, L.J. (1998). Reminiscence as autobiographical memory: A catalyst for reminiscence theory development. *Ageing and Society*, *18*, 185–208.

Brewer, W. (1986). What is autobiographical memory? In D.C. Rubin (Ed.), *Autobiographical memory*. New York: Cambridge University Press.

Bruce, D. (1985). The how and why of ecological memory. *Journal of Experimental Psychology: General*, *114*, 78–90.

Bruce, D. (1991). Mechanistic and functional explanations of memory. *American Psychologist*, *46*(1), 46–48.

Butler, R.N. (1963). The life review: An interpretation of reminiscence in the aged. *Psychiatry*, *26*, 65–76.

Cappeliez, P., & O'Rourke, N. (2002). Personality traits and existential concerns as predictors of the functions of reminiscence in older adults. *Journal of Gerontology: Psychological Sciences*, *57*, P116–P123.

Cohen, G. (1998). The effects of aging on autobiographical memory. In C.P. Thompson, D.J. Herrmann, D. Bruce, D.J. Read, D.G. Payne, & M.P. Toglia (Eds.), *Autobiographical memory: Theoretical and applied perspectives* (pp. 105–123). Mahwah, NJ: Lawrence Erlbaum Associates Inc.

Coleman, P.G. (1974). Measuring reminiscence characteristics from conversation as adaptive features of old age. *International Journal of Aging and Human Development*, *5*, 281–294.

Conway, M.A. (1990). *Autobiographical memory: An introduction*. Buckingham, UK: Open University Press.

Conway, M.A., & Pleydell-Pearce, C.W. (2000). The construction of autobiographical memories in the self-memory system. *Psychological Review*, *107*, 261–288.

Culley, J.A., LaVoie, D., & Gfeller, J. (2001). Reminiscence, personality, and psychological functioning in older adults. *The Gerontologist*, *41*, 89–95.

Dixon, R.A., & Gould, O.N. (1996). Adults telling and retelling stories collaboratively. In P.B. Baltes & U.M. Staudinger (Eds.), *Interactive minds: Life-span perspectives on the social foundation of cognition* (pp. 221–241). Melbourne, Australia: Cambridge University Press.

Eakin, P.J. (2000). Autobiography, identity, and the fictions of memory. In D.L. Schacter & E. Scarry (Eds.), *Memory, brain, and belief* (pp. 290–306). Cambridge, MA: Harvard University Press.

Fitzgerald, J.M. (1996). Intersecting meanings of reminiscence in adult development and aging. In D.C. Rubin (Ed.), *Remembering our past: Studies in autobiographical memory* (pp. 360–383). New York: Cambridge University Press.

Fitzgerald, J.M. (1999). Autobiographical memory and social cognition: Development of the remembered self in adulthood. In T.M. Hess & F. Blanchard-Fields (Eds.), *Social cognition and aging*. San Diego: Academic Press.

Fivush, R. (1991). The social construction of personal narrative. *Merrill-Palmer Quarterly, 37,* 59–82.

Fivush, R., & Reese, E. (2002). Reminiscing and relating: The development of parent–child talk about the past. In J.D. Webster & B.K. Haight (Eds.), *Critical advances in reminiscence work: From theory to application.* New York: Springer Publishing Company.

Freeman, M. (1993). *Rewriting the self: History, memory, narrative.* London: Routledge.

Habermas, T., & Bluck, S. (2000). Getting a life: The emergence of the life story in adolescence. *Psychological Bulletin, 126,* 748–769.

Havighurst, R., & Glasser, R. (1972). An exploratory study of reminiscence. *Journal of Gerontology, 27,* 245–253.

Holland, J.L. (1985). *Making vocational choices: A theory of vocational personalities and work environments* (2nd ed.). Englewood Cliffs, NJ: Prentice-Hall.

Hyman, I.E., & Faries, J.M. (1992). The functions of autobiographical memory. In M.A. Conway, D.C. Rubin, H. Spinnler, & W.A. Wagenaar (Eds.), *Theoretical perspectives on autobiographical memory* (pp. 207–221). Dordrecht, The Netherlands: Kluwer Academic Publishers.

Kovach, C.R. (1995). A qualitative look at reminiscing: Using the autobiographical memory coding tool. In B.K. Haight & J.D. Webster (Eds.), *The art and science of reminiscing: Theory, research, methods, and applications* (pp. 103–122). Washington, DC: Taylor & Francis.

LoGerfo, M. (1981). Three ways of reminiscence in theory and practice. *International Journal of Aging and Human Development, 12,* 39–47.

McMahon, A., & Rhudick, P. (1967). Reminiscing in the aged: An adaptational response. In S. Levin & R. Kahana (Eds.), *Psychodynamic studies on aging: Creativity, reminiscing, and dying.* New York: International University Press.

Merriam, S.B. (1993). The uses of reminiscence in older adulthood. *Educational Gerontology, 19,* 441–450.

Michaels, A. (1996). *Fugitive pieces.* Toronto, Ontario: McClelland & Stewart Inc.

Mikulincer, M., Florian, V., & Tolmacz, R. (1990). Attachment styles and fear of personal death: A case study of affect regulation. *Journal of Personality and Social Psychology, 58,* 273–280.

Neisser, U. (1988). Five kinds of self-knowledge. *Philosophical Psychology, 1,* 35–59.

Nelson, K. (1993). The psychological and social origins of autobiographical memory. *Psychological Science, 4,* 7–14.

Nelson, K. (2000). Memory and belief in development. In D.L. Schacter & E. Scarry (Eds.), *Memory, brain, and belief.* Cambridge, MA: Harvard University Press.

Norman, M.L., Harris, J.L., & Webster, J.D. (2001). *Psychosocial correlates of reminiscence functions in Caucasian and African American adults.* Poster presented at the 17th Congress of the International Association of Gerontology, Vancouver, Canada, 1–6 July.

Pasupathi, M. (2002). The social construction of the personal past and its implications for adult development. *Psychological Bulletin, 127,* 651–672.

Pasupathi, M., Lucas, S., & Coombs, A. (2002). Conversational functions of autobiographical memory: Long-married couples talk about conflicts and pleasant topics. *Discourse Processes, 34,* 163–190.

Pillemer, D.B. (1998). *Momentous events, vivid memories: How unforgettable moments help us understand the meaning of our lives.* Cambridge, MA: Harvard University Press.

Plutchik, R. (1997). The circumplex as a general model of the structure of emotions and personality. In R. Plutchik & H.R. Conte (Eds.), *Circumplex models of personality and emotions.* Washington, DC: American Psychological Association.

Romaniuk, M., & Romaniuk, J.G. (1981). Looking back: An analysis of reminiscence functions and triggers. *Experimental Aging Research, 7,* 477–489.

Ross, M., & Wilson, A.E. (2000). Constructing and appraising past selves. In D.L. Schacter & E. Scarry (Eds.), *Memory, brain, and belief.* Cambridge, MA: Harvard University Press.

Rybash, J.M., & Hrubi, K.L. (1997). Psychometric and psychodynamic correlates of first memories in younger and older adults. *The Gerontologist, 37,* 581–587.

Santor, D.A., & Zuroff, D.C. (1994). Depressive symptoms: Effects of negative affectivity and failing to accept the past. *Journal of Personality Assessment, 63*(2), 294–312.

Saucier, G., Ostendorf, F., & Peabody, D. (2001). The non-evaluative circumplex of personality adjectives. *Journal of Personality, 69,* 537–582.

Schank, R.C. (1990). *Tell me a story: A new look at real and artificial memory.* New York: Charles Scribner & Sons.

Sherman, E. (1995). Differential effects of oral and written reminiscence in the elderly. In B.K. Haight & J.D. Webster (Eds.), *The art and science of reminiscing: Theory, research, methods, and applications.* Washington, DC: Taylor & Francis.

Tracey, T.J.G. & Rounds, J.B. (1997). Circular structure of vocational interests. In R. Plutchik & H.R. Conte (Eds.), *Circumplex models of personality and emotions.* Washington, DC: American Psychological Association.

Watt, L., & Wong, P.T.P. (1991). A taxonomy of reminiscence and therapeutic implications. *Journal of Mental Health Counseling, 12,* 270–278.

Webster, J.D. (1993). Construction and validation of the Reminiscence Functions Scale. *Journal of Gerontology: Psychological Sciences, 48,* 256–262.

Webster, J.D. (1994). Predictors of reminiscence: A lifespan perspective. *Canadian Journal on Aging, 13,* 66–78.

Webster, J.D. (1997). The Reminiscence Functions Scale: A replication. *International Journal of Aging and Human Development, 44,* 137–148.

Webster, J.D. (1999). World views and narrative gerontology: Situating reminiscence behavior within a lifespan perspective. *Journal of Aging Studies, 13,* 29–42.

Webster, J. D. (2001). The future of the past: Continuing challenges for reminiscence research. In G. Kenyon, P. Clark, & B. de Vries (Eds.), *Narrative gerontology: Theory, research, and practice.* New York: Springer Publishing Company.

Webster, J.D. (2002). Reminiscence functions in adulthood: Age, race, and family dynamics correlates. In J.D. Webster & B.K. Haight (Eds.), *Critical advances in reminiscence work: From theory to application.* New York: Springer Publishing Company.

Webster, J.D., & Cappeliez, P. (1993). Reminiscence and autobiographical memory: Complementary contexts for cognitive aging research. *Developmental Review, 13,* 54–91.

Webster, J.D., & Haight, B.K. (1995). Memory lane milestones: Progress in reminiscence definition and classification. In B.K. Haight & J.D. Webster (Eds.), *The art and science of reminiscing: Theory, research, methods, and applications.* Washington, DC: Taylor & Francis.

Webster, J.D., & McCall, M. (1999). Reminiscence functions across adulthood: A replication and extension. *Journal of Adult Development, 6,* 73–85.

Webster, J.D., & Young, R.A. (1988). Process variables of the life review: Counseling implications. *International Journal of Aging and Human Development, 26,* 315–323.

Wiggens, J.S. (1979). A psychological taxonomy of trait-descriptive terms: The interpersona domain. *Journal of Personality and Social Psychology, 37,* 395–412.

Wiggens, J.S., & Trobst, K.K. (1997). When is a circumplex an "interpersonal circumplex"? The case of supportive actions. In R. Plutchik & H.R. Conte (Eds.), *Circumplex models of personality and emotions.* Washington, DC: American Psychological Association.

MEMORY, 2003, *11* (2), 217–224

Commentary
Cognitive–affective mechanisms and processes in autobiographical memory

Martin A. Conway

University of Durham, UK

This commentary highlights some of the interesting points to emerge from the preceding papers about the self, social, and directive functions of autobiographical memory. Additionally some cognitive functions are also considered and especially the way in which autobiographical memory supports, constrains, and maintains the goals of the self. Directions for future research into the self, social, directive, and cognitive–affective functions and processes of autobiographical memory are reviewed. Emphasis is placed on future research into the function of autobiographical memory in representations of attachment.

This special issue of *Memory* on the functions of autobiographical memory provides the most comprehensive testament yet that autobiographical memory is central to a wide range of fundamentally important forms of cognition and behaviour. Bluck in her overview groups specific functions into the broader categories of self, social, and directive, and the papers that follow describe specific functions within these domains. Thus, Nelson focuses on the contribution of autobiographical memory to supporting and defining individuality and argues persuasively for the rise of individuality in Western societies and what she terms the "personalisation of culture". Current thinking from several traditions converges on the view that in these societies the structures and belief systems that supported and constrained the self have been eroded, devalued, or lost altogether, perhaps in response to a rise in the 'cult' of the individual, and because of this the self is now more reliant on or more defined by a detailed personal history. Indeed it may even be the case that this (over)emphasis on the individual predisposes people to stress-related mental dis-

orders. Autobiographical memory, however, can also serve to counter such pressures—indeed Robinson noted over a decade ago (1992) that autobiographical memory might function as a "resource" in times of stress and threat. As Wilson and Ross show, favourable comparisons of the current self with past selves, reflected in specific autobiographical memories, can serve to create a positive appraisal of the current self—appraisals that are perhaps overvaluations (in previous work a similar bias in memory to recall positive materials was dubbed the "Pollyanna principle", Matlin & Stang, 1978). In a related vein autobiographical memories might be used to regulate emotions, and Pasupathi reports interesting new data showing how shared recall can modulate negative moods. However, this type of emotion regulation is complex and influenced by individual differences and contextual factors.

Alea and Bluck are explicitly concerned with the social function of autobiographical memory and review the evidence that sharing autobiographical memories can function to develop or maintain intimacy, teach and inform, and establish

Requests for reprints should be sent to Martin A. Conway, University of Durham, Department of Psychology, Science Laboratories, South Road, Durham DH1 3LE, UK. Email: M.A.Conway@durham.ac.uk

This work was supported by an Economic and Social Research council Grant (R000239395) and is part of a larger project directed by the author into the nature of autobiographical memory. The author thanks Susan Bluck for insightful comments on an earlier version of this paper.

DOI:10.1080/09658210344000017

empathy. Presumably as sharing specific auto-biographical memories is a form of self-disclosure such "memory talk" might also function, possibly strategically, to inculcate in a listener a particular impression of the self doing the remembering. Thus, another social function of the recall and sharing of memories might be in impression management. Yet another social function of sharing memories is described by Fivush and her co-workers and demonstrated by new findings. Of interest to this group was the way in which children discuss memories of emotional events with adults, and especially mother. Their data indicate that recalling and reworking emotional memories may have beneficial effects on the development of the self. Related to this, in a welcome attempt to bring together reminiscence and autobiographical memory research, Webster reports an analysis which proposes that the functions of reminiscence can be located in a two-dimensional circumplex model. The two dimensions are *Individuality* with the poles Self versus Social and what I would call *Goals*, with the poles reactive/loss versus pro-active/growth. Reminiscence then serves to develop aspects of the individual or group, or is focused on lack of attainment of goals or attainment and goal development. It might be noted here that these dimensions relate quite closely to the Eriksonian psychosocial stages of identity formation and development of intimacy in the case of individuality, and generativity in the case of goals. The link back to Alea and Bluck's emphasis on the use of autobiographical memories to promote intimacy is also evident.

Finally (although not in terms of order) Pillemer develops his important work on the directive function of autobiographical memories. Pillemer is especially interested in how the content of what he terms "personal event memories" can be used to constrain and guide behaviour. Personal event memories are memories of specific moments in time and I usually refer to them simply as "specific autobiographical memories". The valuable point of Pillemer's work is to show how these memories can act as powerful guides to future behaviour. To give a trivial example: having once forgotten to take a pound coin to my local supermarket, and so being unable to collect a trolley, I have never done so since and have never failed to recall the occasion on a subsequent shopping trip. For more profound examples of the directive function of autobiographical memory see Pillemer's paper which explores the directive functions of traumatic memories. Although the directive function may often appear helpful it is perhaps worth noting that it may also have a negative side. Can we escape the diktats of memory? To take an extreme example, patients suffering from post-traumatic stress disorder are often disabled by the intense anxiety induced by the recall of specific autobiographical memories of trauma. Moreover, specific autobiographical memories might lead a person to repeat the past, to become locked into a characteristic way of responding, and so to behave inflexibly and, possibly, in dysfunctional and disruptive ways (see MacAdams, Reynolds, Lewis, Patten, & Bowman, 2001).

The self, social, and directive functions of autobiographical memory are covered well in this volume. However, as Pillemer points out, it is not always a simple matter to isolate these functions and often an act of recall will serve functions in all three categories. Their utility may then lie more in organising our thinking about the functions of autobiographical memory than in applications to specific episodes of recall. Furthermore, it is clear that self, social, and directive functions, and other functions too, are mediated by cognitive–affective mechanisms and processes that underpin the varied uses of autobiographical memory. Cognitive–affective mechanisms allow or facilitate certain types of processing. For example, goal evaluation and generation, creation of models of the self, connectedness to reality, a sense of continuity and integrity or dissolution, and sustaining particular patterns of attachment. In the sections that follow these aspects of autobiographical memory will be briefly considered in more detail and I start by describing some of the mechanisms and processes we have identified as critical to autobiographical remembering. And it might be noted that this view leads to a rather different evolutionary account of the development of autobiographical memory from that subscribed to in several of the earlier papers.

EPISODIC MEMORIES: IMAGES OF THE PAST

In a revision of Tulving's (1972) original characterisation of episodic memories, we have proposed that episodic memories represent sensory–perceptual–affective information and knowledge of recent conceptual processing (Conway, 2001; Conway, Pleydell-Pearce, Whitecross, & Sharpe, 2002). This information is abstracted from comparatively short time slices of experience. We postulate that when a working self goal structure changes, e.g., from writing to making a cup of tea, from thinking about episodic memory to thinking about a visit to a school, and from feeling elated to feeling something else, then at that point an episodic memory, or possibly set of episodic memories, is formed. An episodic memory contains records of representations created by the episodic buffer—a subsystem of working memory (see Baddeley, 2000). The episodic buffer configures the output of other working memory systems into a relational representation. Perhaps one way to conceive of this is that representations in the episodic buffer, other patterns of activation over knowledge structures in long-term memory, and activation in the goal hierarchy of the working self (Conway & Pleydell-Pearce, 2000), as well as affective states, constitute a mental model (Johnson-Laird, 1983) of current experience, conscious as well as nonconscious. The same mental model may remain in a stable state and modulate processing and behaviour until the goal structure of the task requires generation of a new or radically altered mental model. Note that we do not postulate that succeeding mental models of current experience necessarily entail the dysfacilitation of the preceding mental model. This may occur when two mental models are very similar, e.g., switching from writing one paper to writing another, or from one conversation to another, but it seems more likely to us that multiple mental models may be accessible at any one time and switching between them appropriately and fluently is one of the major tasks of executive processes. The episodic memories that result from switches between mental models of current experiences are highly detailed, experience-near, records of recent processing sequences. They are, in our view, sensory–perceptual–affective–conceptual short-time slice records of experience.

One implication of this view is, of course, the generation of numerous episodic memories, perhaps in the order of hundreds every day. This would require an unfeasibly large storage medium, not to mention insoluble access problems. In any case, what use could such a literal representation of experience ever be? One possibility is that it might be very useful, from a survival point of view, to have quite detailed records of *recent* progress with goals. This would require records that represented with some degree of accuracy (if they are to be of survival value) the intersection of a mental model with reality. Which

is exactly how we conceive of episodic memories. In this conception, however, episodic memories are transient representations that are rapidly lost. Retention of an experience-near sensory–perceptual–affective–conceptual episodic memory of successes in making and drinking a cup of tea earlier is (mercifully) retained for only a short while. Episodic memories may be being formed and lost all within the same day with more widespread loss over a sleep period. Episodic memories are only retained for longer periods if they become attached to durable pre-existing long-term knowledge or if they lead to the formation of such knowledge (see Conway, Gardiner, Perfect, Anderson, & Cohen, 1997). Episodic memories are then a sort of "sample" of past experience or a sample of a past self that created the episodic record. Finally we also suggest that the sample is sparse and that relative to the numbers formed every day very few episodic memories are in fact retained for longer than 24 hours.

This view of "experience-near" episodic memories leads to a rather different set of proposals about the evolution of episodic memory. In contrast to Tulving (1983), who viewed episodic memories as a late and possibly uniquely human development, we view them as an early development, the product of a phylogenetically older memory system, and quite possibly common to many animals. Neuroimaging studies of autobiographical memory suggest that the episodic component (typically in the form of visual images) in the construction of an autobiographical memory may be mediated by posterior networks that represent their sensory–perceptual–affective–conceptual content (see Conway et al., 2002). A possibility here is, then, that episodic memory is mediated by an older temporo-occipital memory system, which is highly sensitive to cues and in which retrieval is along a temporal line or by memory content (encoding-specificity, Tulving & Thompson, 1973). Such a memory system would serve well an animal whose behaviour was largely stimulus-driven and provide a detailed record of recent experience that was highly accessible. Of course there would be little in the way of more abstract autobiographical knowledge, schematic knowledge, or other semantic knowledge, so very few episodic memories would ever be retained. But this in itself is probably of little significance to the survival of such an animal. No doubt there would be some schematic representations of habitual actions, knowledge of at least some others, goal structures, and so some limited possibility to retain at least a few episodic memories. But as the extensive long-term knowledge structures needed to retain potentially representative samples of episodic memories are not present, a full autobiographical memory cannot be developed.

AUTOBIOGRAPHICAL KNOWLEDGE: UNIQUELY HUMAN?

By our view, a uniquely human and phylogenetically late developing fronto-temporal memory system represents conceptually organised autobiographical knowledge that provides a context or setting for episodic memories. Indeed, we have suggested that this system controls the output of the episodic system by directly inhibiting/activating it and by selecting and modifying the cues used to access it (Conway & Pleydell-Pearce, 2000). By cue generation and elaboration the autobiographical knowledge system can control the formation of patterns of activation in the episodic system during memory construction. The autobiographical knowledge system also provides stable and enduring knowledge structures to which episodic memories may become linked and, consequently, retained for periods longer than they would otherwise. One way in which we have conceptualised autobiographical knowledge is in terms of event specificity, and two broad types of autobiographical knowledge we (and others) have identified along this dimension are *general events* and *lifetime periods* (cf. Conway & Pleydell-Pearce, 2000). We have also suggested, on the basis of studies of impairment to autobiographical memory following brain injury, that general event knowledge structures might be represented in temporal lobe networks, whereas lifetime periods might be localised to frontal networks (possibly dorsolateral prefrontal cortex).

General events, as the term implies, are more strongly event-specific than lifetime periods but not as event-specific as sensory–perceptual episodic memories that are directly derived from actual experience (Conway, 2001). General events refer to a variety of autobiographical knowledge structures such as single events, e.g., the day we went to Blackpool (a seaside town in the northwest of England), repeated events, e.g., work meetings, and extended events, e.g., holiday in Spain. General events may themselves be organised in several different ways. For example, there may be mini-histories structured around detailed

and sometimes vivid memories of goal attainment in developing skills, knowledge, and personal relationships (see Robinson, 1992). Some general events may be of experiences of particular directive significance for the self (Pillemer, 1998; Singer & Salovey, 1993) and act as reference points for other associated general events. Yet other general events may be grouped because of their emotional similarity (see McAdams et al., 2001). However, the research currently available indicates that organisation of autobiographical knowledge at the level of general events is extensive and it appears virtually always to refer to progress in the attainment of highly self-relevant goals. General events, then, contain knowledge about locations, others, activities, feelings, and goals. This autobiographical knowledge may be represented in several different ways and consist of (visual) images, feelings, verbal statements, associated together in a mental model. The evidence, however, indicates that autobiographical knowledge in general events predominantly takes the form of generic visual images, i.e., images derived from repeated experiences, (Brewer, 1986; Conway, 1996; Rubin & Greenberg, 1998). General event autobiographical knowledge can be used to access associated episodic memories and when it is used in this way a specific and detailed autobiographical memory can be formed. Thus, a specific autobiographical memory will usually, if not always, contain some general event knowledge and this will often be in the form of generic images.

General event autobiographical knowledge can also be used to access related lifetime periods that contain associated knowledge. Lifetime periods, like general events, contain representations of locations, others, activities, feelings, and goals common to the period they represent. They effectively encapsulate a period in memory and is so doing provide ways in which access can be limited, channelled, or managed in other ways by the working self. There is also evidence that lifetime periods contain evaluative knowledge, negative and positive, of progress in goal attainment (Beike & Landoll, 2000), and it seems likely that lifetime periods play an important role in what Bluck and Habermas (2000) call the *life story*. A life story is some more or less coherent theme or set of themes that characterise, identify, and give meaning to a whole life. A life story consists of several life story schema which associate together selective autobiographical knowledge to define a theme (Bluck & Habermas, 2000). Lifetime periods might provide the auto-biographical knowledge that can be used to form life story schema and thus support the generation of themes, and this may be particularly so because of the goal-evaluative information they contain. These lifetime period evaluations access related general events and, in turn, episodic memories which, when formed, provide the "evidence" jus-tifying the evaluations (see Beike & Landoll, 2000, and Conway & Pleydell-Pearce, 2000, for more on how autobiographical knowledge "grounds" the self in memories of experience). Thus, lifetime period autobiographical knowledge is less event-specific than general event autobiographical knowledge, it is also more conceptual and abstract, it encapsulates significant parts of the life story, and may form an important bridge from autobiographical memory to core aspects of the self. In particular, general events and lifetime period knowledge may support the generation of "possible selves" (Markus & Nurius, 1986) or models of the self and these are represented in what we have termed the "working self". The working self is conceived of as a set self images and beliefs, and a complex goal hierarchy, which function to control the construction of memories and the encoding of new knowledge.

COGNITIVE–AFFECTIVE PROCESSES MEDIATE FUNCTION

Goals

An autobiographical memory—one or more epi-sodic memories contextualised by auto-biographical knowledge—contains information about past goals. About what they were, although this may be implicit rather than explicit (especially for childhood memories), and what progress had been made in achieving them. In the Conway and Pleydell-Pearce (2000) model, autobiographical memories are said to be "saturated" with goal-relevant knowledge because they are thought to be encoded through the goal hierarchy of the working self. Autobiographical memories then support evaluation of one's goal history. This might take the form of feelings about the past, evaluative judgements, or cognitive–affective reactions to memories. Memories, however, also have a powerful connection to the current work-ing self goal hierarchy. They constrain what goals can be held, in that they support, contradict, or are

neutral with respect to current goals. For example, a vivid memory—a "personal event memory" in Pillemer's terminology—of receiving an award for achieving a difficult task might support a current goal to achieve in another difficult enterprise, or it might negate or challenge a decision not to engage in a difficult pursuit, or it may simply be neutral and neither support nor negate current goals.

Autobiographical memories function both to reduce discrepancies *and* to maintain them, and in so doing provide dynamism to the goal system of the working self. Woike's work (2003) on the role of the motives in facilitating access to auto-biographical memories provides some of the best evidence for this. In her work, people with agentic self-focus typically retrieve self-defining mem-ories congruent with themes relating to power (or lack of it). In contrast, individuals with a com-munal self-focus retrieve personal event mem-ories associated with themes of relating and interacting. Thus, the goal system appears to render congruent memories more accessible than incongruent memories. On the other hand, goal-incongruent memories can be retrieved and when this occurs, dissonance-reducing reactions, such as justifying or dismissing the event, may result (see Beike & Landoll, 2000). To take an extreme example, a serial killer reminded of one of his murders snatched up a can and read the ingre-dients list from it repeatedly aloud until the dis-sonant memories had "passed" (Christianson & Engleberg, 1997). In other, also extreme, cases such as mental illness and following brain damage (see Conway & Fthenaki, 2000 for a review) it is often the case that people hold (deluded) beliefs that are contradicted by autobiographical know-ledge and by specific memories. For instance, a young schizophrenic man believed himself to be a famous rock guitarist even though he knew he could not play a guitar (Baddeley, Thornton, Chua, & McKenna, 1996); a confabulating patient repeatedly recalled a bitter argument with his father the previous evening even though he could also recall attending his father's funeral some years earlier (Downes & Mayes, 1995); and an elderly female patient confabulated memories about her grandson, which she apparently believed, even though other memories rendered the confabulations wholly implausible (Conway & Tacchi, 1996). These disconnections of memory from the self all illustrate the critically important contribution of autobiographical memory to the current self. Indeed, it is particularly interesting, but not formally investigated, that patients who have badly disrupted autobiographical memory following brain damage often suffer a general loss of motivation. Autobiographical memory may then help to define a particular motive focus and maintain the dynamism of the self by providing a database of experience that facilitates appropriate goal generation and construction of models of the self or self-images.

Reality testing

Models of human memory are sometimes considered to fall into one of two camps: correspondence or coherence theories. Correspondence theories assume that memories represent experience or reality. Coherence theories, on the other hand, do not make this assumption and instead focus on how knowledge coheres to form meanings for the individual. The papers in this issue quite clearly lean more to the coherence than correspondence camp, in emphasis at least. I do not imply that the authors are unconcerned with correspondence issues. It is, however, implausible that a memory system could have evolved that did not represent reality and represent it with some degree of accuracy. An animal that recalled its fantasy of food at the waterhole and acted on this as though it were memory would not survive for long. On the other hand being able to daydream about food and where it could be found might be both pleasurable and also useful as a basis for later action. My point is that a theory of auto-biographical memory will have to include mechanisms and processes that support both cor-respondence *and* coherence.

In our view the main mechanism that represents reality is the temporo-occipital episodic memory system. Episodic memories are the "hard data" of the memory system and although they might be forgotten, incompletely recalled in fragments, and subject to many different inter-pretations, even constructed in many different memories, they always represent the sensory–perceptual–affective–conceptual knowledge that was originally processed. In other words they are an accurate record of experience. Of course, it does not follow from this that an experience was an accurate record of reality. Nevertheless, we argue that experience should in the main (and in health) accurately represent reality and, conse-quently, episodic memories should do so too. We believe that because of their "experience-near" nature episodic memories have the special prop-erty of inducing recollective experience when they are incorporated in a memory construction (see Wheeler, Stuss, & Tulving, 1997, for a more extensive account). They support the "cognitive feeling" of remembering, the sense of the self in past, and this feeling of recollection is a signal that one is remembering rather than fantasising, dreaming, or in some other state. Episodic mem-ories also make memories specific, they link them to a specific point in time and a specific location, and so define Pillemer's "personal event memories".

In our thinking about autobiographical mem-ory, then, episodic memories play a special and fairly well-defined role: they connect the remem-berer with a past reality and bring about recol-lective experience. It does not follow from this that other types of knowledge, e.g., general events, lifetime periods, generic images, etc., do not also represent reality. On the contrary we believe they do but they cannot bring about recollective experience. Also it seems possible that this con-ceptual autobiographical knowledge might be more predisposed to the construction of false memories and false life stories or "personal myths" as Kris (1956/1975) called them (see Conway, Pleydell-Pearce, Whitecross, & Sharpe, 2003, for some recent evidence on this).

Mental models

Finally, I would like to briefly consider the role of autobiographical memory in supporting the development, maintenance, and breakdown of relationships. Of especial interest here, although not yet researched, is how episodic memories and autobiographical knowledge might feature in core mental models of the self-system such as those that modulate attachment behaviour. Early experiences and the mental representations to which they give rise determine attachment type (secure, dismissive, disorganised, etc.). According to Bowlby (1969/1982) this occurs progessively over the first five years of life and takes the form of the establishment in long-term memory of an *internal working model* (IWM) of attachment. What content and structure this mental model contains is unknown, but the nature of early childhood memories when recalled by adults is predictive of attachment type (George, Kaplan, & Main, 1985; Ijzendoorn, 1995). Thus, early auto-biographical memories are probably part of or indexed by an attachment IWM. By our earlier reasoning an IWM should contain some goal-related knowledge but exactly what form this might be in is unknown. Assuming that the IWN is first formed in the preverbal period below about 2 years of age and then modified, changed, and developed into some more stable and enduring representation over the beginning of the verbal period, then the initial representation must be nonverbal. As preverbal infants are known to have quite complex memories and certainly have episodic memories (Rovee-Collier, 1997) it would seem reasonable to assume that an initial attachment IWM would contain some sensory–perceptual–affective knowledge. And also, perhaps, some conceptual knowledge or least a precursor of this, possibly in the form of generic images (from a range of modalities). Because the working self goal structure of the infant is elemental in many respects, driven largely by limbic system drives not yet embedded in complex goal hierarchies, the memory representations that arise when encoded through the infant working self may well be inaccessible to later more complex, verbal, and developed (adult) versions of the working self goal hierarchy. Nevertheless, investigating infant and childhood memories in adults from an attachment point of view may lead to interesting developments in our theoretical thinking about autobiographical memory. For example, we have found (unpublished data) that people are able to bring to mind images from infancy that they claim predate their earliest memories, but which are not themselves localisable to any unique event. Exploration of these sorts of mental representations may provide insight into one of the earliest autobiographical structures: the IWM of attachment.

AUTOBIOGRAPHICAL MEMORY: THE FUTURE

This special issue of *Memory* gives an exciting and wide-ranging view of the self, social, and directive functions of autobiographical memory. The editor and contributors have made an important contribution to deepening our understanding of one the major forms of higher-order cognition: autobiographical memory. In this closing commentary I have tried to show that cognitive–affective mechanisms and processes that mediate autobiographical memory may serve functions that are more internal to the entire system, and which are to do with motivation, coherence of the self,

accuracy and connectedness to reality, cognitive feelings, and attachment. These internal features of autobiographical memory feed into and underpin the more overt uses of autobiographical memory in disclosing the self, affect regulation in self and others, developing meaning over the lifespan, and in shaping courses of action. One of the tasks that faces autobiographical memory researchers is to unify the cognitive–affective account of mechanisms and processes of autobiographical memory with the use of memories in everyday life: this special issue will stimulate progress towards that unified account.

REFERENCES

Baddeley, A. D. (2000). The episodic buffer: A new component of working memory? *Trends in Cognitive Science, 4,* 417–423.

Baddeley, A. D., Thornton, A., Chua, S. E., & McKenna, P. (1996). Schizophrenic delusions and the construction of autobiographical memory. In D. C. Rubin (Ed.), *Remembering our past: Studies in autobiographical memory* (pp. 384–428). Cambridge, MA: Cambridge University Press.

Beike, D. R., & Landoll, S. L. (2000). Striving for a consistent life story: Cognitive reactions to autobiographical memories. *Social Cognition, 18,* 292–318.

Bluck, S., & Habermas, T. (2000). The life story schema. *Motivation and Emotion, 24,* 121–147.

Bowlby, J. (1969/1982). *Attachment and loss: Vol. 1: Attachment.* London: Hogarth Press.

Brewer, W. F. (1986). What is autobiographical memory? In D. C. Rubin, (Ed.), *Autobiographical memory* (pp. 25–49). Cambridge: Cambridge University Press.

Christianson, S-A., & Engelberg, E. (1997). Remembering and forgetting traumatic experiences: A matter of survival. In M. A. Conway (Ed.), *False and recovered memories* (pp. 230–250). Oxford: Oxford University Press.

Conway, M. A. (1996). Autobiographical memories and autobiographical knowledge. In D. C. Rubin (Ed.), *Remembering our past: Studies in autobiographical memory* (pp. 67–93). Cambridge: Cambridge University Press.

Conway, M. A. (2001). Sensory perceptual episodic memory and its context: Autobiographical memory. *Philosophical Transactions of the Royal Society, London, 356,* 1297–1306.

Conway, M. A., & Fthenaki, A. (2000). Disruption and loss of autobiographical memory. In L. S. Cermak (Ed.), *Handbook of neuropsychology, 2nd Edition: Memory and its disorders* (pp. 281–312). Amsterdam: Elsevier.

Conway, M. A., Gardiner, J. M., Perfect, T. J., Anderson, S. J., & Cohen, G. M. (1997). Changes in memory awareness during learning: The acquisition of knowledge by psychology undergraduates. *Journal of Experimental Psychology: General, 126(4), 1–21.

Conway, M. A., & Pleydell-Pearce, C. W. (2000). The construction of autobiographical memories in the self memory system. Psychological Review, 107, 261–288.

Conway, M. A., Pleydell-Pearce, C. W., Whitecross, S., & Sharpe, H. (2002). Brain imaging autobiographical memory. The Psychology of Learning and Motivation, 41, 229–264.

Conway, M. A., Pleydell-Pearce, C. W., Whitecross, S., & Sharpe, H. (2003). Neurophysiological correlates of autobiographical memory for experienced and imagined events. Neuropsychologia, 41(3), 334–340.

Conway, M. A., & Tacchi, P. C. (1996). Motivated confabulation. Neurocase, 2, 325–339.

Downes, J. J., & Mayes, A. R. (1995). How bad memories can sometimes lead to fantastic beliefs and strange visions. In R. Campbell & M. A. Conway (Eds.), Broken memories: Case studies in the neuropsychology of memory (pp. 115–123). Oxford: Blackwell.

George, C., Kaplan, N., & Main, M. (1985). The Adult Attachment Interview. Unpublished manuscript, University of California at Berkeley, USA.

Ijzendoorn, M. H. (1995). Adult attachment representations, parental responsiveness, and infant attachment: A meta-analysis on the predictive validy of the adult attachment interview. Psychological Bulletin, 117(3), 387–403.

Johnson-Laird, P. N. (1983). Mental models. Cambridge, MA: Havard University Press.

Kris, E. (1956). The personal myth: A problem in psychoanalytic technique. In The selected papers of Ernst Kris (1975). New Haven, CT: Yale University Press.

Markus, H., & Nurius, P. (1986). Possible selves. American Psychologist, 41, 954–969.

Matlin, M., & Stang, D. (1978). The Pollyanna principle. Cambridge, MA: Schenkman.

McAdams, D. P., Reynolds, J., Lewis, M. L., Patten, A., & Bowman, P. T. (2001). When bad things turn good and good things turn bad: Sequences of redemption and contamination in life narrative, and their relation to psychosocial adaptation in midlife adults and in students. Personality and Social Psychology Bulletin, 27, 472–483.

Pillemer, D. B. (1998). Momentous events, vivid memories. Cambridge, MA: Harvard University Press.

Robinson, J. A. (1992). First experience memories: Contexts and function in personal histories. In M. A. Conway, D. C. Rubin, H. Spinnler, & W. Wagenaar (Eds.), Theoretical perspectives on autobiographical memory (pp. 223–239). Dordrecht, The Netherlands: Kluwer Academic Publishers.

Rovee-Collier, C. (1997). Dissociations in infant memory: Rethinking the development of implicit and explicit memory. Psychological Review, 104(3), 467–498.

Rubin, D. C., & Greenberg, D. L. (1998). Visual-memory-deficit amnesia: A distinct amnesic presentation and etiology. Proceeedings of the National Academy of Sciences, 95, 1–4.

Singer, J. A., & Salovey, P. (1993). The remembered self. New York: The Free Press.

Tulving, E. (1972). Episodic and semantic memory. In E. Tulving & W. Donaldson (Eds.), Organization of memory (pp. 382–403). New York: Academic Press.

Tulving, E. (1983). Elements of episodic memory. Oxford: Claredon Press.

Tulving, E., & Thomson, D. M. (1973). Encoding specificity and retrieval processes in episodic memory. Psychological Review, 80, 353–373.

Wheeler, M. A., Stuss, D. T., & Tulving, E. (1997). Towards a theory of episodic memory: The frontal lobes and autonoetic consciousness. Psychological Bulletin, 121, 351–354.

Woike, B. (2003). The influence of implicit and explicit motives on autobiographical memory. Manuscript submitted for publication.

Subject Index

Adaptive function, 114, 116, 167, 169, 174
Adolescence, self-continuity, 114
Affect, 145–146
Age, social function, 170, 174–175
Agentic self-focus, 221
Animals, episodic memory, 219
Appraisal, 140–141, 143, 217
Appraisal support, 161
Attachment style
   mental representations, 222–223
   relationship valence, 173
Attitude development, 115
Audiences, 152
Autobiographical knowledge, 220–221
Autobiographical memory
   conceptual classifications, 204
   disconnected, 221–222
   empirical taxonomies, 203
   historical perspective, 115–116
   as a resource, 217
Autobiographical self, 130–131
Autobiography, 117, 128, 130–131
Autonoesis, 126

"Baby Boomers", 132
Biography, 128

Change, 114, 116, 138
Child-rearing practices, 132
Children
   attachment style and mental
     representations, 222–223
   distancing, 145
   emotional self-concept, 180
   encouraging to narrativise memory, 134

   episodic memories, 223
   nurturing, 116
   reminiscing, 186
   self-continuity, 114
   see also Parent–child reminiscence
Circumplex model, 120, 203–215, 218
Cognitive–affective mechanisms and
   processes, 217–224
Coherence, 114, 116–117, 222
Collective narratives, 115–116
Collectivistic societies, 116
Communal self-focus, 221
Conceptual model, social function, 118,
   165–178
Confabulation, 221
Connections, 180
Consistency, 138, 140
Context, 121
Continuity, 114, 116
Contrast effects, 117
Conversation, 114, 151–163
   listener behaviour, 156, 157, 158–159, 161,
     171–172, 175
   mother–child, 186–188
Coping, 180, 181, 190
Correspondence theory, 222
Couple expertise, 173
Couples, remembering, 153
'Cult' of the individual, 217
Cultural myths, 127
Cultural narratives, 126–127, 132–133
Cultural stories, 125
Cultural variations
   autobiographical memory use, 116,
     131–132, 134

Author Index

hypothesised functions fit into one of three categories. These categories are well represented in Pillemer's (1992) formulation of AM as having self (self-continuity, psychodynamic integrity), communicative (social bonding), and directive functions (planning for present and future behaviours). To expand this scope a little, I refer to these three more generally as self, social, and directive functions (Bluck & Alea, 2002).

A REVIEW OF THREE FUNCTIONS: SELF, SOCIAL, DIRECTIVE

I provide here a brief review of the three theorised functions of AM to set the stage for the collection of papers that follows. Each function is presented as a discrete category for the purpose of organisation. This also reflects how individuals have gone about research thus far (that is, with a focus on one type of function). Although these three functions have discrete labels they do not necessarily represent discrete categories in everyday behaviour or mental life. For example, one may remember a past success (e.g., a talk that was well received at a conference) in order to serve the directive function of preparing for an upcoming engagement. Concurrently, however, that same memory may serve a social function of relationship development or maintenance as one recalls new and old relationships with those who were at the conference. It is clearly a challenge, one that sometimes emerges in the papers that follow (e.g., particularly Pasupathi's, and Pillemer's contributions) to consider the overlap between functions of memory, how they are served in combination, and if one may be said to be more fundamental, or have primacy, over the others.

Self

Knowledge of the self in the past, and as projected into the future, has been seen as one critical type of self-knowledge (Neisser, 1988). Many theoretical formulations emphasise the function of AM in the continuity of the self. Although these share a similarity to Pillemer's (1992) "psychodynamic function" that emphasises the psychological and emotional importance for the self of recalling one's own past, AM researchers have not necessarily embraced the psychodynamic aspect of the self function. Conway (1996) claims that the adequacy of autobiographical knowledge depends on its ability to support and promote continuity and

development of the self. Similarly, a hypothesised function of the personal past is to preserve a sense of being a coherent person over time (Barclay, 1996). Fivush (1998) describes how this coherent sense of self-over-time develops in young children, and Habermas and Bluck (2001) outline a trajectory for this continued development of biographical identity through adolescence (see also McAdams, 1985). Most researchers agree that self-continuity through adulthood is maintained by the interdependent relation of self and autobiographical memory (Bluck & Levine, 1998; Brewer, 1986).

Autobiographical knowledge may be especially important when the self is in adverse conditions requiring self-change (Robinson, 1986). Regardless of challenges to the self, however, self functions such as emotion-regulation (see Pasupathi, 2003 this issue), and self-concept preservation and enhancement (Ross, 1989, 1991; Wilson & Ross, 2003 this issue) have also been suggested as useful aspects of self-regulation (Cohen, 1998).

Social

Neisser (1988) claims that the social function of AM is the most fundamental function. AM provides material for conversation thus facilitating social interaction in general (Cohen, 1998). Sharing personal memories also makes the conversation seem more truthful, thus more believable and persuasive (Pillemer, 1992) and thereby offers an avenue for teaching and informing others. This teaching function may be particularly important in certain relationships, for example, that between parents and their children (Fivush, Berlin, Sales, Mennuti-Washburn, & Cassidy, 2003 this issue).

AM also allows us to better understand and empathise with others (Cohen, 1998). For instance, sharing personal memories can engage the listener in a story and elicit empathic responses, especially if the listener responds with their own personal memory (Pillemer, 1992). The importance of AM in developing, maintaining, and strengthening social bonds has been repeatedly noted (e.g., Pillemer, 1998) and sometimes tied to its potential evolutionary adaptive value (Neisser, 1988; Nelson, 1993, 2003 this issue). When episodic remembering is impaired, social relationships can suffer, thus highlighting the importance that autobiographical memories can serve for social bonding (Robinson & Swanson, 1990). Sharing AMs with someone who was not

MEMORY, 2003, *11* (2), 113–123

Autobiographical memory: Exploring its functions in everyday life

Susan Bluck

Institute on Aging and Psychology Department, University of Florida, USA

This special issue of *Memory* spotlights research that uses a functional approach to investigate autobiographical memory (AM) in everyday life. This approach relies on studying cognition, in this case AM, taking into account the psychological, social, or cultural-historic context in which it occurs. Areas of interest include understanding to what ends AM is used by individuals and in social relationships, how it is related to other cognitive abilities and emotional states, and how memory represents our inner and outer world. One insight gained by taking this approach is that levels and types of accuracy need not always be regarded as memory "failures" but are sometimes integral to a self-memory system that serves a variety of meaningful ends of human activity. Previously hypothesised functions of AM fall into three broad domains: self, social, and directive. Each of the contributions addresses how AM serves one or more of these functions and thereby examines the usefulness and adequacy of this trio.

The aim of this special issue of *Memory* is to present current empirical and theoretical work on the functions of autobiographical memory (AM). An explosion of work over the last decade in the AM literature has been concerned with the important task of examining memory performance in everyday life. The literature has been crowded with debates concerning how much we remember about, and how well we remember, the events of our lives (e.g., eyewitness testimony, repressed/false memories). The focus on function in this special issue provides another area to spotlight: the primary concern is not with how much or how well humans remember their personal past (although those features often play some role), but instead with *why and how* humans remember both mundane and significant life events. What functions does it serve for people to remember, reflect on, and share with others, the experiences of their lives?

Various researchers have described the benefits of a functional approach to memory (Baddeley, 1987; Bruce, 1989; Neisser, 1978). Certainly, partial accounts and embellished accounts are included when researchers examine the memories people have and the stories they inevitably tell. The functional approach, however, does not particularly attempt to label information as correct or in error, actual or biased, but tries instead to understand how the memory system operates during person–environment interactions (i.e., life), by understanding why individuals recall things the way that they do.

Autobiographical remembering implicitly involves thinking about the past in the present. So why do we do it? A number of theoretical writings suggest the general importance of the expansion of one's present perspective through an extended temporal view of self and life (e.g., Lewin, 1926; Neisser, 1988; Neugarten, 1979; Staudinger & Bluck, 2002). Beyond recognising this general utility of considering the present as framed by the past (and the future), researchers have also more particularly addressed why remembering and thinking about the past occurs in everyday life— that is, the functions of autobiographical memory.

Although researchers have identified different specific functions, or subsets of functions, most

---

Requests for reprints should be sent to Susan Bluck, Institute on Aging, McCarty C, 5th Floor, PO Box 115911, Gainesville, FL, USA, 32611-5911. Email: bluck@ufl.edu